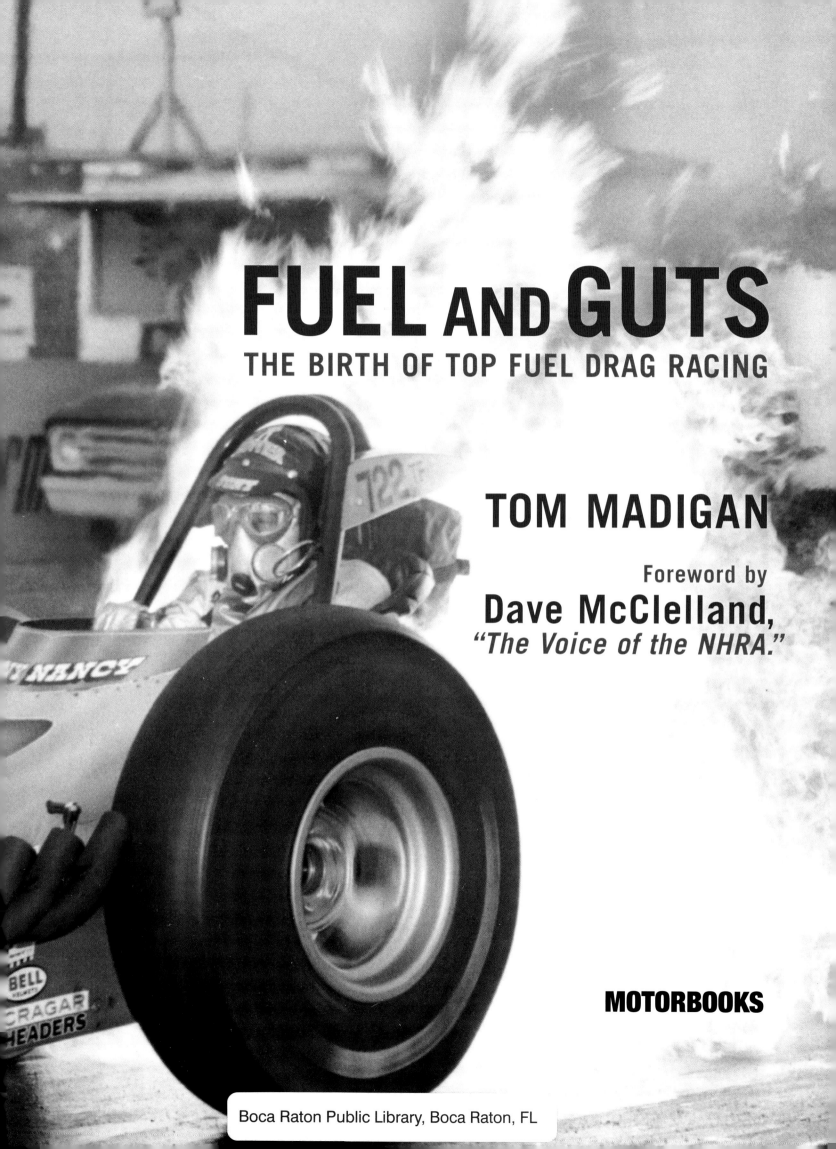

FUEL AND GUTS
THE BIRTH OF TOP FUEL DRAG RACING

TOM MADIGAN

Foreword by
Dave McClelland,
"The Voice of the NHRA."

MOTORBOOKS

THIS BOOK IS DEDICATED TO THE MEMORY OF TONY "The Loner" NANCY,
MY FRIEND AND LEGENDARY CALIFORNIA TOP FUEL DRIVER.

First published in 2007 by Motorbooks, an imprint of MBI Publishing Company, Galtier Plaza, Suite 200, 380 Jackson Street, St. Paul, MN 55101 USA

Motorbooks titles are also available at discounts in bulk quantity for industrial or sales-promotional use. For details write to Special Sales Manager at MBI Publishing Company, Galtier Plaza, Suite 200, 380 Jackson Street, St. Paul, MN 55101 USA.

To find out more about our books, join us online at www.motorbooks.com.

Library of Congress Cataloging-in-Publication Data

Madigan, Tom, 1938-
  Fuel and guts : the birth of top fuel drag racing / by Tom Madigan.
    p. cm.
  Includes index.
  ISBN-13: 978-0-7603-2697-8 (hardbound w/ jacket)
  ISBN-10: 0-7603-2697-5 (hardbound w/ jacket)
  1. Drag racing--History. I. Title. II. Title: Fuel and guts.
  GV1029.3.M23 2007
  796.72--dc22
                                        2007018068

Editor: James Manning Michels
Designer: Mandy Iverson

Printed in Hong Kong

On the cover: Shown on the cover is Dave West's recreation of the dragster with which John "The Zookeeper" Mulligan and Tim "Chops" Beebe won the 1969 NHRA Winternationals. Later that year, the Zookeeper drove the Beebe & Mulligan car to first place in qualifying at the U.S. Nationals with the quickest elapsed time yet recorded in drag racing history, 6.43 seconds. Mulligan faced Tommy Ivo in the first round of eliminations; at the 1,000-foot mark, the clutch exploded and a violent fire ensued. A badly burned Mulligan was thrown from the car. For three weeks, he made a valiant effort to stay alive, but finally succumbed to his injuries. The well-liked Zookeeper's death was a turning point in the evolution of drag racing. *Tom Madigan*

On the endpapers:
Front: By the mid-1960s, NHRA National Drag Racing had become a mainstream, major-league auto racing series. This aerial view of the 1964 Indy Nationals offers an idea as to drag racing's popularity. *Don Brown*

Back: Jim "Jazzy" Nelson was a master of running nitro. He worked closely with Vic Edelbrock Sr. and Ed Iskenderian. Later, he and Dode Martin started Dragmasters. Dragmasters was one of the first companies to market everything from a chassis to a turn-key dragster. All a racer had to do was open their catalog and choose. *Author's collection, courtesy of the Edelbrock Corporation*

On the frontispiece: Ford Motor Company got into the Top Fuel arena in the late 1960s with their 427-SOHC engine, run by several top names, including Lou Baney. Baney's engine was built by Ed Pink, and once Tom McEwen got it running right, the car was driven by Don Prudhomme. To everyone's benefit, a budding rivalry blossomed. Hot Rod/Motor Trend *Archives*

On the title page: Always the showman, Tony Nancy didn't mind giving the crowd a thrill with a firey burnout. Although Tony ran Top Fuel for only a few years, he made the top dogs sit up and take notice. *Steve Reyes*

CONTENTS

FOREWORD	LIGHTING THE 1,000-FOOT FUSE	6
CHAPTER 1	GOLETA	10
CHAPTER 2	THE NEXT LEVEL	18
CHAPTER 3	INCUBATION	24
CHAPTER 4	STRAIGHT SHOOTER	30
CHAPTER 5	THE CAMFATHER	38
CHAPTER 6	GETTING SERIOUS	48
CHAPTER 7	HAND GRENADE HARRY AND THE POND	60
CHAPTER 8	DUEL IN THE DEW	82
CHAPTER 9	WHAT IS IT ABOUT FLOYD?	102
CHAPTER 10	GETTING HIP	116
CHAPTER 11	THE ROCKING '60S	126
CHAPTER 12	RACING AT THE RAINBOW	142
CHAPTER 13	RUN WHAT YOU BRUNG, AND BE SURE YOU BRUNG ENOUGH	154
CHAPTER 14	OH NO, HERE COMES GARLITS	162
CHAPTER 15	WHAT'S UP, BRO?	176
CHAPTER 16	BIG MONEY IS COMING	190
CHAPTER 17	WORKING CLASS RACERS	200
CHAPTER 18	THE LONER	228
ACKNOWLEDGMENTS		237
INDEX		239

LIGHTING THE 1,000-FOOT FUSE

Picture this if you will….a teenaged high schooler from a small town in Missouri, attending his first drag race. It was an event staged by the original NHRA Drag Safari in 1955 in Kansas City, MO. From that day forward, my life took a decidedly different direction. Much to the chagrin of my more conventional parents, I eagerly plunged into the world of drag racing with a passion that lingers to this day. From that first event, I had the desire to be a part of a great and growing sport….and ended up devoting an entire lifetime and career to it.

Drag racing in its infancy was a difficult sport to categorize and to understand, as evidenced by my reluctant parents. On the surface, it is so simple….two cars, side by side, competing from a standing start over a straight-line quarter mile. First one to the finish line wins. But, oh, the ultimate complexity of accomplishing that simple goal. It's not as easy as it looks!

The sport got its start on the dry lakes of Southern California, where the race course was measured in miles…not 1320 feet. But when the coupes, roadsters, belly tankers, and streamliners on the West Coast started attracting attention and interest in other parts of the country, it was obvious a different race course had to be found. Thus…the quarter mile drag strip that quickly became the standard nationwide.

When you went to a drag race in those early days, the innovation and creativity of the owner/builder/driver just overwhelmed you. From the simplest hot rod—a coupe, roadster or even the infrequent sedan—to the purpose built first dragsters…it was a gearhead's delight.

Race tracks were cropping up all across the country, providing an ever-increasing supply of race cars that defied description. Innovation was king and, if you went to the races as often as you could, you marveled at the changes in the cars that seemed to be happening right before your eyes. You never knew what you were going to see!

Some wild creations have been attempted over the years, all in search of that ever-quicker elapsed time through the quarter mile. Some were just improvements on the original idea of a front-engine dragster but others bordered on the fringes of reality. Multiple engines, up to as many as four; aircraft engines, including piston, turbine and jet; plus a propeller-driven machine or two as well; sidewinders, or cross-engine mounting, plus rear-engine dragsters; compressed air powered dragsters; three-wheel, four-wheel, and even six-wheel dragsters; you get the idea. In those days anything was acceptable.

Shortly after my first experience as a spectator, I ventured into the world of race announcing, starting in 1959. This allowed me the opportunity to become a part of the national scene when I announced my first NHRA National event at Indianapolis in 1961, and that set me on the road which eventually gave me the chance to come to the mecca of drag racing, Southern California.

It was the NHRA Winternationals, 1964, and I thought I was in heaven. I had been on the national event trail, announcing the Nationals at Indy since 1961, but this was CALIFORNIA, the place where it all started, where it seemed there were race cars in every garage, parked in every driveway, even driven on the street. At this point, there was no turning back for me.

I was no different than so many people of the era, caught up with the speed, the competition, and the friendships. But the one factor that stands out among all the other attributes of this great sport is the absolute drive and determination of the competitors to do it their way, letting their own creativity rise to the top. Whether the ideas worked or not was determined on the race track, not in a conference room jammed with rule makers.

Sure, there were some rules that dealt primarily with the safety of the driver and spectator, which has been of paramount interest to the NHRA since the beginning of the sport. But in the early days, on the performance front, it was pretty much let your mind, your abilities, and your pocketbook rule.

I have often described the sport of Drag Racing as the "People's Motorsport" because with the rules allowing a broad mix of cars to compete, from the vehicle you drove to the track to the most exotic, nitro-burning machine ever built, there was some place for anyone on any size budget to compete. This was, and still is, totally different from almost any other form of racing in existence and, coupled with the minimal restrictions of the early days, allowed for the creation of the unbelievably unique machines.

When you added the highly volatile nitro-methane fuel mix to the equation, it definitely changed the landscape. While the dragsters were impressive on gasoline or methanol, the use of nitro not only increased the performance, but the ground-shaking, explosive sound and indescribable physical sensation enjoyed with the multi-thousand-horse-power machines battling over the quarter mile raised spectator appeal as well. There were thrills and spills, some that had tragic overtones, but that did not alter the progress of the sport. The crowds kept getting larger and larger and more and more people became enthralled with these daring young men and their thundering machines.

The inexorable march of improved performance came on many different fronts: in car design, increased horsepower, improved clutches and drive trains, and, probably as important as any, improved tires. From the very first, it was apparent that the tires used on the street were not the "hot setup" for a high-horsepower acceleration device known as a dragster. First came the recapped street tires with the slick tread, then the purpose-built

Above and below: Dave McClelland has been involved with drag racing since 1955. He first announced the NHRA U.S. Nationals in 1961, and has been known as "the voice of the NHRA" ever since. *Dave McClelland collection*

drag tire, and on to the 17-inch-wide monsters in use today. And through it all, the tuner could, and still can, overpower any tire at any time, turning a good run into a quarter mile of tire smoke and burning rubber.

Speeds climbed rapidly, from the very low 100's to 200 mph and eventually topping 330 mph. Is there an end in sight? If so, it will be either the result of rulemaking to keep the cars and drivers from going faster, or from tire limitations. Because one thing has never changed in the more than half decade of this sport: the ability of the builder/tuner/driver to extract even greater performance. It may come at a

It all started with guys like these. A group of hot rodders, a stripped down body mounted on Model A frame rails, a seat, steering wheel, running gear, and an engine. It didn't take long for progress to take hold. Hot Rod/Motor Trend *Archives*

Shown here is an example of the last generation of front-engine Top Fuel dragsters. California produced many a great top fuel driver, and the late Tony "The Loner" Nancy was among the best of them. Tony had his best year in 1970, setting top speed records and winning the Bakersfield U.S. Fuel & Gas Championships. *Ed Justice Jr.*

slower pace today than in years past, but I have yet to see an attempt to slow down a dragster that has ultimately been successful. Of course, draconian measures have yet to be employed and that remains for the future to determine.

From a wide eyed teenager in Missouri to a senior citizen in California, it has been quite a ride. But I, like so many of my contemporaries in the sport of drag racing, consider myself to be one of the luckiest people in the world. I had a chance to grow up as an active participant in a sport that was maturing as I did. It was the opportunity to earn a living doing something I had

done for fun, to become close friends with my heroes, to hopefully make a small contribution to the overall success of the sport, but most important of all, to have been there and played a role during what was truly the "Golden Era of Drag Racing". Those days of the 1950's and 60's are a time to be cherished, a time that reveals the ingenuity in action that is the mantra of the American Hot Rodder, talents and skills that continue to this day. It was truly a time when innovation ruled supreme in the sport of drag racing.

Dave McClelland

CHAPTER ONE

GOLETA

Long before fancy staging and timing lights, there was no Christmas tree starting system; only a human standing in front of two roaring race cars. Green flag in hand, the starter would point to each competitor and mouth the question, "Are you ready?" then leap into the air and the race was on. *Don Brown*

Long before the first official drag race, California had a history of wild and crazy motorheads kicking up dust on the dry lake beds of the Mojave Desert. California was a land of plenty, and yearlong good weather nurtured the seeds of automobile racing. California also offered freedom and an unconventional lifestyle not experienced in the rest of the country. So it was with drag racing. Drag racing moved from the dry lakes to the streets, where it became an outlaw with a tarnished reputation, a stepchild of traditional, accepted forms of auto racing.

Eventually, it would overcome its tumultuous birth and unruly adolescence to become accepted. But the process would take time.

It is begging for a fistfight to offer opposition to the notion that the first drag race was contested somewhere other than California. Racers from the East will state flatly that drag racing could have started in plenty of other places, and their hypothesis does have merit. But, with all due respect, this yarn is about California, and is limited in scope to a narrow frame of time. With that prerequisite understood, I chose to begin in a place and time that was real and actual. Hopefully we can avoid the undue controversies often found when dealing with historical events whose origins prove difficult to determine conclusively.

For years, the Ford flathead V-8 was the engine of choice for Hot Rodders on the dry lakes and the early days of drag strips. Then, in 1951, Chrysler introduced the 331-cubic inch Hemi V-8 and drag racing was changed forever. Dragsters adopted the Hemi as soon as they could get one. Hot Rod/Motor Trend *Archives*

To the casual observer, the most often-told account of drag racing in California centers around a small airfield in Orange County, near the town of Santa Ana, and a friendly, charismatic man named Cloyce Hart or "C.J." Hart, a.k.a. Pappy. Hart had the vision not only to organize drag racing, but to make it a commercial enterprise, charging spectators admission and participants entry fees. C.J. Hart was a pioneer and Santa Ana was an exciting time, but they are not the beginning of our story.

Staying true to our story's premise, our version of drag racing's roots comes firsthand from someone who lived the experience. There will be no rumors or innuendo, only facts remembered by one man offering his wisdom.

It was spring of 1949, and the United States was finally overcoming the effects of the Great War. Everyone was looking forward, anticipating a new decade, a decade that would become known as the Fabulous 50s. For some unexplained reason, California seemed even more alluring than it had during the gold rush years a century before. Jobs were abundant, the economy blossomed in the spring air, and,

unlike the days of the Depression, the borders of the state were no longer lined with club-wielding police whose job was to turn back the hordes of settlers from the East. Young men were returning, and their pockets were filled with military service pay. The terrible effects of the war were being overcome. Although hundreds of thousands of our country's young people had died and over a million were wounded, it was time to move on.

Major manufacturing companies that had earlier given up civilian production for the war effort were now free to build a new economy. The automobile was again the focus of every young man, and for many that focus became a passion—to have a fast car, a machine to match the freedom of California, personal transportation with attitude. Young men wanted fast cars to perform a new kind of mating ritual that included drive-in eateries, car clubs, and tempting the gods by engaging in street racing. Yes, California had it all—palm

Rolling out of San Diego, the Bean Bandits, led by Joaquin Arnett, made drag racing history in the early 1950s. Once a racer on the dry lakes of the Mojave Desert, Arnett turned to drag racing. One of the first to use Nitro, he and his crew raced on a shoestring budget but still beat the best of the day. The car was first powered by a Ford flathead and later an Ardun overhead valve V-8. *Author's collection/ Courtesy of Edelbrock Corporation*

If you ran a fuel burning dragster in the mid-1950s your goal would be to have a Chrysler Hemi with a Potvin style supercharger set-up and a full-body to project a real race-car look. Just behind this dragster sits the fuel burning Fiat coupe of Jim "Jazzy" Nelson. Hot Rod/Motor Trend *Archives*

trees, beaches, Hollywood, fast cars, and time to enjoy life. The year 1949 was a great time to be a hot rodder.

Tossed into this scenario of rebirth was a young man who had served his country and returned to Santa Barbara, California, to open a small, two-pump Texaco station with a tiny service garage. He had raced the dry lakes before the war and, in 1949, he wanted nothing more than to earn an honest living and build himself a fast car. The young man's name was Bob Joehnck. Bob was a member of the Whistlers Car Club and a participant in a new, fast-moving culture called hot rodding.

By turning his garage into a speed shop, Joehnck became a ground-floor pioneer in the newest business opportunity of the day—building high-performance engines using products called "speed equipment." Disciples of the dry lakes days, a small but growing group of talented mechanical wizards began turning experience and expertise they had gathered before the war into an enterprise, manufacturing performance products for profit. Joehnck knew instantly that producing parts that could be sold over the counter to customers who lacked the talent or ability to manufacture equipment on their own was a great idea. He learned quickly, and became one of the very first dealers to buy in bulk from performance pioneer Vic Edelbrock, Sr., stocking the manifolds, heads, and carburetors he made for Ford flathead engines.

Joehnck began building engines for club members and local racers. He soon gained a reputation as a talent, not a mouth. It didn't take long for someone as bright as Joehnck to realize that racing on the streets, be it in Santa Barbara or Los Angeles, was not the answer to building the speed equipment industry. Everyday citizens hated hot rodders, and if the status quo continued, police departments would be forced to declare an all-out war on anyone driving a hot car. So, Joehnck and a group of fellow racers organized to confront the problem. They took racing off of the streets and established a controlled environment in which it could mature. A new form of racing was about to be born in California.

I met Bob Joehnck a few years ago while doing research for a book titled *Edelbrock: Made in the USA*, a history of the Edelbrock Corporation. From day one, Joehnck impressed me with his straightforward manner, candor, and sometimes cutting remarks. He knew his stuff, he didn't care what other people thought, and he regarded anyone who tried to con him or lie to him as a worthless son of a bitch.

In 2006, Joehnck agreed to do an interview with me to discuss his involvement in the earliest days of drag racing. The actual interview was conducted in Bob's shop, which is located on a quiet, tree-lined street in Santa Barbara. The coastal community was, as always, filled with tourists on holiday, high-priced estates, and even higher-priced celebrity residents. Sand, sun, and money was, is, and forever will be the lifestyle.

In his mid-eighties at the time, Bob Joehnck projected a stern demeanor, his handshake relayed a strong physical posture, and he quickly established the fact that he was ready to express his personal views without much provocation. From the dry lakes of California to the salt of Bonneville, from engine builder at the drag strip to crew chief for one of the original four Corvette Z06 Sting Rays to race at Riverside in 1962, Joehnck has put together a remarkable 60-year career. He designed manifolds and created engine-building methods that are still used today. He learned his trade from some of the greatest pioneers in the business, including Ed Winfield and Vic Edelbrock, Sr.

As we were about to begin, Bob stated his prerequisite before telling the story. "Tell the people the real story or I don't want to be involved. I'm not a bullshit artist, and I don't like exaggeration. Back in the early days we were doing what we had to do to race, nothing more. Just tell the truth or leave the story alone."

A transformation seemed to take place as Joehnck leaned forward and began to tell the first of many tales that populate this book. He relaxed, a thin haze of a smile became visible, and his spirit drifted back to days long buried in his memory.

BOB JOEHNCK

The whole hot rod movement actually began to come together before the war. In the late 1930s up to 1940, the car business in California was substantial and people began buying new cars. They may not have had extra money for anything else, but the lure of owning a new automobile was strong. The result of this growth meant that the junkyards began filling up with old models. In turn, this exchange provided a gold strike for young guys looking to acquire used Ford Model As and early flathead engines.

Remember, the first flathead engines were produced in 1932, so by the end of the decade there were plenty available. The result was hot rodders, with little in the way of disposable income, began scrounging the wrecking yards in search of a deal. Another much overlooked item to be found in discarded junk were hydraulic brake systems. So, the formula for a hot rod in the late 30s until the war became a Model A frame fitted with a flathead V-8 and hydraulic brakes. All of this stuff was a bolt-on deal. Guys could build a car in their backyard using simple equipment like a cutting torch, hand tools, and one friend who could weld.

Basically, the hot rod scene began to change at this time. In the very early days, the racers would go to the dry lakes and were paid little attention. Nearly all of the speed equipment was handmade by racers with a high level of mechanical skills. It was a personal thing. The average person on the street paid little or no attention to the lakes—they only knew circle track racing at local fairgrounds or some bull ring track in town. But things changed and kids started building stripped-down hot rods for the street. Just before the war, things began to get crazy. Street racing was out of control and guys were crashing into innocent people, with many deaths blamed on hot rodders. The cops, especially in Los Angeles, and the newspapers began an all-out war against street racers. Adding to the controversy was the fact that the first of the speed equipment manufacturers began selling parts over the counter to make cars go faster.

Of course, the lid on all this was slammed shut in 1941, when the war started. Everything, circle track racing and new car manufacturing and most of the dry lakes, was shut down as a result of the war. We all went into the service.

It is very difficult for people living today to understand that a whole segment of society was gone. Nearly every young man and many young girls, 18 to 24 years old, would be away from home fighting and dying on foreign soil for four to five years. They were in their prime, giving themselves up to defend their country. Thousands would never see their home again.

Overseas, between the fighting, all we ever talked about was girls, beer, and cars. When the war ended, the hot rod scene exploded. Everyone came home and wanted to pick up the pieces. Hot cars were at the top of the list. It didn't take long before the same old situation started over—guys racing on the streets, and the cops and newspapers trying to stop it with overkill and brutality. In Los Angeles, it got ugly. Up north, we street raced but there were far fewer cars. And, yes, the cops jumped all over us, but they were small-town officers who knew us all and didn't use excess force when they cracked down.

And, unlike the big city, we knew that something had to be done, because it was our town, too, and we all lived in close proximity. The one advantage we had was the fact that Santa Barbara was still very rural, and outside of town nobody really paid attention to what was going on.

The Goleta Airport was a small, private landing field, rarely used before the war. When the war started, the Marines moved in and made it into a training center for fighter pilots. After the war, the government just left and the airport reverted back to a state of near abandonment. The military had left behind several buildings and a network of roads at one end of the property, surrounded by a cluster of bunkers used for ammunition storage. Aside from the bunkers and buildings, there was nothing but open space.

At the time, I belonged to a local car club called the Whistlers. The name came from the fact that we had a lot of '32 Fords, and when you went fast the grille bars on a '32 would whistle like a tea kettle. At any rate, we started going out to the airport and driving around on the roads bordering the runway. Nothing serious, just screwing around, racing and choosing each other off. Over a period of time, we discovered that we could go out to the airport on Sunday after church and race around with nobody really caring. It wasn't long before word got out and guys started showing up to do some serious racing.

Freeways and super highways did not exist in the 1940s, and traffic on Highway 101 was minimal.

Unlike today, when Sunday on 101 North in Santa Barbara is a complete pain in the butt, back then it was a two-lane country road and we would simply turn off onto the airport road, drawing little attention. At first, it was quiet enough. Most of the cars had mufflers of some type. But once we had more than eight or ten cars show up, it was time to organize.

We were not running on the airport runway itself. The road we used ran parallel, and we would go as far away from the hangars or parked airplanes as we could get. The road went due west toward the ocean and it was as straight as an arrow. It crossed over a small bridge and came to a dead end at a gate. We would open the gate and, after a run, the driver could turn right after the gate and return to the starting area by using one of the auxiliary roads.

We had gotten the blessing of the airport manager, a man named Swain, about using the straight road and the return roads as long as we cleaned up after the meets. One problem did crop up soon after

Drag Racing in California did not begin on a drag strip. It began on the dry lake beds of the Mojave Desert and then moved to the streets of Los Angeles. As it did, battles with police and an outcry from citizens forced the demon hot rodders to get creative. The Goleta Airport in Santa Barbara California lays claim to the first organized drag race in California. Here, pioneer racer Bob Joehnck, in his '29 Ford roadster, is getting ready to make run. *Tom Madigan collection/Bob Joehnck photo*

Close but no cigar. The California Competition Body Shop Special driven by Bob Alsenz was runner-up to Melvin Heath at the 1956 NHRA Nationals. But, the team won a new Chrysler engine for posting the fastest time of the event. Hot Rod/Motor Trend *Archives*

we began running. Mr. Swain saw no problem in us using the property, but he did want us to provide proof of insurance. That became a key issue. So, we formed a club called the Santa Barbara Acceleration Association. I knew an insurance agent in town, and we put together a policy with Lloyds of London for about fifty bucks.

The bottom line to our effort was one of the first, if not *the* first, place where you could come in off the street and run your car on private land and be covered by some type of insurance. Technically, although we didn't know it at the time, we were an organized drag strip with two vital components: permission and insurance. For us, it was just a place to run without getting into trouble.

Our time at Goleta was pure fun. Guys and their girlfriends would show up with picnic lunches packed. We marked a starting line with white paint and the cars would roll up and take off. We raced down the road to a bridge, which was approximately a quarter-mile. There was a dip in the road right before the bridge and the cars would hit that dip and bounce. Back at the starting line, we could all tell who won by the first car to bounce in the air. We never started from a standing position because we had narrow, stock, tread tires. Neither the rear end gears nor rear axles would tolerate dropping the clutch and trying to spin the tires. Nobody wanted to get towed home.

For the first couple of months, participants would race each other until the fastest car was left unbeaten. Then more and more cars showed up, so we separated entrants into loose-fitting classes: roadsters, coupes, and cars with and without fenders. There were no timing lights or actual officials. One member would start the cars by waving an arm. We even tried a starting pistol. At one point, the girls would go to the end of the road and wave frantically over the lane of the winning car.

Many times after a lunch break, the guys turned their cars over to girlfriends or wives, and they would show the boys some tough racing. There was an old, abandoned warehouse near the starting line, and it had a huge wooden dock. The guys would climb up on the dock and yell their heads off when their girls would bounce in the air at the bridge.

Sunday afternoon racing at Goleta became the event of the week for local racers and eventually entries reached 25 to 30 cars. One old man would show up with a pickup truck. He'd bring a barbeque grill and cases of soda pop packed in blocks of ice. He'd cook up hot dogs and hamburgers for ten cents or something like that. He'd give the club a cut of the profits and we'd pass the hat around to get enough money to buy a couple of trophies for the winners. Then we'd buy the trophies back for five bucks and use them the following weekend.

Old man Swain let us run the taxiway once. I can't remember the reason, but it was the best race we ever had because the strip was long and wide, and you didn't have to worry about the bump on the bridge.

One thing stands out in my mind about those days at Goleta: we all wanted the same thing. We just raced and had fun. No drinking, fighting, or vandalism. We didn't have gangs, we had clubs. The racers respected each other, the property they raced on, and the idea of fair play and sportsmanship.

Racing went on hot and heavy for a year or so, then airport management began getting cold feet about racing cars on their property. The number of cars kept growing and it became more difficult to control the situation. By that time, other drag strips were being created and the racers started going to other places, some better equipped. Goleta had its day in the sun, but it didn't just fade into the annals of bench-racing storytelling without a big finish. This story has been told about a million times and every time it seems to be a little different. I was there and here is my version, take or leave it!

For a long time I had been a dealer for Vic Edelbrock, Sr., selling his manifolds and cylinder heads. Senior was one of the smartest men I ever met. He was honest, a man of his word, and would never back down from a challenge. Street racing in Los Angeles after the war was a big deal; everybody did it, but some guys were just stupid. They crashed their cars, hurt themselves and other people, pissed off the cops, and gave the newspapers plenty of headlines.

Vic Sr. and his crew, Bobby Meeks, Don Towle, and Fran Hernandez, did their share, but Vic was also worried about his name getting tainted if one of his guys screwed up. His business depended on the average hot rodder on the street buying his equipment, so he was careful about what he and his crew did. But you know how some people just can't leave things alone and have to create controversy? Some local street squirrels, not real racers, started trash talking how a certain Los Angeles racer could blow the doors off the Edelbrock shop car.

At first, Vic ignored the rumors and would toss anyone who started shooting their mouth off out of his shop. But the yapping didn't stop, and finally Vic had enough. The local racer at the center of the story was a fellow named Tom Cobbs, who lived in Santa Monica. Cobbs was not your typical hot rodder. His family had money—they were part of the American Tobacco Company fortune.

Here's where the true story differs from the bull-shit tale everybody tells: Tom Cobbs was a real racer. He ran the dry lakes, and he was one of the first hot rodders to use a GMC 4-71 supercharger on his engine. He ran a '31 Ford Model-A sedan with a blown flathead, and he used Evans heads, not Edelbrock.

On one of my trips into Los Angeles to pick up my order of heads and manifolds, Vic invited me into his private office, a trailer behind his shop, for a bourbon and Coke. I started telling him about what we were doing in Goleta. As we went on, the conversation got around to the badmouthing between Cobbs and Edelbrock. He suddenly turned serious, and muttered something to the effect that this thing had to get settled. Before I left, I filled in Bobby Meeks and Fran Hernandez about Goleta and what I had told Vic.

I can't remember how the whole deal got put together, but the short version is that Vic had enough of the talk and told Meeks and Towle to put the shop engine into Fran's '32 coupe and set up a race between the Edelbrock car and Cobbs.

One Sunday morning, Cobbs and several of his buddies showed up at our strip. A short time later, here comes Vic Sr., Meeks, Towle, Fran, another employee named Bob Bradford, and Vic's son, Vic Junior. They had the coupe in tow behind the shop pickup truck. You couldn't believe the buzz. People were running around in a frenzy talking about the grudge race that was about to happen.

Vic Sr. decided to have Don Towle drive the car instead of Fran. I have no idea why. So, they line up, Cobbs with his blown flathead, and Towle running the shop engine loaded with nitromethane. Before you can blink, it's over and Towle blows the doors off of Cobbs' sedan. Towle doesn't wait for a second. He comes back to the pickup, Vic hooks the car up, and the whole gang goes out of the track. Vic had proved his point. Towle had beat Cobbs fair and square and that was that. Some of the onlookers started yelling "you cheaters," but Vic just waved goodbye.

Over the years, that story has gotten so blown out of proportion that it has become mythology. It was no big deal. Two racers had it out and one guy won. Tom Cobbs is a very nice man and he never was part of the trash talk. Through the years, he would only say that it was good racing. That's the way it was in the old days—guys raced each other because they wanted to see who was best. You always have people who don't know their ass from third base shooting off, saying things that aren't true. I hate that crap. If you want to prove how good you are, just race. Losers should have done better.

CHAPTER TWO

THE NEXT LEVEL

In the late 1950s and early 1960s, Top Fuel cars came in all shapes and sizes—for example, Texan Jack Moss and his lightweight, short-wheelbase, blown Chevy digger. Check out those front wheels. *Don Brown*

Goleta had proven that a wild bunch of hot rodders could organize and conduct what was arguably the first legal drag race on private property. But, the question remained: would the idea grow or die on the vine?` The answer to the question would be a resounding yes….

Unless you have been visiting another planet for the last half century, the story of Santa Ana airport and a man named Cloyce "C.J." Hart has been told at least a thousand times, in every book and magazine story about the history of drag racing.

In 1950, Hart and his wonderful wife, Peggy, took their roles in drag racing history to a tiny Orange County, California, town called Santa Ana. Hart had been a dry lakes racer before the war, and returned to Southern California afterward to continue his efforts. However, the times had changed and the dry lakes had lost some of their appeal. So Hart came up with the idea of creating a local venue for racing.

The whole idea started with the use of an old Navy base in Orange County. He originally started running drag races on an abandoned airstrip and blimp base the locals called "Mile Square," because it was a huge chunk of flat concrete (more on this from Jim Nelson later). Mile Square didn't work, so Hart tried another angle: the airport proper. Hart joined forces with two partners, Creighton Hunter and Frank Stilwell and, together with Peggy (who later became a very competitive drag racer), they started running events at the Santa Ana airport on one of the old military strips that had been abandoned after the war.

There were two profound differences between Goleta and the C.J. Hart endeavor. First, Hart charged an admission of 50 cents to start. Second, he installed timing clocks. For the first time, drag racers could get accurate speeds and times on their runs. Hart also had a real pit area, restrooms, primitive grandstands, the basic racer food groups of hot dogs and soda pop, and parking for spectators. Santa Ana was a commercial business.

With the onset of Santa Ana, drag racing in California took off like one of the state's infamous wildfires.

Nearly all of the pioneers of drag racing ran the asphalt of Santa Ana: Art Chrisman; Jim Nelson and Dode Martin (the Dragmasters); Jim Jazzy Nelson; Joaquin Arnett and his Bean Bandits; Paul Pfaff; Calvin Rice; Don Yates; Lou Baney; and many more. Mr. Hart had lit the fuse, and there would be no stopping the burn.

The idea of a commercial drag strip kicked off a host of new ventures in 1951. Paradise Mesa near San Diego opened. The Pomona Valley Timing Association joined the list by opening Pomona. Two of the all-time great racing pioneers from Southern California teamed up to open a drag strip in Saugus: Lou Baney, dry lakes veteran, engine builder, car owner, and one of the greatest men you could ever meet, partnered with Lou Senter, co-founder of Ansen Automotive, owner and driver of every type of American race car you can think of. Senter was a mentor to many Top Fuel drivers and, like Baney, a man everyone respects and loves as one of the founding fathers of drag racing.

Next on the list came Fontana in 1952, then San Fernando and Long Beach in 1955, San Gabriel (first version) in 1956, and Irwindale (first version) in 1957. Northern California sported its own list of drag strips like Cotati, Half Moon Bay, Lodi, Kingdon, and Vacaville.

The same factors that had stimulated racing on the dry lakes and made California the nucleus of the performance parts industry in the 1940s allowed for the growth of fuel dragster development in the 1950s—great weather, a tremendous pool of experimentation, and racers working hand in hand with manufacturers.

The story of Top Fuel drag racing in California between 1950 and 1970 must contain the name of Art Chrisman. Chrisman was a racer to be reckoned with, a pioneer in developing Top Fuel dragsters. He began his climb to fame behind the wheel of his Number 25 dragster, shown in this photo after going 140 mph at Santa Ana drag strip. The car was built in the 1930s for the dry lakes then converted into a dragster in the 1950s. *Tom Madigan*

Looking down on a state-of-the-art 1950s fuel dragster, owned by Ken Lindley and driven by Bob Alsenz. The car was powered by a Potvin-style supercharged Chrysler Hemi and ran consistently over 150 mph. Although "Competition Body Shop Special" was painted on the side, the crew affectionately referred to the dragster as Miss Fire. Hot Rod/Motor Trend *Archives*

It is reasonable to assume that not every participant in the rise of Top Fuel racing in California was a daring, unbridled warrior sitting behind the wheel of a monster machine. Many who played vital roles were not drivers, car builders, or creators of revolutionary pieces of equipment, but, nevertheless, they made contributions considered critical to the history of the sport.

When reviewing the history of drag racing in California, two names consistently waft through like a breeze in summer. One was a cross between an old-time Hollywood movie-star agent and a Fortune 500 entrepreneur. The other was a pioneer of the dry lakes and the birth of hot rodding. Both were visionaries. Together, the late Robert E. Petersen and Wally Parks changed the complexion and character of drag racing in California and the rest of the country, with their most prominent impact occurring in the period between 1950 and 1970.

Singlehandedly, these two men raised drag racing from a street-racing endeavor of outlaws, disdained by the general public, to a legitimate automobile racing category that became recognized around the world. But, more important was the fact

that, through their efforts, drag racing established itself, like NASCAR and dirt track, as an All-American form of racing. Homegrown in the USA, open to anyone who wanted to race.

Robert E. Petersen, nicknamed Pete, is a California native. He was born in Boyle Heights, a suburb of Los Angeles, in 1926. At the time, Boyle Heights was a predominantly Jewish neighborhood, and Petersen once remarked, "It was a great place to grow up because all of the mothers on the block watched out for the kids and they made sure we were fed. We were never hungry, no matter how tough the times."

At the height of the Depression, the Petersen family moved to the desert town of Palmdale, and it was there that Pete got his introduction to the dry lakes and fast cars. Young Pete would hitchhike to

During the 60s, Top Fuel was open to new ideas and innovations. The cars were all different, not like the cookie-cutter models we have today. Many Top Fuel cars ran two engines; this one even ran four rear tires, each set powered by its own engine.
Steve Reyes

There is no such thing as being handicapped in Top Fuel racing, you simply overcame the obstacles. Joe Winter lays down burn-out bleach for his Top Fuel car, Swinger I, as the driver gets ready to heat the tires. *Steve Reyes*

the lakes, riding with names like Bobby Meeks, Vic Edelbrock Sr., Ak Miller, and a teenaged Wally Parks. When he was old enough, he built his own ride and actually started racing.

As the times grew more difficult, the Petersen family was forced to give up the desert and return to the city, this time to Hollywood. Young Robert E. found work at MGM Studios. He started as an errand boy and then became a guide or, as Petersen puts it, "I would take big stars around and show them where everything was located, including the bathrooms."

With hard work and a lot of smiles, Petersen hit the big time and moved up to the Public Relations Department, where he became a publicist. Then the bright lights went out in 1941.

World War II put Robert E. in the skies over Europe as a reconnaissance photographer. While in the Army Air Force, he noted one undeniable fact—the young men fighting the war had two things on their minds: girls and hot cars.

Petersen received a life lesson when the war ended. Serving your country did not guarantee your old job would be waiting when you got back. The studio informed Pete that his services were no longer required. Petersen took up with a gang of ex-publicists who shared the same fate, and formed a loose-knit alliance called Hollywood Publicity Associates.

Petersen's life took an unpredictable turn as he struggled with the insanity of Hollywood. His buddy, then-President of the SCTA (Southern California Timing Association) Wally Parks, was feeling pressure from law enforcement and the

Some early drag strips did not offer much in the way of safety precautions. Wally Parks and the NHRA were pioneers in the improvement of safety conditions at strips around the country. With their Safety Safari, they had a traveling crew capable of setting up a portable drag strip, complete with timing lights and technical inspectors, to put on events across the country. They did this not only to promote drag racing, but safe drag racing. *Don Brown*

In an effort to "spread the gospel of safe hot rodding," Wally Parks and the NHRA created the Safety Safari, a team of officials who traveled the country setting up drag racing events and teaching the rules of safe racing. Sometimes things didn't go according to plan. *Author's collection/Eric Rickman photo*

National Safety Council to voice opposition to illegal street racing. It got so bad that the Los Angeles Police Department and the Safety Council tried to close the dry lakes to racing of any kind.

Hot rodding was at a crossroads. It might have been banned or legislated out of existence, the industry we enjoy today dying as a dream. But, Wally Parks took the fight to the invaders and began to lobby for hot rodding. He was the evangelist of hot cars, and he preached safe driving, club membership, and racing at the lakes. Parks convinced his friend, Bob Petersen, to join the fight and become a spokesman for the SCTA and its newsletter, of which Wally was editor. Petersen agreed, and soon the rally cry was "Safety First." "Drive Carefully, Save a Life" became a motto.

In order to help improve the hot rodder profile, a car show produced by Wally Parks called the Hot Rod Exposition was held at the National Guard Armory in Los Angeles. The show went off without a hitch. Indeed, it proved to be a block buster, and the pieces of a complex puzzle fell into place in a very short period of time.

Prior to the car show, Robert Petersen decided that a magazine for hot rodders would go a long way toward improving the plight of the enthusiast. He joined forces with a fellow MGM expatriate

named Bob Lindsay and the two pieced together a concept for a magazine dedicated to hot rods. The idea gained momentum and, with the help of Wally Parks, Petersen and Lindsay succeeded in producing a magazine specifically for the hot rod enthusiast.

The staff consisted of Parks, Petersen, Lindsay, Richard Sobotka, Lee Blaisdell, Don Miller, Hugh Gilbert, and two eastern reporters named John Lelis and Anthony "Andy" Granatelli. The first bound issue of *Hot Rod* magazine, dated January 1948, was ready for delivery as the Hot Rod Exposition opened its doors. From that historic moment, the sport of drag racing and *Hot Rod* magazine would be forever linked.

Wally Parks became editor of *Hot Rod* magazine in 1949. But, Parks had his own vision, and in 1951, along with legendary racer Ak Miller and a friend named Marvin Lee, founded and became president of a fledgling organization called the National Hot Rod Association. The NHRA and Top Fuel drag racing in California, as did *Hot Rod* magazine and Top Fuel drag racing, would grow into a relationship that, like marriage, would have good times and bad times. However, history should show that without Robert E. Petersen and Wally Parks, drag racing in California, and across the nation, may have played out in a very different way.

CHAPTER THREE

INCUBATION

Your humble author in 1964, learning the fuel dragster ropes. The car is a Fuller chassis with a Pfaff & Sowins small-block Chevy motor. *Dave Sowins*

As author and contriver of this story, I feel, considering I was also present during the period, that it is both acceptable and justifiable to describe my personal experiences and memories of what went on during the time period of 1950 through 1970 with regards to drag racing and its growth.

Being a teenager in southern California as the 1950s hit their midrange was as near to living a dream as the human spirit can endure without getting into illusion. California offered a feeling of optimism.

Los Angeles was a cool place to live and there was plenty to do. For teenage boys, the automobile offered the key to everything exciting—drive-in movies; drive-in restaurants; and girls in tight angora sweaters, poodle skirts, and saddle shoes who giggled with anticipation at the thought of Cruising the Boulevard in a hot car. Most importantly, if you had a car, you could go drag racing.

To a California teenager, drag racing had several advantages over other types of motor racing.

The most obvious was that anyone with a valid driver's license could participate, even if the car you were driving was a dog-stock sled that belonged to your grandmother.

Also, teens of the 1950s were beginning to rebel from the traditional roles teens had played in the past. Drag racing offered a rebellious image—after all, it had come from the streets and was disfavored by parents, police departments, and major city newspapers. Rock and roll music had entered the

Pomona California, 1967. The NHRA Winternationals featured a wild-looking and awesome-running Top Fuel car called "Yellow Fang," owned by Ed "Big Daddy" Roth. *Steve Reyes*

youth environment. Hollywood popularized the seedy side of hot rodding with movies featuring crazy teens on rampages of speed and reckless behavior. James Dean became a cult hero, blending hot rods and hormones together.

And, for the first time since the war years, teens had disposable income. The marketplace began to cater to youth. Teens worked in gas stations, at movie theaters, and in grocery stores. Babysitting became a career move for young girls.

Although wages averaged about a dollar an hour, teenagers were likely to spend more freely than their parents. Life was not very expensive: gas was 23 cents per gallon, movies cost 50 cents, and a great burger topped with fries and a milkshake averaged about two dollars. Teens spent their money on 45-rpm records, magazines, and clothes. The girls wanted to dress like Patti Page and Brigitte Bardot, and the boys leaned toward leather jackets, T-shirts, and engineer boots. And, every red-blooded young rebel envisioned his car as a hot rod, no matter how far from reality that might be.

Those of us who were caught up in drag racing had many options. By 1955, drag strips had blossomed all over Southern California. Of course, there was Santa Ana, but now there were others, including Pomona, Saugus, San Fernando, Riverside, and Long Beach. No one saw drag racing as a billion-dollar industry or as a form of motorsport to rival

any in the world. It was new and not like other auto racing events.

For one thing, every ticket was a pit pass. Once at the track, you were free to wander the pits, inhaling the odors, and feeling the pulse of the cars. The price for most drag strips was between 50 cents and a buck and a half, with an additional charge for a driver's pass, which indicated that you were more than a spectator. You could spend the entire day going from pits to trackside and back. And, unlike circle track racing, the results of the contest came quickly; start to finish, winner and loser determined in seconds. For young spectators, the idea of fast was appealing.

Clear recollections of my first few visits to a drag strip have become faded and dull with age, but there remain a few incandescent flashes that light the way into my memory. For me, the act of going to the drags, be they at Santa Ana or Long Beach, was in every way a considerable adventure.

In Los Angeles and its surrounding cities, the freeway system was barely off the drawing board and most drag strips were located in rural areas. During the drive, there always seemed to be time for telling dirty jokes, listening to the hottest songs on the radio, and bragging about girls. Once at the strip, the most vivid sensory perceptions were the smells and sounds that filled the air.

The pit area reeked of gear oil, gasoline, over-heated clutches, and the faint odor of burnt rubber.

When Ontario Motor Speedway opened in 1970, it offered not only a 2 1/2-mile oval, but also a state-of-the-art drag strip. The NHRA was quick to seize the moment and began running major events there. *Don Brown*

By the late 1960s tire technology had reached the point where the "burn out" became part of the starting line ritual. A crew member looks on as the Glen & Schultz Top Fuel dragster heats the slicks before a run at Lions. *Ed Justice Jr.*

And, of course, there's no mistaking the eye-burning, soul-addicting fumes of nitromethane. Once inhaled, the effects of nitro vapors last a lifetime.

There was also the noise. All types of cars would warm for battle in the pits, producing an oscillating staccato that phased between the sharp piercing scream of a six-cylinder GMC, the rasping growl of a flathead Ford, and the deep roar of a Chrysler Hemi. Then, transcending all the other sounds, the thundering fuel burners were heard.

There were no fancy trailers or motorhomes. Racers either towed cars behind pickup trucks or mounted them on simple open haulers. Most of the pit areas were a combination of poorly laid asphalt or hard packed gravel. The crews worked in the open, without the benefit of sun protection. Tool boxes were stationed on tailgates, and most teams drafted wives or girlfriends to make up a food supply.

Of the many drag strips I attended as a teenager, all had one common attribute: the camaraderie between competitors was that of a family. Everyone was willing to help when needed and then compete when the time was right. Whenever the old-timers talk about the 1950s, one subject remembered with fondness is how racers gave to one another so they could compete on a level field.

In the early days, drag races were conducted in a less restricted atmosphere than today. Most of the cars were push started, then would roll into position for the race. Drivers and crews had to watch out for their own safety. *Ed Justice Jr.*

Then there were the cars. Over the period of a year or two, certainly before I finished high school in 1956, I was lucky enough to witness firsthand nearly all the big-name dragsters running in Southern California at the time. Words fall short when recollecting the dragsters of the period and the effects they had on those of us who stood along the strip of black pavement, spellbound by their splendor.

Five decades after those summer days, what remains vivid in my memory are the sights and sounds created by cars that seemed malformed, yet strangely compelling. Chills traversed my spine when Lloyd Scott and the Bustle Bomb staged at the starting line. The Weiand Manifold-sponsored monster had two powerful engines: a Cadillac and an Oldsmobile, front and rear. Scott drove from the middle, clad in Levis, T-shirt, Cromwell crash helmet, and goggles. He was protected by only a lap belt and a very primitive roll bar. The car was unpredictable. Sometimes it ran on both engines and blasted down the strip; sometimes it ran with one engine stumbling and

then correcting as the second engine balked, lurching the beast down the track like a twin-engine bucking bronco and drawing a collective gasp from the crowd.

The second monster I remember inspiring a wide-eyed stare was a car driven by a fellow named Manny Coelho. Manny was a popular driver in the mid-1950s. His creation, as I recall, featured two engines: one a flathead Ford and the other a Chrysler Hemi. The chassis resembled a bridge girder, on some occasions covered by a handmade, rudimental body. More often than not, though, Manny sat exposed to the elements, protected by nothing more than his helmet.

Of course, other cars and other racers sparked intense reactions from fanatics like me. The Bean Bandits; Cook & Bedwell; Calvin Rice; Ed and Roy Cortopassi and their Glass Slipper; Romeo Palamides and his full-bodied dragster; and the tiny, unreal Fiat coupe of Jim Jazzy Nelson all made spectators stare in wonder. Throughout the 1950s, change and the wonder of invention was as much a part of drag racing as anything else.

Calvin Rice and the J.E. Riley & Sons dragster was the car to watch when the big dogs ran at places like Santa Ana. Calvin dusted off many of the hot racers of the day including Mickey Thompson, Art Chrisman, Jazzy Nelson, and the Bean Bandits. The car started out with a Mercury flathead but ended up with a Chrysler Hemi. Hot Rod/Motor Trend *Archives*

By the mid-to-late 1950s, Fuel-burning dragsters began to evolve rapidly. Mickey Thompson's version of the slingshot-style dragster, Buddy Sampson and Lefty Mudersbach and the Money Olds digger, and the Nesbitt's Orange car all were being built from tubing rather than rail. The Chevy small-block engine, introduced in 1955, would prove to be one of the most popular engines ever used in drag racing.

Then, to the mortification of the California racers, fuel-burning dragsters began coming from other parts of the country and making their marks. There was much too much happening, as dragsters began to defy reality. Speeds increased to the point where experts just shut up and shook their collective heads.

Admittedly, the fuel-burning dragsters were my favorite cars to watch, but there was one exception. A car that made my head swirl and my heart pound, and it wasn't even a dragster. It was built by and raced by two men who would later write many chapters in the Top Fuel history book. But the car of which I speak came before the pair would set their marks.

The two men were Frank Cannon and Art Chrisman, and the car was a 1955 Ford Thunderbird powered by a Chrysler Hemi. Let me tell you, back in 1950s when that T-Bird would roll to the starting line, all eyes focused on the machine. The car was loud and usually ran rich; it created bellows of nitro fumes as it got ready to launch. When Chrisman unloaded the clutch, the grandstands would shake and all of your emotions went off the chart.

One of the first sponsorship deals in California drag racing was created when Bob Armstrong and Maurice Richer actually received a few bucks from a soda pop company called Nesbitt's Orange. Hot Rod/Motor Trend *Archives*

Chrisman and Cannon teamed on many projects after the T-Bird. Everyone knows the most famous, the car called Hustler One; in the days when Top Fuel competition began to exceed the 180-mile-per-hour mark, Hustler One became the car by which others were judged, in both results and image.

CHAPTER FOUR

STRAIGHT SHOOTER

King of Top Fuel in the late 1950s and early 1960s was the team of Chrisman Brothers & Cannon, with their fuel burning monster, Hustler I. The car was driven by Art Chrisman, shown dressed in the uniform of the era: leather pants and jacket. Art proved himself to be a champion driver, one of the all-time greats in California Top Fuel history. *Bob Muravez Collection*

When it came time to bench race about the days when Top Fuel began to rise up and be recognized, I picked Art Chrisman to offer his comments. Having told the stories over and over through the years, Chrisman wondered out loud if telling them again was a good idea. I convinced him that history needed to be recounted one more time.

Chrisman and I had crossed paths in the late 1960s and early 1970s when, as a journalist, I covered events and press junkets offered by the Ford Motor Company and the Autolite Spark Plug Company. At the time, the two were affiliated, and many of their programs became joint ventures. One occasion in particular was the running of the Autolite Lead Wedge, a battery-powered streamliner that ran at the Bonneville Salt Flats. Chrisman was part of the team, and he allowed journalists, including myself, to drive the car.

During the years in which Chrisman and I came in contact, I was impressed by his character in several ways. He was ever the gentleman, treating everyone equally, regardless of status. He never over-reacted to situations, and he carried a sense of calm no matter how hectic the moment. And, as a racer, Chrisman never elaborated on any accomplishment he attained during his career. To him, it was just racing and that's what he wanted to do, so whatever came of it was no big deal.

We met at CARS, a restoration shop owned by Art and his son Mike. Although in his seventies, Art

One of California Drag Racing's greatest photographers captures one of the most famous California dragsters. Eric Rickman, pioneer lensman for *Hot Rod* magazine snaps Art Chrisman in the fabled Number 25 car at Santa Ana drag strip. *Author's collection/Rickman photo*

Chrisman shows little sign of the ravages of age. We sat in the middle of the shop, surrounded by some of the most stunning and desirable street rods and vintage race cars the mind can imagine. I wanted to know about the days when the Hustler was new and drag racing was evolving.

The Chrismans came to California from Arkansas, trying, like many families, to overcome the pain and suffering of the Dust Bowl and the Great Depression. It was little wonder that California appeared as the Promised Land. As it turned out, the Chrisman clan landed in Compton. The family patriarch was Everett Chrisman. He had two sons, Art and Lloyd, plus a younger brother named Jack. Everett found work as a welder in the shipyards located in San Pedro, but later joined the war effort, enlisting in the Navy. The oldest of Everett's sons, Lloyd, was drafted. Young Art, only 13 years old at the time,

remained in Compton with his grandparents until Everett returned from his tour of duty.

After the war, Everett returned home, as did Lloyd. Lloyd and Art suggested to their dad that they should open a small auto repair shop. Everett agreed, and the Chrisman & Sons Garage began making history. The really cool aspect of Chrisman & Sons was the fact that Everett's younger brother, Lloyd and Art's Uncle Jack, opened a gas station in front of the shop. Thus did Compton, California, become home to the Chrisman clan and a part of hot rodding history. Hot cars were but a quick step away for the Chrisman boys.

Throughout the history of hot rodding, drag racing, and even going back to the early days of the dry lakes, certain characters within the sport possessed an innate ability to build fast cars, to produce flawless work while doing the job, and to always be able to find the answers and go faster than a competitor. Art Chrisman is one of those characters. Between Art, Lloyd, and Uncle Jack, racing machines exploded from the tiny Compton Garage. There were coupes and roadsters; cars for the lakes, Bonneville Salt Flats, and drags strips; personal cars; and customer cars. Chrisman-built racing machines were sought after and the garage became a focal point where the fast guys converged.

It would take industrial-sized archives to chronicle all of the incredible cars built by the Chrisman team. So a choice was made, and two legendary cars were selected for our purposes. Both cars are historic, and both have Art as the driver of record. Before getting to the machines, one interesting point should be considered about the Chrisman history.

Although the family worked together building cars, they never really raced as a team. Art and Lloyd took one direction, and Uncle Jack went in another. Jack became a National Champion dragster driver. He created one of the very first Funny Cars and he suffered two of the most horrific injuries a dragster driver could suffer. There will be more on Uncle Jack as our story unfolds. For now, it is the 1950s and Art Chrisman was to become a player.

NUMBER 25

Art Chrisman entered the world of fuel-burning dragsters in 1953, behind the wheel of the first of the two cars that would establish his legacy. Everyone who knows anything about the history of drag racing has heard of the car. It is simply remembered as Number 25. Art and Number 25 were the first to break the 140-mile-per-hour barrier at Santa Ana, and they would go on to race at the first-ever NHRA Championship. Today, the tiny digger is preserved for posterity within the confines of the NHRA Motorsports Museum in Pomona, California. Number 25, a modified-roadster-turned-dragster, remains one of a handful of machines created in the 1950s to which Drag Racing owes its genealogy.

According to Dean Batchelor in his book *The American Hot Rod*, Number 25 was conceived by a man named Harry Lewis in the mid-1930s to be run at the dry lakes, powered by a Rajo T engine. Later, the car was sold to several owners, including Ernie McAfee. The Rajo engine was replaced by a Ford flathead and the car continued running the lakes. More changes of ownership finally brought the car to pioneer hot rodder and race car owner Leroy Neumayer.

By the time Number 25 reached Neumayer, it had been modified and repainted and changed from lakes racer to street machine and back again. Neumayer was about to get serious about racing the car when the Korean War stepped in, and he was drafted. Before Leroy went to war, he turned the responsibility for the car over to his friend, Art Chrisman. Art picks up the story of Number 25.

ART CHRISMAN

My whole drag racing thing got started in the early 1950s with a '36 Ford sedan that I built as a custom car for racing on the streets. The guys would race at night, but back then the cops were pretty cool. Most of them would turn their siren and red lights on about two miles before they would get to us, and we had plenty of time to disappear. But street racing was still a problem and a lot of guys got hurt.

Then C.J. Hart opened up Santa Ana Drag Strip, and I took the sedan out and ran 101 miles per hour, which was fast for a bold, old tub. When Leroy got this old modified roadster, we took the engine out of my '36 and we started running as a team. After Leroy was drafted, I continued running the car. I extended the wheelbase out to 110 inches to make it handle better.

At the time, fuel (nitro) was a big issue, and I had learned a lot about it from Tony Capanna. Tony was a dry lakes pioneer, superb engine builder, and, along with partner Red Wilson, had a shop known by all who wanted to go fast, called Wil-Cap. The shop specialized in dynamometer testing and racing fuel sales. We started upping the percentage of nitro until we were the first fuel-burning dragster to go 140 miles per hour.

But, all that joy was short lived. It didn't take long before we all began to realize that the Ford flathead was not going to live much longer. The Chrysler Hemi was on the horizon, but for a few moments in time, the guys running the Hemi didn't know how to get the power out of the engine. And when they did, the car lost traction from tire spin.

In 1955, we took the 25 car back to Great Bend, Kansas, for the very first NHRA Nationals. Before heading east, we replaced the flathead with a Chrysler. We ran 149 miles per hour in qualifying and won a brand-new Chrysler engine, complete in a crate. It was the biggest thing I had ever won. Our luck didn't last. During eliminations, we discovered our weakness. We were still running a Ford three-speed transmission, and it wouldn't take the power. Every time I yanked it into high gear, the transmission would come apart and we would have to change it for a replacement. Finally, I got beat by the Bean Bandits.

The kicker to the race was the fact that it rained out the finals. So, the first complete National event was later, in Phoenix, Arizona, when Calvin Rice, who had run a Chrysler at Great Bend, swapped back to a flathead and beat Fritz Voight in the final race. Although Calvin won with a flathead, it didn't take a rocket scientist to figure out the flathead was dead. The Hemi would become king of Top Fuel and none of us really understood just how big a deal the small block Chevy would become.

THE HUSTLERS

Art continued to race, both at drag races and at Bonneville. The 1950s rocked on, and drag racing grew in popularity and in the performance of the cars. Drag strips were going nationwide, and names from back east headed west. The legendary Setto Postoian came west and other non-California racers started setting records and winning national events. Out of Ohio, Art Arfons was running an airplane engine in a dragster. Melvin Heath, from Rush Springs, Oklahoma, won the 1956 Nationals.

And there was another name being bandied about, someone to look out for. The rumors flew: this guy from the swamps of Florida was a real runner. His name was Garlits, and he was building his own cars and setting records at drag strips all over the southeast. But talk was cheap. Word in California was that Garlits ran short strips, tracks with questionable clocks, and he was a one-man band. California racers had no fear of Don Garlits.

California racers had their head in the sand, say some historians. Drag racing was becoming a monster, and new strips were appearing everywhere: Texas, Florida, Colorado, Ohio, Michigan, Illinois, Arizona, Oregon, Oklahoma, and the list was growing. Fuel-burning dragsters were growing in numbers like a family of rabbits. Still, California remained the leader in the production of speed equipment and drag racing technology, and was still home to the biggest names in the fuel-burning class.

For Art Chrisman, drag racing had become a part-time occupation, second to running his shop. The occasional blast across the Salt Flats of

The late top Fuel drag racing champion Calvin Rice gave California something to cheer about in 1955 when he won the first-ever NHRA Top Eliminator title at the Nationals in Great Bend, Kansas (rain delayed the finish so the event concluded in Phoenix, Arizona). Rice ran the J.E. Riley & Sons dragster with both a Ford flathead and a Chrysler Hemi (shown here), and always on fuel. Hot Rod/Motor Trend *Archives*

Not all of the early dragsters were powered by a single engine or a conventional V-8. Here, driver Art Arfons smokes the tires of his Green Monster I, powered by an Allison airplane engine. The Monster was too heavy and slow (and, apparently, smoked the tires too much) to overcome the quickness of Jack Moss and his twin-engine dragster. *Don Brown*

Bonneville, coupled with a few quarter-mile events, were satisfying enough—until he had a meeting with a customer named Frank Cannon. Mr. Cannon had two passions: drilling core holes through solid rock for oil exploration, and racing fast cars. Cannon's latest project was a 1955 Ford Thunderbird running a Y-block Ford engine with a supercharger.

Art and Frank hit it off from the beginning, because both had the same goal: going faster than anyone else. Frank had a few bucks in his pocket and Art had all the talent they needed. Combined, they made a great team.

First, they pitched the Y-block in favor of a 450-cubic-inch Chrysler Hemi. The result was a jaw-dropper. Those who saw the T-Bird run, myself included, have never forgotten the blast from the

exhaust as the Bird blasted down the drag strip. But, Cannon and Chrisman were not satisfied with fast, they wanted faster. The partners decided to go outside the box and create something bigger and better. The result of their dream became the second of the mythological Chrisman cars.

If forced to make a list of images that best represented the Top Fuel dragster as the 1950s ended and the 1960s began, the Chrisman & Cannon Hustler One would be at the top. Art picks up the story of Hustler One from his own recollections.

ART CHRISMAN
When the slingshot dragster design was first created by guys like Calvin Rice and Mickey Thompson, it was plain as day that dragsters like

Number 25 were rendered obsolete in a heartbeat. Those cars showed up at Great Bend, Kansas, and I could see the handwriting on the wall. The sit-up-straight style car, with the driver over the rear axle, was not the way to go. I talked things over with my brother Lloyd and Frank; it was a unanimous decision that we would build a purpose-built slingshot-style dragster.

Lloyd and I built a tube chassis in a slingshot design, and along the way we integrated all of the features we thought would work, including a safe roll bar and a comfortable seating position. When the chassis was completed, we pulled the Chrysler out of Cannon's T-Bird and we ran a couple of meets. But the results were just not there, because our first setup had the engine running gasoline using Hilborn injectors.

In 1958, we changed the configuration to a Chuck Potvin-style front-mounted blower, and we had a Z-drive gearbox out of a boat between the engine and the blower so we could overdrive the supercharger. The car was also sporting a fully enclosed body, running from the front axle to the driver's compartment. We took the car to Oklahoma City for the NHRA Nationals. We won the Best Engineered Car award, and figured we had a chance of dusting off the competition during eliminations.

The night before the final eliminations, one of the crew decided that we needed to put more power in the engine. So he decided that changing the gear ratio in the blower overdrive was a great idea. That may have been good news in his mind, but the bad news was he couldn't see very well, as instead of raising the ratio 10 percent, he upped it 40 percent. The change made so much power that the car was unmanageable. The second I lit the engine, I knew we were in trouble. We raced Cyr and Hopper, and Ted Cyr blew my doors off because the tires smoked the length of the track.

After that meet, we came back to California and rented Riverside Raceway and did some testing to get a handle of what was needed to make the car run strong. The decision was made to put the blower on top of the engine so the car would get better traction. The problem became the lack of a manifold to use with a top-mounted blower. Because we used a GMC 6-71 blower, there wasn't a production manifold available to fit, so we took a Weiand casting and machined our own custom manifold.

With the new system in place, Hustler One became the first fuel dragster to run 180 miles per hour on the West Coast. We became overnight heroes, and every drag strip in California wanted us to run. With Cannon paying the bills, we cleaned up our act and started to look like a professional team.

With a full body, leather cockpit area, beautiful paint job, and that big Hemi and top-mounted blower, the Hustler put on a real show. Not only did the car run hard, but it sounded loud and the fans loved it. We even started wearing matching uniforms and looked like an Indy-car team when we would show up at a track. I feel that we were a forerunner to the modern team.

We continued to make changes on Hustler One every week. It went from running a Halibrand quick-change rear end with a two-speed transmission to an Oldsmobile rear end and a direct-drive unit with high gear only. We worked hard to cut weight, and continued to up the nitro percentages until it was over 50 percent.

In 1959, the Smokers Car Club in Bakersfield decided to promote a drag race based on the East vs. West rivalry that had become such a big deal. All of the Eastern racers wanted to come to California and kick our butts to prove that they could run as hard as we did. I'm sure that the story of Bakersfield will be brought up plenty before this book is over. Anyway, the race was to feature Top Fuel cars, and so the first U.S. Fuel & Gas Championships was born.

Don Garlits had run 180 miles per hour back East, and he wanted to come out to California and prove himself. The Smokers paid him appearance money to show up. He shows up with an unblown car with six carburetors. We just stared and thought no way is this guy going to beat us. Well, Garlits broke or something happened, I don't remember, but we ended up winning the meet and he went back to Tampa leaving his carburetors behind and taking a blower with him. We sent him home with his butt kicked, but he would come back to do some butt-kicking of his own.

After the 59 Smokers meet, Frank wanted to drive too, so we built a second dragster called Hustler II, but it was a space-frame car, lighter, and used a smaller engine. Frank turned out to be a good driver, but he never liked Hustler One. We went back to Bakersfield in 1960 and '61, finishing runner-up both years.

By 1962, Hustler One had run its course and became obsolete. At the same time, I went to work for Ford's Autolite division, and Hustler One ended up parked on the side of my shop. Many years later, I restored it and put it in the NHRA Museum, but we pull it out from time to time to run at vintage events.

As for Uncle Jack, he accomplished more as a driver than I ever thought about doing. He drove for Mickey Thompson, won the first NHRA

Not every run was a perfect run. In the early days, crashes were common as chassis builders and drivers used trial and error to explore the outer limits of going fast. Sometimes the results were happier than others. *Don Brown*

Winternationals in the Howard Cams Twin Bear Chevy. Uncle Jack broke new ground when he drove the rear-engine Sidewinder and the fantastic Chuck Jones/Kent Fuller Magwinder, two cars way ahead of their time. Jack was one of the first Funny Car racers with his GT-1 SOHC 427 Mercury factory experimental machine. Uncle Jack liked to tour and he traveled all over the country running major events. He was one of the greats.

There was a tragic side to his life that haunted him until he quit racing. Old Uncle Jack had two of the worst crashes you could ever imagine. The rear end housing on a dragster he was driving broke loose and spun around inside the driver's cockpit. The front part of the rear end caught Jack between the legs, and he received absolutely terrible damage to his vital

organs. Later, while he was driving the Magwinder, a rear-engine dragster with a chassis constructed from magnesium tubing, its push bar broke and the pickup truck pushing the car came over the top of the roll bar and tore Uncle Jack's helmet off.

As for myself, I was gone from Top Fuel racing by 1962 and would never return to competition. Uncle Jack, my brother Lloyd, who never really got the credit he deserved as a car builder, and Frank Cannon are all gone. All I can say about the period we raced was it was a time when the drag racing business was new and everything we did was exciting. Mostly, it was the friendships and the close-knit feeling of family that we all had about racing.

Today, it's all about money. Back then, it was all about racing.

CHAPTER FIVE

THE CAMFATHER

Whether or not fuel-burning dragsters originated in California, other parts of the country still had a share in the early development. Jack Moss (Jack the Giant Killer) came from Texas to whip many a California hotshot. Moss, like all racers in the old days, built everything on his own. *Don Brown*

Automobile racing in California constantly seemed to exploit one advantage it had over the rest of the country: it was the nucleus for the manufacturing of speed equipment. Since the days of the dry lakes, the pioneers in the creation of performance parts had roots in California. This is not to say that all manufacturing came from California, but certainly a large percentage of the well-known names in racing called the Garden State home.

There were two reasons behind California's performance parts production advantage. One, of course, was the weather. The other centered on skills learned in the aircraft business, which blossomed in California during World War II. Not to belabor the issue, but agreement can be reached that many of the products synonymous with speed got their start in California.

Not every hero in the Old-West was a gunfighter, wore a sheriff's badge, or rode a white horse. Similarly, as we discussed earlier, not every hero in the history of California drag racing was a driver blazing down the strip and leaving a trail of tire smoke. Some of the great characters in the story of drag racing stayed in the background, away from the roaring crowd. But, without the innovations and contributions of those who preferred to avoid public adoration, the daring deeds of our racing heroes would have been far more difficult to accomplish.

Ed Iskenderian is one such behind-the-scenes character. Born in 1921 to Armenian parents, baby Ed spent his first few years on a vineyard in Tulare

If California Top Fuel drivers could use only one image to project the personality of a hard running, independent racer, it might very well be that of 60s driver Dennis Baca. A tough competitor who always brought a strong-running car, Dennis marched to his own drummer and took on any challenger. *Steve Reyes*

County near Fresno, California. The vineyard was part of a sizeable farming community in the region. However, farming was not in the cards for the Iskenderians, and several years of bad weather forced the closure of their vineyard. The family moved to Los Angeles in search of a better life. Young Ed found that Los Angeles provided a breeding ground for the cultivation of his greatest interest. Not growing crops, but a fascination with hot cars and racing. Racing would become his life's work.

As a teenager, Ed built his own roadster and went to the dry lakes, like most young men of his time. But the urge to drive faster than anyone else was never a priority. What Ed found most intriguing was the mechanical workings of fast cars. Due to his Armenian heritage, Ed also placed a high value on making a living. He never wanted to relive the days on the farm when crops were lost and the bills came due.

Iskenderian worked hard at learning the world of racing, and he would become one of the best-known names in the creation of racing camshafts. Nicknamed "The Camfather," Iskenderian played a huge role in the development of drag racing in the years between 1950 and 1970, especially in the ranks of Top Fuel machines.

His friends refer to Ed Iskenderian as Isky, and it is simply a fact that you can feel nothing but warmth for the man when you spend time in his company. Isky is not an overpowering person, but his mannerisms allow you to feel comfortable and he seems to pull you into the conversation with his soft, reassuring voice. Without realizing the cause, you focus on the words coming from the man and you take everything spoken as the truth. Not that you are overwhelmed, but you want to listen because there is so much wisdom in his words.

I met Ed Iskenderian in 1964 while building my fuel digger. He offered to help me and asked his foreman at the time, Sig Erson (Erson would become a noted cam manufacturer in later years), to come up with a camshaft and kit for my Chevy small block. I never forgot the kindness, so when it came time to choose my list of those who lived the California drag racing story, Ed Iskenderian jumped onto our pages.

The interview took place in the lobby of his manufacturing facility in Los Angeles. In business since 1946, the company moved into its present location in 1966.

The very act of interviewing Isky is an experience that only happens once in a lifetime. Ed is a "keeper," which means that every scrap of information, every catalog, magazine, order invoice, note, letter, engine combination, and tidbit of memorabilia ever to pass through his hands has been preserved. His warehouse is filled with tools, machines, engines, furniture, collectables, a Model A coupe, countless stray cats, and one 1950 black & white TV. Even more amazing is the fact that he can recall the location of every item that fills the vastness of the complex.

Ed and I decided to fast-forward through the years and try to extract as many details as possible concerning drag racing from its start in the 1950s and its growth through the 1960s. As we settled into our position at a table in the center of the lobby, customers, racers, salesmen, and employees continued to conduct business as usual. Ed, with his trademark cigar secured in place, began to hold court, sharing his stories with anyone who wanted to listen.

Now in his eighties, Isky has the mind of a much younger man. In a voice soft but filled with expression, Isky was about to condense 60 years of hot rodding into a single tape recording. He seemed to enjoy going back to his beginnings, so he started with his childhood.

I was born in Cutler, California, a small town located in the central part of the state, but we moved to Southern California when I was still a young boy. Back in those days, cars were every boy's dream and we would ride our bicycles as fast as we could, making believe that we were driving a real car. Every once in a while, something would go zipping up and we would all yell, "Wow, what was that?" It would be a Model T, or maybe a Chevy, all stripped down, no fenders. Back then we called them "Gow Jobs" or "Hot Irons." There weren't any hot rods back then.

One day, we were at a friend of mine's house when a guy named Jack Andrews comes wheeling up in his "Gow Job." It was a Model T with an SR Frontenac (Fronty) high-performance engine, Winfield carburetors, a Franklin front axle, a Ruckstell two-speed rear axle, and Rocky Mountain brakes. We just stared in wonder at this wild machine, and when he took off there was a roar and a cloud of dust and I thought, "Boy, what could be more fun than that?"

In those days, it was up to your own imagination. There were so many cars in junkyards and you could buy parts really cheap. You could build a "Gow Job" to your own specifications. I remember building cars were my daydreams. I would sit on our porch and think about what I would build if I had money. But we didn't have much money, so it was just fun to dream.

Sometimes the older guys would ask us kids if we wanted to go to the dry lakes. Oh man, what a thrill. We would save up a dollar or two and tag along. I remember the open space of the lakes, and the hot, dry winds, and all of the cars. You could smell the gear oil and fuel mixed with the desert air, and there would be cars from all over the state. It was a grand feeling for a young kid.

You could learn so much because the guys would tell you whatever you wanted to know. The racers saw us kids as the next generation of competitors.

When I finally built my first car, Ed Winfield ground the camshaft, and he was nice enough to show me his cam grinder, with his own rocker bar attachment. He took a liking to me for some reason, and he explained his methods, and I learned the difference between duration and lift. Winfield was known for his carburetor work, but he was also a pioneer in camshaft design. Sometimes I look back on those days and marvel that I learned something from Ed Winfield.

When I got out of the Army, I decided to follow in the footsteps of the great Ed Winfield. In my mind, he had given cam grinding special status, because he knew more about engines and racing cars than anyone we had ever heard of, so he was a hero to those of us who loved cars. Winfield made cam grinding sound like a very sophisticated art form, and you got a lot of respect if you told people you were a cam grinder, so I wanted to make cam grinding my life's work.

Just by luck, I started experimenting by trial and error and hit on a pretty good design for the Ford flathead. At first, I thought I was horning in on Winfield's business, but I kept going. Then Clay Smith started grinding cams. He had learned from another famous pioneer, named Perrie Bertrand, who had created a cam grinding machine from a lawn-mower-blade sharpener. Clay was a partner with Bill Stroppe, and they were doing a lot of racing using the flathead Ford. Clay told me there was plenty of room in the cam grinding business for everyone.

I started trying different lift and duration combinations. My first cams were very noisy because I made them without clearance ramps. It became somewhat of a joke that my noise problem with the tappets was so bad that you could hear a car running my cam coming down the street from a block away. I didn't realize that I had found something in my designs. I was just trying everything that came into my mind. None of the speed shops would buy my cams. Finally, Karl Orr, the famous dry lakes racer and speed shop owner in Culver City, gave me an order. Karl was a racer first and a shop owner second, so he supported me because he thought I was on to something.

The only way I could sell cams in any kind of number was to the local kids building their first flathead. As a bonus for buying one of my cams, I would help them build the engine.

But, for some reason, I started building up a small inventory, and new customers appeared one at a time. Then one day, I get a phone call from a race team called S&S Stock Car Racers in North Carolina. Bill France had NASCAR going strong down South, and these guys were short-track racers. The team wanted to buy two cams and have the order sent air mail. It seems they liked my cams because they had good low-end and mid-range power, so they could pass cars coming out of corners on the short dirt tracks they raced on. Suddenly, I was popular with the good old boys down South, and selling to those Southern racers put me on the map.

I moved into a larger building just across the street from Vic Edelbrock, Sr., on Jefferson Boulevard in Los Angeles. Well, it turned out to be the best move of my life because Vic would come over and ask me to grind special cam profiles and then test them on his dynamometer. Edelbrock was a great man, and one of the best engine builders ever.

Oh, I have to tell a very interesting Edelbrock story. In 1955, Chevrolet sent out some of their new small-block V-8 engines to various engine builders and asked them to see what they could do with the performance. I think Vic got three engines, Smokey Yunick and Junior Johnson each got several, with the idea that they could develop their own ideas without factory interference.

Well, Vic invited a few cam grinders to profile a cam for the new engine. He wanted to see which cam would work best. In the end, he wouldn't tell who did the best job, but I found out later that my design worked the best. That's the kind of man Vic was—he didn't want to embarrass anyone.

Big changes happened when the OHV V-8 engines from Cadillac and Oldsmobile came out. The writing was on the wall for the flathead. I started working with the drag racers as early as 1950 trying to get more power out of the new V-8 engines, but

there weren't that many available. Junkyards were not getting many, so the racers were still using the six-cylinder GMC, and most of the rest remained loyal to the flathead.

But all that was short-lived. Racers wanted more power and the OHV V-8 was the answer. We all knew that Chrysler was coming out with a Hemi in 1951; what was it like and how would it work were the questions. Everyone had a story. Ed Winfield told me that he had heard Chrysler had hired several new engineers, and most had come from a hot rod background. He also heard that the engineers were told that Chrysler wanted an OHV V-8 like Olds and Cadillac had, but with heads like an Ardun (the OHV conversion created by Arkus-Duntov for the flathead Ford). Thus, the Hemi was conceived.

Racers had two problems with the Hemi: it was expensive to buy new from a dealer, and there just weren't any in the junkyards. As luck would have it, a Chrysler dealer in Bakersfield, California, got a new Chrysler with a pin hole in the block casting, and had

Above and opposite page: When the Funny Car craze took the spotlight from the Top Fuel dragsters, many of the big names either switched outright or added a Funny Car to their team. Funny Cars had fan appeal, and when it got dark at night, they could put on a big show. *Tom Madigan*

to replace the engine. He called Ernie Hashim, a local tire supplier and serious drag racer, and asked if he wanted the engine to put in a dragster.

Other types of racing had already recognized the potential of the Hemi engine. The Pan-American Road Race in Mexico was one example. Tony Bettenhausen of Indy 500 fame, he drove a 1951 Chrysler Saratoga for Karl Kiekhaefer of Mercury Outboard motor fame. American sports car racer

Briggs Cunningham used the new Chrysler Hemi for his 1951 Le Mans 24-hour race effort.

Ernie came to me and wanted a cam ground for his new Hemi. I jumped at the chance. I had profiled a lot of cams for the OHV GMC and Chevy six-cylinder engine, so I followed that train of thinking for the Hemi. Actually, back then, everything we tried was done by-gosh & by-golly. We didn't have a clue of what would work. As soon as

If one 1950s dragster team had to be determined as the most exposed across the pages of *Hot Rod* magazine, it would be the team of Cook & Bedwell. Camshaft manufacturer Ed Iskenderian took full advantage of Emery Cook and Cliff Bedwell in his ads after their dragster shattered the quarter-mile record with a blast of 8.89 ET and 166.97 mph in 1957. Hot Rod/Motor Trend *Archives*

we got the first cam profiles complete, the next step was to add a 6-71 GMC blower mounted out front of the engine and start racing the Fuel Dragster class at the Bakersfield drag strip.

Back in those days, Bakersfield hadn't come up with the big championship event they would become famous for, but it was a popular strip, and all of the really fast teams would haul up from Los Angeles.

When it came to fuel, the guy to beat was old Joaquin Arnett and the Bean Bandit. He had learned about nitro at the dry lakes and he was slick when it came to using it. Arnett gave us some ideas, and within a short period of time Ernie's car started running hard, and I made up an ad featuring his car and the speeds he was turning. It worked; we started getting inquiries from all over.

The Chrysler Hemi got popular in a big hurry, but they were still hard to get. However, I discovered something that very few people know. It's been kind of a secret all these years.

I found out that, down in Texas, some of the oil drillers were buying Chrysler Hemi engines from the factory in bulk and using them to run well pumps. They ran the engines 24 hours a day and used really poor gasoline. The valve seats couldn't take the abuse and would go bad. The oil companies would just yank the engine and put in a new one. We started buying the old engines as fast as we could and reselling them to racers. Those Texas oil boys never knew how much they did for drag racing.

Fuel-burning dragsters got more and more popular and, by the mid to late '50s, I had a good busi-

ness going, but I was always looking for more.

I was fascinated with great advertising, and always wanted to one-up my competition. One great story happened when a fellow named Scotty Fenn called me to say that he was depressed and tired of the hassle of running his business (Chassis Research), and he wanted to leave California. Scotty was the first dragster chassis builder to offer a dragster chassis you could buy over the counter. He had a shop in Los Angeles, and was actually a very bright guy, and had a chassis that worked very well and allowed the average race team to buy his chassis and bolt together a car without much trouble.

Scotty had his own personal dragster chassis that he ended up selling to the team of Emery Cook and Cliff Bedwell down in San Diego. They took the Chassis Research chassis, installed a Chrysler Hemi with a Crower U-Fab manifold, six carburetors, and one of my camshafts. Cook and Bedwell started breaking records and kicking butt. In 1957, they set a record of 166.97 miles per hour with an 8.89 ET. Scotty Fenn had a mind change and decided to stay in the chassis business for a while longer.

I wanted to use Cook and Bedwell in my ads, but how? Again, it was Scotty Fenn who played a role. He and I were talking, and he asked if I had heard about the Italian Formula One teams talking about a five-cycle cam for their racing engines. I had no knowledge but thought, "Wow, what a concept." I could have a five-cycle cam while all the others had a four cycle.

We started making ads featuring the Cook and Bedwell dragster running an Isky five-cycle cam. It worked great. Boy, all of the other manufacturers were really mad, but we were selling cams like crazy. The more I advertised, the more the other cam grinders hated what I was doing. I figured the best thing to do was come up with more ads and start a war.

Going through a popular magazine of the day, I came across an ad featuring a crazy musician named Spike Jones. If you don't remember, Spike Jones made records using all kinds of wild sound effects and noises, crazy stuff, very risqué for the day. This ad showed a table with three statue heads on it: Jones in the center, and on one side was Mozart and the other side was Beethoven looking cross-eyed

The fearless dragster drivers of the early 1950s could never have imagined cars going 300 mph in a quarter mile. They just wanted to have fun. Scientists of the era proclaimed that if cars surpassed 140 mph in a quarter-mile from a standing start the drivers would pass out from shock. Hot Rod/Motor Trend *Archives*

wondering what is this fool doing on our table. I had an idea. I got my artist to draw up an ad with me and Albert Einstein looking cross-eyed. The ad read, "Albert Einstein discovered the fourth dimension and Isky discovered the fifth cycle."

Howard Johansen (Howard's Cams) got so mad they made up an ad showing five bicycle riders. Four had really cool racing bikes, and the fifth rider was wearing a clown suit and a dunce cap, riding an old bike. The idea was to make fun out of the fifth cycle. We counterattacked when one of our sponsored cars won a Top Eliminator. I had Pete Millard (famous cartoonist) draw up a clown driving a pickup truck, towing a race car with an old bike in the truck bed. The clown is holding a trophy out of the window and the caption reads, "Five Cycle wins again."

It was in the late 50s that I really got involved in the Top Fuel dragster craze. I was partial to the little teams, where three or four guys would build a car and share expenses. We initiated a program to lend out cams and kits to these teams. They could trade cams at any time, and we would help with their engine development programs. Once we would get someone running really strong, the other cam grinders would say, "Hey, we can get these guys away from Isky if we give them some money. Isky isn't giving any money."

Engine position became an issue during the late 60s and builders were torn between tilting the engine downward and keeping it level. *Steve Reyes*

So, I would lose a team to other cam grinders over a few bucks.

One of our best early sponsorship deals developed when I got a phone call from Don Garlits. When Ernie started going faster, I made up an ad featuring his car, and Garlits saw the ad. He was running a Hemi, and we sent him the same cam that Ernie was using. Pretty quick Garlits is turning speeds around 180 miles per hour.

I started touting Garlits in my ads, and the California guys got really mad. They would tell me, "Garlits is running on concrete strips and they are way smoother than our strips." Or they said, "The timing lights at the tracks he runs are bogus." The stronger Garlits ran, the madder the California racers got.

Finally, the Smokers Car Club in Bakersfield realized that if they paid Garlits and some of the other Eastern top fuel racers to come out west, they could have a big meet with a lot of paying spectators. It happened in 1959. Garlits wanted $1,500 to come out. The problem was that he had been cheated by some track owners out of his appearance money, and he didn't trust anyone. So, he asked me if I would help. I agreed and I had the Smokers make out a cashier's check for $1,500 and I called Garlits and told him I was holding his money, so he could come out.

I remember that the meet was so big that the crowd trying to get in stretched for miles. I had to ride a bicycle to get in. Somebody told me that the track promoters had so much money coming in that they were putting it into fruit boxes. The promoters never expected so many people. Everyone wanted to see the California racers and the teams from back east fight it out. The fans hated Garlits. He was the Swamp Rat.

With the rocking 60s came a new breed of Top Fuel car. Inventive chassis builders like Ken Fuller, Don Long, Frank Huszar, Woody Gilmore, and Roy Steen joined forces with body sculptors like Bob Sorrel, Doug Kruse, Tom Hanna, and Wayne Ewing to produce works of art posing as race cars. *Don Brown*

What the world knew as a California Top Fuel car improved dramatically by the mid to late 1960s. The major upgrades included a longer wheelbase, far better tires and much-improved clutch combinations. *Ed Justice Jr.*

Garlits ran our cams for a while, then one day I heard that he had a Ray Giovannoni cam box in his push truck. I heard the same story several times, so I called him up and said, "Hey, you're supposed to be running my cam, how come you got that Giovannoni stuff in your push truck?" He said, "Yeah, well, I did that on purpose so you would hear about it. I heard that some of the guys on the west coast are getting more help than I am." And I said, "Well, sometimes when they blow an engine or something, I feel sorry for them and give them some help. Would you like to have some money to run our cams?" He replied, "Boy, that sure would be nice." We settled on $1,000 a year.

But, after a period of time, Giovannoni offered him more than I could afford and he left. Later he went to Crower, and then came back to running our cam. But later still, he went back to Crower and stayed with them for a long time. I never took his moving around personally, because Garlits earned his living racing and he needed the best deals he could find. People don't realize how hard he had it in the early years. Garlits was a super racer, but he also built the cars and tuned the engines. He had to be very tough.

As the '60s came on, Top Fuel cars got longer, the bodies were more aerodynamic, the engines put out increasing power, and the tires had better grip. We found that it was not a good idea to smoke the tires from start to finish, so I worked hard on making cams with longer duration, and with more duration the drivers could flat-foot the throttle off the line and not smoke the tires so bad, and the car would run strong at the top end.

Top Fuel made Iskenderian a big name in the sport. Although most of our sales were to the street builder or the sportsman racer, it was the dragsters that made our name. We had some really awesome cars back then, starting with Ernie Hashim, Cook & Bedwell, Pfaff & Sowins, Cyr & Hopper, Jazzy Nelson, The Greek, Tommy Ivo, Tony Nancy. Mickey Thompson won Top Eliminator at the 1962 NHRA Nationals with Jack Chrisman driving. We got a lot of good ideas from our customers, especially the Fuel racers. Through it all, I always loved the sound and fury of the Top Fuel cars, and my weak spot was teams that were under-funded and needed help. I loved the underdog.

The cam business was very competitive in the 1960s, and I had to fight the competition at every step. So, advertising was a big factor and it was my second love in the business. Fun is the name of the game and, in the 1960s, my great joy was to one-up the competition. I have two great examples.

Dave Zeuschel, who was building the meanest Fuel motors in California, came to me and said, "Ed, I want you to grind me a Super Leggera cam." And I said, "Hey that sounds great, but what is it?" Zeuschel says, "Oh, it's Italian and it means super light." (It was actually a trademark name for an Italian Coach Builder who made bodies for Ferrari.) So, we started advertising a Super Leggera Cam. It drove the other cam grinders nuts.

Another time, the great Keith Black ran a match race with his driver, Tom McEwen, against The Greek, Chris Karamesines, who was running my cam. When it came to the final run, McEwen's engine wouldn't fire and The Greek won. We came up with an ad showing Keith Black with a huge cigarette lighter pointing to McEwen and the caption read, "Keep it lit."

We made good products and the racers knew it, but what was so great about the '50s, '60s, and into the 70s, was the innovation. If any one thing stands out in my mind about the dragsters of the 1950s and 60s, it was the fact that there were so many different types of engines. Ford flatheads, GMC six cylinders, Pontiacs, Lincolns, Chryslers, the small-block Chevy, Cadillacs, DeSotos; it was something new every week. And then there were the racers from back East coming out to battle the California teams, and they brought their own ideas.

Many, many times, what the Top Fuel racers accomplished was done for the first time ever. Everyone wanted to experiment. And first times only happen once.

CHAPTER SIX

GETTING SERIOUS

This was the classic California Top Fuel dragster of the mid-1960s: light chassis, hand formed aluminum body and blown Hemi power. Here Ted Lemond gets ready for a burn-out in The Spoiler. *Steve Reyes*

According to Ed Iskenderian, Scotty Fenn had all but given up on trying to build production dragster chassis—until the chassis he sold to Cook & Bedwell set a top speed record for dragsters. So Fenn opened Chassis Research in Los Angeles and began selling ready-made chassis. Scotty is no longer around to tell his wild tales, but I spoke to Roger Wolford, who worked for Scotty when production was at its peak.

ROGER WOLFORD

Scotty was the first to realize that dragsters needed safer chassis design. He came up with a lot of innovations and made it easy for the average racer to afford a good chassis. The backyard racer knew that something had to be done. The cars were going faster and most guys really didn't know how to design a chassis.

Scotty's first design, the TE-440 (Top Eliminator/four hundred forty yards), had a hoop roll bar design. It was made of 1020 mild steel with a 3-inch bottom tube,

1-1/2-inch top tube, and a 1-1/2inch x 0.120-wall roll bar. His idea with the hoop chassis, or skid-bar as some called it, was a design to absorb energy in a crash. And, he figured that the hoop bar wouldn't catch onto railings or fences in the event of a rollover. Even the firewall hoop was designed to disperse energy.

He was the first chassis builder to include roller-bearing safety hubs, so if you broke an axle it wouldn't fly out of the housing. His K-88, or square-back, design was even more improved and some of the

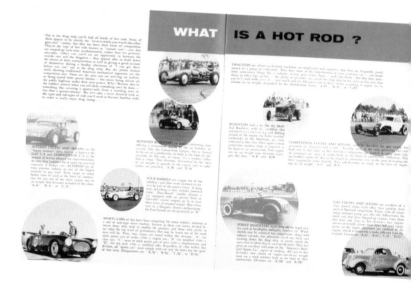

really fast guys started using them. Scotty had a good product, the best deal for the time, and he offered a cheap price. You could buy a complete chassis for 300 bucks, or a kit you weld yourself for less than 200 bucks.

I worked for him nearly three years, and in the end we had our differences, but during his time, he saved a lot of drivers from getting hurt or worse.

THE DRAG MASTERS

Scotty Fenn may have been the first over-the-counter chassis builder, but he would be far from the last. While collecting research material for this book, I discovered a catalog buried deep in a musty cardboard box. Long forgotten, its cover brought back memories and its contents showed just how far drag racing has come.

The catalog was that of a company called Dragmaster, owned and operated by two racers named Dode Martin and Jim Nelson. Once, in the early 1960s, I had talked to Nelson about buying a rolling chassis in order to build a finished dragster. As things worked out, I did not get the Dragmaster chassis, but I did keep the catalog.

In their heyday, the Dragmaster guys offered a customer the opportunity to take pencil to pad and choose the parts and pieces needed to build a complete and ready-to-run race car right off the catalog pages. For example, Martin and Nelson offered their top-of-the–line, 112-inch wheelbase Dragmaster Dart chassis made of mild steel for $450. Or, the same chassis could be had in chrome-moly tubing for $525. A complete magnesium rear-end assembly went for $618 and a complete front end made from chrome-moly steel cost $210.

Martin and Nelson took the guesswork out of building a dragster. You told them what you wanted, and they told you if it would work. If needed, Dragmasters would build a complete car that was ready to run. What made things even better was the fact that Martin and Nelson played no favorites when it came to choosing equipment. They offered the customer an unrestricted selection of parts: six brands of racing tires; five types of wheels; eleven cam grinders; three types of injectors;

every major manufacturer of pistons, rods, and crankshafts; and even several choices of drag chutes.

The Dragmasters made building a dragster as simple and easy as making a telephone call. If any two men were responsible for the growth of dragster racing in California, as well as the rest of the country, it was the team of Dode Martin and Jim Nelson. They had to be part of our story.

I sat down with Dode Martin and Jim Nelson at Martin's shop located on his ranch in Fallbrook, California. The shop is straight out of the 1950s. Set in the center of an orange grove, it is filled with

Building a dragster in the '50s was a do-it-yourself venture until Jim Nelson and Dode Martin created a commercially available dragster catalog, offering buyers everything from a bare chassis to a turnkey, ready-to-run car. Scotty Fenn already offered a ready-made chassis from his company, Chassis Research, but Martin and Nelson's Dragmaster company took things one step further—they raced their own cars. *Don Brown*

Drag Racing left the streets and arrived on a strip around 1950. Fuel-burning dragsters evolved from modified roadsters and stripped-down dry-lakes machines, called "Lakesters." Safety was not a priority—in the early days racers ran with a helmet and goggles, lap belt and maybe a roll bar. Hot Rod/Motor Trend *Archives*

early drag racing memorabilia. As for the orange grove, Martin confirms that the trees have been bearing fruit since the 1890s.

At the time of our meeting, Dode was in the process of restoring, actually recreating, two of the team's most famous cars: the Mooneyes dragster and the Two Thing dragster. Both cars were strong contenders in the Top Gas dragster class during the 1960s.

Just watching Dode Martin, at age eighty-something, welding tubes with the grace of an artist was a sight to behold. Dode volunteered to offer his side of the Dragmaster story first, claiming that he was short of memory and that Jim would do a far better job. Before any recording work could be done, however, Martin had to fill a cardboard box with some of his prized oranges.

There is another obstacle to be overcome before the tale of the Dragmaster team can be told, and it has nothing to do with oranges. The question arises: what is a team noted for building and racing Top Gas dragsters doing in a book about the history of Top Fuel dragsters in California between 1950 and

1970? It's a question that will arise from time to time throughout our story, and one that must be addressed for the sake of good historical value and consistent storytelling.

First, Top Gas dragsters played a very important role in the decades between 1950 and 1970. At one time, Top Gas dragsters were of equal importance as the fuel burners. From 1957 to 1962, there was a fuel ban in effect covering NHRA-sanctioned tracks. In California, Mickey Thompson banned fuel at Long Beach even before the NHRA's ban.

Also, many of the drivers who would set many of the Top Fuel records began their apprenticeship in gas dragsters. This brings us back to the story of the Dragmasters. Their connection to the history of Top Fuel racing will become very evident as their story unfolds.

DODE MARTIN

I originally wanted to build a car to take to the dry lakes, but old C.J. Hart had started Santa Ana and a bunch of the guys from Fallbrook wanted to go up there and see what was happening.

I was driving a chopped-top coupe with a stout-running Ford flathead engine at the time, so I took it up to Santa Ana and gave drag racing a shot. I couldn't believe how many cars were there, and all of them seemed faster than mine. Then I spotted this contraption, it was a stripped-down roadster with nothing more than a seat, engine, and a little piece of bodywork bent over the firewall acting as a cowling.

The car was called the Bug, and it was owned and driven by a fellow named Dick Kraft. I said to myself, "I can build something better than that," so a week later I came back with a stripped down roadster of my own. Looking back, my version was no better than Kraft's. It was just a frame, engine, and me.

I came back the following week and I had to race another car owned by a fellow named Otto Ryssman. Old Pappy Hart came over to me and said, "What the heck am I going to call your car? It's not a lakester and it's not a roadster. I'm calling it a dragster." He painted a big "D" on the side of both

cars. I'm not sure if that was the first time the term dragster was used, but as far as I'm concerned, dragsters got their name that day.

It didn't take long before dragsters started to develop and get much better in function, but still most were built from Model A or Model B frame rails and guys would wrap some sheet metal around the driver and go racing. The real factor was that the spectators ran to the fences whenever a stripped-down dragster would run. I could see the light, that this type of car was going to be the future of drag racing. Sure enough, like in all styles of racing, development was fast and the racers learned from each other. It wasn't long before dragsters started looking like real race cars.

I built my second dragster at the end of 1953, still using a frame-rail chassis, only this time the car had a complete fiberglass body. When I ran the car, a friend of mine wanted to drive and he promptly crashed it and I had to rethink my design.

My third dragster came from a new concept that was whirling around in my head. The idea was to

Way ahead of their time, Dode Martin and Jim Nelson built a full-bodied, streamlined dragster, called the Dragliner Special. The car used an early-model, small-block Chevy V-8 for power. *Dode Martin Collection*

build a new kind of dragster, a streamliner, a sort of a combination dragster, lakester, and Bonneville car. It would have a full body with a canopy to enclose the driver.

As I bounced around the concept, the big news out of Detroit was the introduction of the Chevy small-block V-8. We all heard that this new engine was a runner and it could turn good rpm and not come apart. The new engine would find a home in my new car. But that's getting ahead of the story.

For years, local hot rodders in the Fallbrook and Oceanside areas frequented a parts house called Masters Automotive to buy speed equipment. The manager was a fellow hot rodder named Jim Nelson. I had seen Jim around at local street races, and had talked to him at Masters. Jim was a member of the Oilers Car Club and I was a member of the Shafters. As I said, we had street raced each other, but were not really friends.

Word got out about my streamliner and Jim, being a racer, stopped by my shop to see what was going on. Again, I had used Model T frame rails for the chassis, but the rest of the car had some tricky innovations. Jim was impressed and said to me, "Hey, I got a Chevy small block, why don't we join forces and run some of the NHRA events?" I jumped at the chance to have some help and we started working together.

As word spread, we started getting help from several manufacturers who were making names in the drag racing business, including Racer Brown, Bell Auto Parts, Vic Edelbrock, Sr., and some of the other racing guys in Los Angeles. We didn't have many manufacturers down south, so we had to come up to Los Angeles to get the latest parts and pieces. I named the car the Dragliner, but it was not a fuel-burning dragster.

I got to say that I know this story centers around fuel burners, but we had started out running the Dragliner on gasoline and were very successful. Then, in 1957, fuel was banned by NHRA and we had no choice but to run gasoline. Also, gas-powered dragsters played a very important part in the development of the dragster as a racing machine, so I feel that gas dragsters like the Dragliner need to be considered right alongside the fuel burners.

We won "Best Engineered" at the NHRA Nationals, and started to get a reputation as being fast. But, we wanted to go faster, so we started looking into the use of aircraft tubing (both mild steel and later 4130 chrome-moly) as material for chassis building. Jim wanted to build something all new. So, Jim and his brother, Tom, and I began designing a chassis. Tom Nelson never got the credit he deserved for his contribution to the project. He did a lot of work on the design.

Our first chassis was made from mild-steel 1-1/2-inch tubing with a 0.049-inch wall thickness and 1-3/4-inch roll bar with 0.009-inch wall thickness. The wheelbase was 94 inches because that's how long the straight tubing was when we got it from Tube Sales. Anyway, the car worked very well and, within a short time, five or six of our racer friends wanted a chassis like the one we were running, so we started a small business. Then a strip manager from back east ordered ten chassis to give away as Top Eliminator awards.

With that order, we started Dragmaster Chassis Company, and I was the first one to quit his day job and become a Dragmaster employee.

Part two of the Dragmaster story is told by Jim Nelson, and it comes from a different perspective than that of Dode Martin. Nelson was a dry lakes racer. He was also, at one time, a technical inspector for Wally Parks and the NHRA. A reason for the Dragmaster team's success may well be the blending of two completely opposite personalities. Martin, shy, reserved, and soft-spoken, admits that Nelson was always the mouthpiece for the company. Nelson, by contrast, is outgoing and offers total openness combined with a great sense of humor.

JIM NELSON

Before I met Dode, I was a dry lakes racer, involved with both the SCTA and Wally Parks shortly after World War II. I ran the lakes with Wally and Akton Ak Miller, who were both officers in the Southern California Timing Association.

Drag racing was something I knew nothing much about until late 1949. Just before the Santa Ana drag strip was established, and about the same time some local racers were running at the Goleta Airport up in Santa Barbara, I was exposed to drag racing when SCTA made a deal with the Navy Blimp Base in Santa Ana.

The base was located right across the street from where C.J. Hart was trying to start a strip at the airport. The location was a gigantic square of pavement with a mammoth blimp hangar in the center. Racers would start at one end of the pavement and race about a quarter mile. The freaky thing was that we ran through the hangar. You would take off in bright sun, then you would go bombing through hangar shade, and *bang* into the sun again. It didn't last long after C.J. started the real Santa Ana.

Jim Nelson, half of the Dragmaster team, had his roots in the days of Dry Lakes racing after World War II. Nelson also spent time as a NHRA Technical Inspector, which explains the close relationship he had with Wally Parks. The Dragmaster cars were perfect for the racer who wanted a simple, comfortable, safe, and inexpensive race car. The Dragmaster chassis was very popular with racers back east, who did not have access to the other California chassis builders. *Dode Martin Collection*

Another reason for my early involvement in drag racing was the fact that Wally Parks, who had been a tremendous influence in the SCTA and was involved as editor of *Hot Rod* magazine, was talking about starting a whole new organization to deal with drag racing. His idea was the formation of the National Hot Rod Association, an organization primarily devoted to safe driving and hot rods, but with an eye to the future, where drag racing was the next big thing in automobile racing. So, when Wally started NHRA in 1951, I jumped at the chance to work as a technical inspector and to help write the rules for the formation of their drag racing program.

After my stint with Wally, I went to work at Paradise Mesa drag strip for the San Diego Timing Association. It was during this time I began to notice Dode as a really good driver and excellent car builder. He built his own cars and even beat Art Chrisman. Back in those days, beating Art, who was considered a heavyweight in drag racing, was a major accomplishment.

Although drag racing was becoming more legitimate by moving onto real race tracks, there was still plenty of street racing going on. There was a place near San Diego called La Casta Flats, a mud flat that would dry out in the summer and offer a surface like the dry lakes. We used to race in the dirt at night when the cops were someplace in town. Everyone would show up, including Dode Martin. I forget the circumstances, but we ended up talking about his Dragliner and I decided to put my Chevy small block in the car. We became great friends and business partners.

After that strip owner bought 10 chassis to give away as prizes, business just kept growing. Jack Williams, of Bakersfield fame, ordered a car, a couple of teams from Texas bought cars, and soon we were selling all we could make. At the same time, we were traveling all over California, and, wherever we raced, our push truck (a station wagon in the early years), had a bare chassis strapped to the roof rack. We rarely left a drag strip with the chassis still on the roof.

Neither, Dode nor I had ever gone to college. We were racers, not businessmen, so we just went with our talent for building things, but on the business end we didn't really know how to price our products. Looking back, we could have made more money if we would have had a business eye. As it turned out, someone would buy a chassis and we would end up helping them put the car together, get them deals on the other parts they needed, and sometimes help them at the track.

Both Dode Martin (left) and Jim Nelson (right) drove their company's race cars. Dode once said, "We took turns, no matter how important the race. If it was my turn, I drove even if Jim was doing better." *Bob Hardee/Dode Martin Collection*

Within a year after opening their shop, the Dragmaster company was selling to customers all over the country. Nelson had quit his day job and joined Martin as a full-time employee. Jim's brother, Tom, also went full-time. For the first time, a customer could buy a ready-to-run dragster on Friday and go racing Saturday night.

Because the Dragmaster team raced every weekend alongside their own customers, the development of new innovations became an ongoing occurrence. Their original 94-inch wheelbase went to 96 inches and then 98 inches. Although they offered mild-steel as a tubing choice, chrome-moly became the material they considered standard.

The team of Dode Martin (left) and Jim Nelson (right) gave the drag racing world lightweight, off-the-shelf dragsters, available as a bare chassis all the way up to a complete, ready-to-run car. The strange quirk about the Dragmaster team is that they never ran Top Fuel. They made their name racing between 1957 and 1962, when the gasoline-only rule was being enforced at NHRA strips. *Dode Martin Collection*

Less than a year after opening their doors, Dragmaster introduced a stunning, lightweight chassis called the Dart. It could be made of chrome-moly or mild steel, had a 110-inch wheelbase, weighed only 60 (chrome-moly) to 90 (mild steel) pounds, and sold for $525 or less. The Dart chassis was far more sophisticated than early models, with a better seating position, safer roll bar design, and more flex in the lower main rails. As an added safety feature, Dragmaster offered all critical welds and joints magnafluxed for maximum safety.

The Dragmaster Company began to influence the whole drag racing scene by offering the California image to the entire country. Teams from any part of the country could order a ready-to-run race car with all of the cool California products installed, hassle free. Nearly every complete package sold by the Dragmaster Company came powered by a Chevrolet small block, which was considered the engine of choice for the budget team. There were exceptions, including Ford, Pontiac, Oldsmobile, Dodge Wedge, and even a few 392-cubic-inch Hemi Chrysler applications.

For a period of time, the Dragmaster Company and their posse of customers dominated the Gas dragster class in NHRA-sanctioned competition.

Gas dragsters lived large, as the fuel ban prevented the nitro teams from running NHRA events. To keep on top of the heap, to stay in front of the pack, Nelson and Martin had to create bigger and better machines. The pinnacle of this challenge was reached with the creation of the famed twin-engine dragster called Two Thing.

The reason for even thinking about such a machine came from the fact that teams running Top Gas were trying to go faster and faster without the benefit of nitro. The result was an uncontrolled lust for power in the form of twin-engined behemoths that looked more like mechanical monsters than race cars.

At the beginning of 1960, Dode laid out the initial design in chalk on the shop floor. The final design ended up being a collaboration of ideas between Dode, Jim, and Jim's brother, Tom. About Tom's contributions, Jim said, "Tom was a big part of this project and all the projects we worked on. He never got the credit he deserved."

The car was to carry a pair of Chevrolet engines run side-by-side with front-mounted superchargers. The chassis featured a 110-inch wheelbase, and was constructed of 4130 chrome-moly tubing. The front end was a heavy-duty version of their conventional design. After some debate, the final decision on the rear end was to use a Halibrand Engineering Indy Car unit made with a cast-aluminum housing.

There was only one driveshaft, offset 7 inches to the right of the driver. The two engines were mounted with a 28-degree offset from perpendicular. Both Chevy engines were built to identical specifications. Stock 283-cubic-inch blocks and 5/8-inch stroker crankshafts from Crankshaft Company in Los Angeles brought the overall displacement to 354 cubic inches per engine, for a total of 708 cubic inches. Each engine was equipped with Mickey Thompson rods and pistons, Racer Brown camshafts, a two-hole Hilborn injector system, and a GMC 6-71 supercharger using a 1-to-1 ratio Chuck Potvin blower drive assembly. Unlike most dragsters of the time, Two Thing used a pair of Spalding Flame Thrower two-coil distributors, operated by a battery, in place of the conventional self-contained magneto.

The right engine carried a Schiefer flywheel and 11-inch, 2-disc clutch. The left engine ran in reverse with a backward firing order and carried only a ring gear that meshed with the right engine's flywheel gear. The 1100-plus horsepower that Two Thing produced was transmitted to the rear end through a Culbert Automotive in-and-out box. Once completed, with Dode behind the wheel, Two Thing was ready for battle against the likes of Tommy Ivo and his twin-engined Buick, Glen Ward and the Howard Cam Special, and a host of other two-motor dragsters.

How did Two Thing perform? In the words of Jim Nelson, "It was awesome."

Two Thing set top speed for Gas Dragsters at the 1960 NHRA Nationals with a 171.10-mile-per-hour blast. It also won Best Engineered Car. It set the top speed the following year at the Nationals with a 177.10-mile-per-hour reading. Dode Martin said, "In 1961, we ran a tour of 12 drag strips around the country as a paid-in car. We broke the speed record at all 12 strips." Two Thing eventually broke into the 180-mile-per-hour range before it was retired.

The big-fish-in-a-little-pond scenario held true for Dragmaster as their reputation grew and more and more teams ran their chassis. As mentioned early on, the Dragmaster team of Martin and Nelson stayed within the confines of the gasoline-powered dragster class. By no means did this choice prevent them from coming into contact with members of the nitromethane cult who were to make headlines in the future.

Danny Ongais began his career driving for the Dragmaster team but later moved on to run Top Fuel with his "bro" Roland Leong, then went to Mickey Thompson and a Funny Car, and finally to the Indy 500 and World Sports Car racing. Proving that Top Fuel drivers can do more than run a quarter-mile, Danny On the Gas did it all. *Steve Reyes*

Mickey Thompson was a regular customer of Dragmaster. Pete Robinson reworked and modified a Martin and Nelson chassis for use in his climb to fame. Of all those who crossed paths with the Dragmaster partners over the years, two personalities stand out more clearly than the rest. Both would go on to fame and fortune in the history of Top Fuel drag racing in America. Of course, in the early 1960s, the two future stars were just a couple of laid-back Hawaiian surf boys named Danny Ongais and Roland Leong.

The story can only be rightfully told by someone who was there. Jim Nelson offers his recollection of drag racing, Hawaiian style.

JIM NELSON

After we won the NHRA Winternationals at Pomona, California, Roland and his mom, Teddy, came down to the shop. He wanted to buy a ready-to-run dragster to race on the island. His mom, on the other hand, wanted Roland to learn how to work and wanted him to stay on the mainland and get a job. Both terms were decided on. Roland would stay and we would build a car. I turned one of my kid's bedrooms into a Roland Leong room and he went to work for us.

We had him doing all of the dirty jobs, from chipping slag off of welds to cleaning parts and cutting tubing. He was only 16 or so years old, and he didn't like working. He was used to the island lifestyle, kicking back and chillin' out. Roland had never really been anyplace off the islands and just going from our shop in Carlsbad to a parts house in Vista, about eight or nine miles, was a huge challenge for him.

But, to his credit, Roland learned to work and he learned the race car business. He ended up taking a complete, ready-to-run Dragmaster car back to Hawaii and spreading the sport through his participation. He made several attempts at driving dragsters, most of which were just short of cataclysmic. He can tell you more about his driving career. In the big picture, Roland turned into a fantastic car builder, owner, and tuner. He has done so much for the sport and, during the 1960s, Roland was a key player in turning Top Fuel into a professional sport.

As for Ongais, he came over a little later, after Roland had been working for us and was about to take his car back home. Danny showed up with a reputation as a champion motorcycle racer. He walked into the shop one day and said he wanted to go to work. So, we put him to work at the same type of crap jobs we had given Roland. And, just like Roland, Danny wasn't keen on hard physical labor, but he didn't let it show and he turned into a good employee. What I liked right away about Danny was his racer mentality. Whenever things got hard and he didn't like what was going on, he just gritted his teeth and didn't say a word.

After Danny became a full-time employee, I started having second thoughts about driving. Although Dode and I had always taken turns driving, things began to wear on me and my family. My wife, Martha, was raising our boys and I was always gone. Racing put a strain on our marriage and I decided that my family was more important.

I had an idea that Danny might make a good replacement. To test my theory, we took the Dragmaster Dart to Irwindale Raceway for a test session and a photo shoot for *Hot Rod* magazine. Danny hated wearing shoes, and I had a tough time talking him into putting on a pair of driving boots. He claimed he wanted to be able to feel the car. He agreed to wear shoes, so we stuck him in the car for a warm-up run. I told him, "Danny, don't be a hero. Only push as hard as you feel comfortable, then back out." Danny climbs in the car, rolls to the starting line, and jumps on the gas. On that first run, he ran as fast, with as good an ET, as I had ever run. From that point on, Danny "On the Gas" was our driver.

Danny was the best natural race driver I ever saw. He would concentrate so hard at the starting line, you could have set a bomb off and he would have never twitched. Danny was the originator of the dragster drivers' code: "never blink, and never lift." He wanted to win. I just think back to 1964 at Riverside Raceway and the *Hot Rod* Magazine Championships. Danny broke at the starting line on a single's run. He jumped out of the car and pushed it a quarter mile so he could win and move to the next round of eliminations. He was one tough race driver.

It became clear by 1965 that Top Fuel would be the future of drag racing. The fuel ban had been dropped, and cars were running faster and quicker than anyone could imagine. Dode and I decided that we didn't want to go Top Fuel racing because of the expenses involved and the hassle of traveling. For my part, things at home were getting worse and I didn't want to push any harder. My wife was very understanding and very patient, but patience can only go so far.

Pushing the limits has always been the Top Fuel driver's code. Sometimes the code dictates you start spitting out parts through the pan, illustrated by Rich Zoucha unloading the bottom end of his engine. *Steve Reyes*

Top Fuel racing was a tough way to make a living in the 1960s and there was more competition in the chassis business. The last straw came when we went to the March Meet at Bakersfield in 1965. Coming through the gate, all we saw were Top Fuel cars—there were close to a hundred. Once qualifying started, the Top Gas dragsters had to sit in the staging lanes for hours to make one run. We were used to going to a track and making as many runs as we wanted. Not any more. Top Fuel cars ruled and Top Gas cars sucked hind tit. I said to Dode, "Are you tired of doing this?" And he said, "Yes, I'm ready to give it up."

We had not changed our design or welding jigs for several years, and had not even thought about a fuel chassis. And we had developed a line of street chassis designs. So, we gave up drag racing, continued to make parts and pieces to service our racing team customers, and retired to a five-day-a-week business.

Drag Racing in the '50s and '60s was good to us, it gave us a living, and allowed us to race as much as we could handle.

CHAPTER SEVEN

HAND GRENADE HARRY AND THE POND

Hand Grenade Harry Hibler gets ready to take a ride in his rear-engine Top Fuel car. What is interesting about this car is that it was once powered by a jet turbine engine, which was soon outlawed for use in a dragster. *Harry Hibler collection*

Santa Ana was the first drag strip with paying customers. Pomona and Fontana helped the sport grow into a California phenomenon. But San Fernando gave drag racing in California its first taste of eccentricity. It was nicknamed "the Pond" because of a flood-control frog pond near the end of the track.

The Pond was a casual place where drivers could learn and be accepted. Although it was a purpose-built drag strip, San Fernando was located next to an airport. Therefore, a misconception has remained in place for decades that it was originally a runway strip. Unlike other Southern California drag strips, San Fernando ran only Sundays, from noon to 3:00 p.m. At least, that is what its use agreement with the city listed.

San Fernando was home base for many of the Southern California hotshoes, so it became a place where teams formed alliances. The Road Kings hung out there. There were Surfers and there were Beach Boys. Tommy Ivo, Tony Nancy, Tom McEwen, the Beaver Brothers, the Adams Brothers, Rick Stuart, Don Prudhomme, Gary Gabelich, and John Wenderski all called the Pond home.

San Fernando remained part of the drag racing scene from 1955 to 1969. In the summer, temperatures would melt the soles off your shoes. The valley racers were used to it and delighted in watching outsiders go mad from the unrelenting sun.

The Pond never got the crowds that came to the Winternationals in Pomona, never accrued the mystique of The Beach. It did not have the grandeur of

Not only did Tommy Ivo prove to be a tremendous driver, he also built his own cars and loved the mechanical side of racing as much as he did the driving. *Tommy Ivo Collection*

Bakersfield. The Pond could be rude to the first-time visitor. The shut-off area went under a bridge, so if you didn't aim correctly, it meant big trouble. There was sand and gravel to be scooped up by drag chutes. The neighbors were always ready to call the police over the noise. Church-going folk hated the place. And, every once in a while, an out-of-control airplane, pilot screaming *Mayday*, would miss the runway and crash land on the drag strip.

During its heyday, San Fernando had several qualified management personnel, including famed Top Fuel chassis builder (Race Car Specialties) Frank Huszar, who put the first races together, and

Darrell Morgan, a retired Los Angeles Police Department officer who took over after Frank. There was Dave Wallace, Sr., who did PR work to promote the track's image for both Huszar and Morgan. And then there was a transplanted native of New Mexico named Harry Hibler.

Hibler came to California as a youngster and fell in love with cars. Says Hibler, "I came to California in 1951, when I was just 16 years old, and started working construction part-time until I got out of high school, then went full-time. I had always been fascinated by hot rods and race cars, and California had it all. Drag racing had just begun to

Old Hand Grenade Harry himself! Harry Hibler managed San Fernando Drag Strip from its early days and, at the same time, built a reputation as a fearless Top Fuel driver. Owners would come to the strip without a driver and simply hire Harry. Sometimes the cars he ended up driving were less than perfect, and Hibler got the "Hand Granade" moniker from his propensity to toss engine parts all over the drag strip. *Harry Hibler Collection/Petersen Publishing*

get organized with the opening of Santa Ana in 1950. Man, I thought I was living in paradise."

I met Harry Hibler in the late 1960s, when he began working at Petersen Publishing Company selling ad space for *Hot Rod* magazine. Through the years, we both became close friends of The Loner, Tony Nancy. When Tony passed away in November of 2004, the loss was felt by the entire drag racing community, his absence leaving a void in the spirit of everyone who knew him. Harry didn't say much, but it was obvious that he suffered serious damage to his heart. I had written a book about Tony in the early 1970s, and Harry and I joked about how small the book was for how big a life I had tried to capture.

When the idea of telling the story of California Top Fuel drag racing in the period between 1950

and 1970 became a reality, Harry Hibler agreed to offer the account of his tenure as manager of San Fernando Drag Strip and his career as a Top Fuel driver. His only stipulation was that I stay true to his words and, at some point in the book, offer a memory of our friend Tony. I agreed.

The difference between Hibler and other management types was the fact that he was a racer first; everything other than racing came second. Harry drove a Top Fuel car with such ferocity that his reputation for either winning or getting off in a spectacular crash-and-burn earned him the nickname Hand Grenade Harry. No driver he faced ever doubted his bravery. Every competitor knew that Hibler would never lift.

As Harry began to collect his thoughts and organize the tales he was about to tell, there was a calming in his demeanor, as if something he'd held back for a long time was about to be released. Harry concluded that, in his experience, the period from 1955 to 1965 was the best time to be in California driving a Top Fuel dragster.

HARRY HIBLER

Once I got to California and saw what was going on, my interest in mechanics became intense. I met a young guy named Chuck Bowles who had the same desire to learn as I did. He had one advantage: Chuck's dad, Charles, was not only a very interesting man, but was an extremely talented mechanic. Charles Senior worked with Admiral Byrd during his flight over the North Pole. He also had been part of the crew at Ryan Aviation, building the *Spirit of St. Louis,* flown by Charles Lindbergh across the Atlantic non-stop.

By then Charles Senior was building cars as a hobby. He took me under his wing, and began teaching me and his son the inner workings of the internal combustion engine. Once we got a little education, Chuck Junior and I joined The Ghost Riders car club and started running at Pomona drag strip.

In 1952, Pomona was just a drag strip; the NHRA Winternationals didn't come there until 1955. Back then, Pomona was a big, flat piece of asphalt without a plethora of amenities. It was so primitive that there was a string running from the return road up to the timing tower office. When you came back from a run, you would stop at the bottom of the tower and the officials would send your timing slip down clipped to the string with a clothespin.

Between racing and working, we would spend the remaining time hanging out at Bob's in Burbank or one of the other popular drive-in spots, talking about cars, looking at girls, and choosing each other off and going street racing. Some of it got downright serious. Guys would race for money or pink slips. Sore losers would want to fight.

One of the advantages we had street racing in Southern California back then were the orange groves. If the cops started chasing us, we would head out in all directions and hide in an orange grove. The cops didn't have a clue, and they would give up after a few minutes and try to catch us later. It was a game of one-upmanship.

Eventually, the Ghost Riders built a fuel-burning '34 altered coupe with a flathead Ford engine. I ended up driving the coupe most of the time, until the club members lost interest in having one driver all of the time.

Once I started driving, it became an obsession. I was fascinated by the idea of fuel-burning dragsters. The Bean Bandits, Art Chrisman, and cars like the Glass Slipper were just unreal to see run. By today's standards, they were primitive, but at the time they were considered really trick. I met a dragster driver named Gary Cagle, a full-time police officer and part-time racer. Cagle became my hero, and I knew I wanted to drive a fuel dragster.

San Fernando Drag Strip opened up in 1955. Frank Huszar, a pioneer in the Top Fuel dragster class who would make his name a legend as a chassis builder, put together the whole program and started running on Sunday afternoons. He hired me as a technical inspector, the guy who checked the cars for safety items like roll bars, seat belts, and helmets. My day job was construction, so Frank had

Drag racing in the early 1950s took place without much in the way of safety precautions. Drivers wore helmets and had a lap belt to hold them in place. Fire suits, drag chutes, clutch covers, and shoulder harnesses were far in the future. Jack Moss, about to make a run at Tradewind Airport in Amarillo, Texas, in his Hemi dragster, demonstrates the era's lack of concern. *Don Brown*

me building anything the track needed, from grandstands to fences.

When Frank left unexpectedly, a Los Angeles police officer named Darrell Morgan took over managing the place. Frankly, Morgan really didn't want to work all that hard and, soon after he took charge, I took over as manager and he would just sign off on whatever needed to be done. He trusted my judgment without question. After a couple of years on the job, Morgan took an appointment as a judge and left the track, and I became the official manager.

Now is where the plot gets a little twisted. I wanted to drive Top Fuel dragsters, but I had my duties at the track, so I was forced to bend the rules. At first, if a driver didn't show up or was late, the car owner would ask me to warm the engine or sometimes make a half-pass down the strip to see how the clutch set-up worked. Pretty quick, I was getting asked to substitute on a regular basis. It didn't take long and suddenly I was a real driver. Everybody knew what I was doing, so the rules kept getting bent. The good news about my situation was the fact that the strip's staff was sort of inbred with dragster drivers, and they didn't care if I drove. As long as they could get their runs in too, it was fine for me to race and manage at the same time.

Mickey Thompson had started Long Beach, but he wasn't much competition for San Fernando because we were only allowed to run on Sundays. At first, we could run from 9:00 a.m. to sundown, but the neighbors bitched and moaned so much the city made us go to a short schedule, starting at noon and going to 3:00 p.m. for cars with open headers.

The curfew actually worked in our favor because the local Top Fuel cars could run Saturday night at Long Beach or Fontana and still have time to go home, regroup, and get to San Fernando by noon on Sunday. After running Sunday, the crews could get home early, which was good because most of the crews and drivers worked regular jobs come Monday

Nitro meant power and with power came danger. The faster Top Fuel cars went, the more dangerous they became. Thank God for the vision of Safety pioneers like Bill Simpson and Jim Deist, who saved many a driver by creating safety equipment of the highest quality. *Ed Justice Jr.*

morning. It was good for the touring cars, too. Teams like the Ridge Route Terrors would come down from Bakersfield on Friday night, run Lions on Saturday night and Fernando on Sunday, then head home. They could make money doing the weekend sweep.

By the late '50s, early '60s, safety became a real issue. I was still in charge of the technical inspections. If I let anyone else on the staff do the job, well, they hated turning down a car for a safety problem and they would let the car go if the driver

Part of the duties of a track manager is dealing with problems. Harry Hibler, in jacket and striped shirt, comes to the aid of an injured driver after a crash at San Fernando Drag Strip. *Harry Hibler Collection*

started complaining. I had to jump in and get hard-nosed if a car was not equipped with the right roll bar, safety harness, clutch can, onboard fire extinguisher, and good tires. And, if the driver didn't have an approved helmet, the car didn't run. Guys would get pissed and want to fight. Mickey had the same problem at Long Beach. I would try and settle things, Mickey would rather fight.

When the '60s took hold, the Top Fuel scene began to get more serious. Cars started going faster, and more teams formed as racers from other classes, like modified roadsters and gas dragsters, abandoned their classes in favor of building a Top Fuel car. As more cars were built,

the chances of something going wrong increased exponentially. The main reasons were superchargers and percentages of nitro.

In the early 60s, drivers wore leather jackets and Levis with a helmet and goggles with plastic lens. Then Tony Nancy came up with the leather facemask attached to goggles with glass lenses. Drivers got style conscious and began using custom-fit leather jackets and leather pants similar to motor-cycle uniforms.

They looked cool, but there was a flaw in the idea. A very well-known Top Fuel driver named Rod Stuckey had a catastrophic engine fire. He was wearing leathers and, when the fire hit, the leather shrank and his bare skin was exposed. However, the doctors found that everyplace Rod had white cotton, like underwear and socks, the burns were less severe. Right away I made drivers wear long johns, white socks, and white sweatshirts. It wasn't much, but it was something.

Despite every effort, the fire problem continued. There was a very simple reason for the increase in fires. Racers learned by trial and error. They were not chemical engineers, scientists, or safety experts. If they wanted to go faster than the next guy, they added more nitro, most of the time using a simple, inaccurate hydrometer to check percentages. If nitro didn't work, then add some hydrazine to the mix.

This conception created horsepower bombs with a driver hoping not to set off an explosion. When a driver lost the gamble, a 180-mile-per-hour flamethrower took direct aim at his face. Thank God for Jim Deist and Bill Simpson (pioneers in safety equipment). They fought to create protective driving suits and face masks that saved many drivers.

If any one thing haunts me when I think of the Pond, it was the three fatalities we had during my time.

Don Nickelson's brother, Harold, was the first. Dyno Don Nickelson was a very famous Funny Car and Pro Stock driver in the 1970s and '80s. Harold was driving a blown flathead dragster when a front wheel broke, a spindle dug into the track, and his car flipped. By today's roll bar standards, I think Harold would have survived.

A driver named Gary Peterson was the second and, by far, my worst memory. Gary just wanted to do some testing, make a 1/8-mile run just to check things out. I said okay. The trouble hit as soon as he left the starting line. Teams had started using triple-disc clutch units, and sometimes the clutch would get so hot it wouldn't disengage. So, the drivers would whack the throttle and disengage the clutch at the same time.

In the early 1960s, safety features were starting to improve the way of life for Top Fuel drivers. In this crash, at San Fernando Drag Strip, the cocoon-style roll cage saved the driver from having a really bad day.

After his years at San Fernando, Harry Hibler went on to become Publisher of Hot Rod magazine and put on special events like the Hot Rod Chili Cook, which featured a country boy named Don Prudhomme (shown) as special guest and official girl watcher. *Harry Hibler Collection*/Hot Rod *Magazine*

When Gary went to shut off, the clutch stuck. So, he hit the throttle hard but the throttle stuck wide open and his clutch remained engaged. It was impossible to estimate how fast the car was going when it crashed into the bridge at the far end of the track, but the tires were smoking until impact and the engine was thrown about 600 feet. It was an awful scene.

A blower explosion caused the final fatal crash. Things did improve, and drivers began walking away from the worst-looking accidents.

Looking at my total career in drag racing, managing San Fernando was just as satisfying as driving Top Fuel cars, and the reason is very simple: the experiences, the stories I have filed in my head. There were so many, but a few stand out and might be of some interest to those reading this book.

A FEW STORIES

The idea of sharing with readers several of Harry's favorite stories had a certain appeal. After all, the purpose of this book is to offer insight into a lost period of time. If Harry could enhance the visualization of years gone by or help rekindle emotions long dormant in those who lived the experience, then creating a bench racing session around the stories seemed apropos. With the flip of a switch, my tape recorder again started rotating with its muffled hum, and Harry Hibler related some of his favorite moments as manager of the San Fernando Drag Strip.

HARRY HIBLER

Every Sunday at the Pond was a new adventure. I made it a habit of positioning myself at about the 1/8-mile mark on the track so I could go in either direction if something went wrong. On this particular Sunday, a Top Fuel driver was getting ready to make a run. I knew the driver, so I had no real concerns as he unloaded the clutch and jumped hard on the throttle. As the car left the starting line, there was a horrific bang. The car lurched to one side and the rear wheels stopped driving, but the engine kept screaming. Suddenly the car was heading straight for my position and I could see the driver thrashing around.

The problem was that the driveshaft had broken when the car launched and was whipping around between the driver's legs, beating on his inner thighs, and tearing his private parts. So, I ran toward the car,

which had slowed to about 20 to 25 miles per hour. When I got close, I jumped onto the cowling of the car and grabbed the magneto wires and starting pulling them out of the spark plugs. Anyone who has ever grabbed a magneto wire knows what happened. I became a dead ground for the magneto. I ended up screaming as loud as the driver, but the engine shut off and we got the guy out of the car.

One of my favorite stories about the Pond happened in the early '60s. We had a group of wild young guys showing up on Sunday mornings, wanting to run their cars in the stock classes. I knew by looking at the cars that they were cheating, so I went over to the technical inspector and warned him not to let these guys run in stock class. They were told to run in the modified class.

They kept coming back, and each week they caused more trouble. Finally, I had enough. I walked

As manager of San Fernando Drag Strip, Harry Hibler was always ready for the unexpected, which happened on a regular basis. Harry would station himself halfway down the strip, perched on a motorcycle and when a crash happened was first on the scene. *Harry Hibler Collection*

"Every once in a while we would have to stop racing and run like hell," Harry Hibler said, "because some pilot screwed up and crashed landed on the drag strip instead of the runway." *Harry Hibler*

over to their group and told the leader to pack up and get out of my racetrack. The guy and some of his friends starting calling me names and threatening me. It got serious, and I figured I was about to get my ass kicked big time. Unknown to me, someone ran to the Top Fuel pits and starting yelling, "Harry is in trouble—help!" Before you could blink, the Top Fuel drivers and crew members came running over and just started swinging at anyone they didn't know. I had to jump in and calm them down. Those troublemakers never came back.

Airplane crashes caused more than one interesting day at the races. I remember several times when we would be running eliminations and two Top Fuel dragsters would be ready to blast off and suddenly you would see people running onto the track waving their arms. I would look up and see a small plane with the engine off coming down at a steep angle, and then *bang* it would hit the track

and go sliding down the strip. More than once, I had to jump in our track ambulance and race to the scene of a crash and pull survivors out of the wreckage before a fire started.

It seems that the planes would always hit the strip and get upside down and we would have to close the track until the police came. The racers would get pissed and complain that airplanes should crash on their own strip and leave the drag strip alone.

One of the most seldom-mentioned sides of Top Fuel dragster racing in the late '50s and throughout much of the 1960s was the close-knit relationship between drivers when they weren't racing each other. Sure, any driver would put you on the trailer in a heartbeat if given the chance. And, yes, you might get a punch in the mouth if you pissed off another driver by doing something stupid. But if you needed parts or help, that same driver would be the first to your side. When the worst would happen,

Above and opposite page: The late 1950s and early 1960s proved to be dangerous times, as Top Fuel dragster drivers went faster but not necessarily safer. The remains of Gary Casel's dragster, after a major incident at Great Bend, Kansas, has a crowd of onlookers inspecting the damage. One of those wondering what happened is the late Lou Cangelose (left, in dark shirt), famous pioneer of the Top Fuel wars. *Roger Wolford Collection*

you could count on the Fuel drivers looking after and taking care of their own.

The Pond was different in many ways from other drag strips, and most of the differences had to do with my method of running the place. For example, during the fuel ban, if someone wanted to run fuel, we would sort of look the other way. You know, don't ask, don't tell!

I realized early on that the crews running dragsters had problems other types of drag racing cars didn't have. It cost more to build them and it cost more to run them. The top fuel cars back in the '60s were evil-handling machines and could kill a driver at any time. Crews were still learning about fuel and blower pressures and chassis design. Every day was something new and, to compensate for the difficulties faced by the dragster teams, I attempted to encourage a feeling of fraternalism among Top Fuel drivers. I didn't want to kill any of the competitive energy drivers had, but I did try to cultivate camaraderie between all of the teams.

It worked especially when the sport began to grow and touring teams from back East would show up to battle the big names in California. What we did at the Pond was offer teams a chance to tune up before running the big tracks like Bakersfield or Pomona. On any given Sunday, the entire time I was manager, guys like Lou Cangelose, Don Garlits, Pete Robinson, Jimmy Nix, Chris Karamesines, Joe Schubeck or Gordon Collett would show up unannounced.

I would let them run as much as they wanted. It was extremely important that the Eastern racers had a chance to tune up and set up for West Coast weather and track conditions. Clutch settings, tires, jetting for the injectors, general tuning all needed to be done. I would always slip them a few bucks to cover expenses, and they appreciated the gesture. Sometimes we would set up match races with local California teams so the touring cars could get a taste of the competition.

Fernando was also a great place to break in a new driver. If a team showed up with a rookie, I would take them aside and spend time offering my

experience. When the driver was ready, he could make several half passes—leave the starting line hard, then shut off at the 1/8-mile mark. Unless you have actually sat in the seat of a front-engined Top Fuel car of the 1960 era and unloaded a clutch and felt the power, you have no concept of how much courage it takes to perform that act. Many times the regulars like Tony Nancy, Tommy Ivo, or Glen Stokey would come over and help a new guy get set up. The Pond was a place to bend, but not break, the rules.

In the days before big money took over, the touring pros from back East had very little in the way of extra money. Sure, guys like Garlits and The Greek or Kalitta would get a grand to show up at one of the California tracks, but money was still tight, so many of the back-East drivers would stay with a California team while on their West Coast tour. All of the racers shared their homes and meals together. Many Sunday nights, long after the track had closed, back-East racers and local California drivers would just stay at the track bench racing and having a beer or two. Not much of that sort of thing happens nowadays.

If beating someone on the track was fun, then playing a practical joke on your fellow competitor was just as much fun. Racers in the '60s took great pleasure in one-upping each other. One of the most notorious jokers of the time was the late "Rocket Man," Gary Gabelich. My turn came one Sunday during Top Fuel eliminations.

During a run, a driver got too close to the timing lights and, when he pulled the chute, it caught one of the top speed lights and tossed it into the weeds. I went down with a new light and started repairs. As

Considered an interesting character by all who knew him, the late Gary Gabelich was best known for his total lack of fear. He drove Top Fuel, funny cars and Bill Fredrick's jet dragster, Valkyrie, shown here at Long Beach. Gabelich even worked with NASA when they began the Mercury Program. *Tom Madigan*

I squatted on the ground fixing the light, I heard two Top Fuel cars fire up at the staging area. I was in the middle of the track, so I figured they were just warming the engines. It was Bob Hightower in his car and Gabelich in the Sandavol Brothers car.

I didn't think much about them until they staged. I froze when I heard the engines start to rev. Then they both blasted from the starting line. There was nothing I could do but stay down and cover my ears. They came by at about 180 miles per hour, and Hightower gave me a salute and Gabelich gave me the finger. They both thought it was the funniest thing they ever saw. Gary had set the whole thing up, including having the first car take out the lights. Could you imagine that happening today?

Dealing with the unanticipated is something that every track manager faces from time to time. It happened to me and it turned out to be one awesome occasion. The whole story starts with bad weather. Contrary to the popular belief of those living east of Phoenix, there is a rainy season in California. One particular Saturday, the Los Angeles basin had a monsoon, and Long Beach and Irindale were blown out of their night racing show by high water.

Sunday morning dawned bright and sunny in the San Fernando Valley. As I started to open the

The late Gary Gabelich divided his time between driving Top Fuel cars, driving a Jet dragster, and driving the Beach Cities Corvette Funny Car, shown here at Long Beach. *Tom Madigan*

track at about 10:00 a.m., suddenly I had 54 Top Fuel cars show up at the gate wanting to race. By 11:00 a.m., all the cars were in the pit area and getting ready. We had from noon to 3:00 p.m. to run all of the Top Fuel cars, plus all the regulars with open headers who, by the way, had also paid their money and wanted to run. Two things were proven that day: racers want to race and, when it comes down to the short strokes, they will work together to solve any problem.

We decided that the fastest eight cars would run the finals, and every car got a chance to run. We had two cars running down the track, two cars staged at the starting line, and two cars pushing down the fire-up road all at the same time. If anybody needed help, all of the crews who were eliminated would dive in and help. The closer it came to 3:00 p.m., the slower our official clock ran. By 3:30 p.m., we

had the cops at the front gate. They were really cool and sort of found things to take up their time while we ran the last couple rounds.

When sitting around remembering my days in Top Fuel, both as a driver and a strip manager, thousands of races jumble and collide in my memory. It is very hard to distinguish one race from another. But, the personal stories are more simply defined. The human side of drag racing stays with a person long after the excitement is gone. To me, the comradeship between the crews and drivers was a real and ongoing part of the sport. They would do everything possible to beat you, but they would be first to help if needed. I have several examples that stick in my mind.

One year at the U.S. Fuel & Gas Championships at Bakersfield, John Smyser and I were running his Top Fuel car. When we got to the front gate on qualifying day, there sat Marvin Schwartz, out of money and no gas for his tow vehicle. Marvin was a very close friend of Don Garlits, and was a tough racer. But, in the early days, Marvin had a tough time trying to make ends meet. It didn't matter to us. Marvin was a racer, and if he wanted to race then it was our obligation to help out. Several crews chipped in and soon Marvin had gas, spare parts, and was able to qualify.

In round one of eliminations, Marvin wins but blows an engine. Round one for us, I get beat but no damage to the engine. So, John tells Marvin, why not put my motor in your car and continue as far as you can. Marvin ends up runner-up. When it was over, John never asked for the round money or the second-place check. He just told Marvin to keep the winnings and someday return the favor.

Drag News had a promotion they called the Mr. Eliminator list, and it was for both Top Fuel and Top Gas. The ten drivers on the list could challenge one another for position, trying to get to number one. The idea was that the cars on the list would draw bigger crowds to the tracks they ran, and the cars making the list always got a few bucks appearance money as a bonus.

At one race for the number one spot, Zane Schubert was running the number two car. The format was best out of three races. First round, Zane wins but blows an engine. The rules stated a car had 30 minutes between rounds or forfeit the race. Zane and his crew start ripping the engine down; pistons, rods, and other parts flying everywhere. The next thing you know, all the other crews are hovering over the car and all you can see are elbows and asses flogging with wrenches flashing. Twenty minutes later, Zane is putting on his fire suit, getting ready to run.

I need to satisfy a personal need, to tell a story about a man who is no longer with us but, in his time, exemplified the type of person it took to run the Top Fuel ranks. His name was Jack Bynum, but Fat Jack was what everyone called him. Jack was a hardcore Top Fuel mechanic. At one point in his career, he served as crew chief for pioneer woman drag racer Paula Murphy during her Funny Car campaign. I knew Jack as a Top Fuel racer who was known throughout the pit area as one tough dude. If you crossed Fat Jack, expect to get the dog piss knocked out of you in a heartbeat. On one occasion,

Top Fuel racing has always been tough on equipment. Look closely and take note of the blower and injectors of this Top Fuel dragster detached and hanging on the side of the engine. *Steve Reyes*

Getting ready to put on their show are the Hot Wheels Team of Don Prudhomme (left) and Tom McEwen (right). The pair raced Top Fuel cars and Funny Cars both, all sponsored by the Mattel toy company. The Snake and Mongoose Mattel deal was the first big sponsor package to come out of California. *Steve Reyes*

Jack told a crew member from another team, who had come after Jack to teach him a lesson, that he should go and get several more friends because he didn't have what it took to provide a decent fight.

However, my recollection of Jack Bynum is of a bear of a man who proved to be a hero whenever there was a crash or somebody needed help. He would dive into a fire to save a driver. He was extremely strong. I remember Jack getting to the scene of a crash with a car upside down and grabbing the chassis and flipping the car right side up and tending to the driver. If ever a crowd of spectators interfered with the safety crews aiding a driver, old Jack would start tossing people out of the way. During the 1960s, Top Fuel drag racing was a tough and dangerous business, and the sport needed friends like Fat Jack.

By the mid-60s, Top Fuel drivers took on a new image, and some of them started believing their own press clippings. The match race, or promotion race, became the rage: Ivo vs. McEwen, The Snake vs. Garlits, and Gabelich vs. anyone. Money became a factor. I could see costs going up with the speeds. Some of the teams joined forces, and others gave up. I kept driving for John Smyser, but it was tough. John built big-power motors and the car would either set top speed or blow. About every other run, I would get a mouthful of hot oil and fill the air with shrapnel.

As costs escalated, owners started building engines with used parts, and began pushing the envelope with large doses of nitro, a yard of lead in the magneto, and low rear-end gears twisting the motor to extremely high rpm. The result, most of the time, was a blower lifting off at the 1,000-foot mark. One time, Smyser told me he had bought a blower from Frank Pedregon. Old Flaming Frank was known for using discarded parts. I knew I was about to light a 1,000-foot fuse when we pushed down the track to fire the engine. But it didn't blow, and we set top speed of the meet.

There was no avoiding the fact that sponsor money was needed to continue making progress in Top Fuel. California was home to many of the pioneer manufacturers of speed equipment, so several began throwing money into sponsorships. Of course, everything changed when McEwen and Prudhomme put together their Hot Wheels deal.

Corporate sponsorship was born in the late '60s. But, with sponsor money came a real split between some of the Top Fuel teams. Take Tony Nancy, for example. He had several local sponsors, and even some help from Chrysler Corporation, but he never wanted to give up his freedom or his independence. If a sponsor wanted Tony to show up for an autograph session or some type of dog-and-pony show and it didn't fit Tony's schedule, he wouldn't go.

Many of the teams felt the same way. And, in some cases, you wouldn't want the drivers giving interviews, anyway. Back in the 60s, Top Fuel drivers were a tough bunch, and some didn't have much in the way of people skills. If you stuck a microphone in their face, you might get a litany of four-letter words. So, some drivers accepted the changes and others wanted the old way. But, only those who became educated would survive. Big Bill France of NASCAR once told me, "Son, I'm not in the race car business. I'm in show business."

Several drivers took to the sponsorship invasion with enthusiasm and began to make a living, or at least paid expenses, in drag racing. Three of the best were TV Tommy Ivo, Prudhomme, and Tom McEwen. Ivo had a movie and TV career before drag racing, so he was very aware of sponsors and how to act in public. Prudhomme, although very shy by nature, understood that if he wanted to make a living he had to become a personality. McEwen, on the other hand, was a performer by nature and became an instant hit with fans and sponsors.

Another sponsor favorite was Jim Busby. He saw the value of someone other than him paying the bills. At one point, Busby hooked up with the Smothers Brothers (TV comics of the 1960s) and ran a very successful program. Bob Muravez, and his Floyd Lippencotte, Jr., alter ego, was extremely popular. Although his car, the John Peters Freight Train, was a Top Gas dragster, it brought in appearance money plus support from local manufacturers.

As for my career, it would not go professional. I was one of those who wanted to keep his independence. After I left San Fernando as manager, I continued to drive Top Fuel until the early '70s, but my heart stayed in the '60s, when every day there was something new going on, and racers still raced for pride.

Harry Hibler ended his management tour at the Pond shortly before it closed in 1969. Harry went to work for Petersen Publishing Company and became publisher of *Hot Rod* magazine. Harry also continued driving Top Fuel for John Smyser until 1972. Harry once told a magazine writer that his favorite place to race was Bakersfield, not San Fernando. He developed a great friendship with James Warren and the Ridge Route Terrors, and claimed that heading over the mountains from Los Angeles to race in the farm lands of Bakersfield were some of his best times.

In 1970, at the Smokers U.S. Fuel & Gas Championships held at Bakersfield, Harry experienced his finest hour. Harry managed to race into the finals, and his opponent was none other than his closest friend, Tony Nancy. Unable to hold the car in the staging lights due to faulty brakes, Hibler red-lighted the championship away and Tony took the title. It would be the last front-engine fuel dragster duel for a win at Bakersfield. For Harry, that race remains his pinnacle.

FLAMING FRANK,
THE WORLD'S FASTEST MEXICAN

Mexican-Americans and California share a heritage that goes back to the days of Spanish Land Grants, the Mother Lode gold rush, and the agricultural birth of the state as the world's food basket. In the world of drag racing, that heritage is very strong, and can be found in the very conception of the sport. Who can forget the contributions made by Joaquin Arnett and the Bean Bandits, Dave Marquez, Fran Hernandez, Bobby Tapia, and Don Enrique.

Hot rodding and Mexico go back to the early 1950s, when Mexico hosted one of the greatest car races in history, the Pan-American Road Race (1950-1954). Among the competitors were California hot rodders Ak Miller, Mickey Thompson, Ray Brock, Clay Smith, and Vern Houle. A little-known fact: 1954 winner Ray Crawford's co-driver was a racer named Enrique Iglesias. Enrique never received much credit because, at the time, there was a wall of prejudice against Mexican-Americans in California.

In Top Fuel drag racing in California between 1950 and 1970, one unusual story stands out that best epitomizes the true spirit of drag racing and the heritage of California and its connection to Mexican culture. The story of Frank Pedregon, Sr., defies reasonable logic as it breaks down every barrier protecting political correctness.

The heritage of Flaming Frank lives on with his sons, Cruz, Tony and Frank Jr. All are professional racers, doing what their father loved best. *Jere Alhadeff*

According to Tony Pedregon, his dad knew the only way for a budget racer to make it was to put on a show and have a gimmick. So, Flaming Frank built a fuel dragster with a Fiat coupe body that became the talk of drag racing. *Jere Alhadeff*

Frank was a racer, and he raced for the pure love of the act. He raced on a shoestring budget, proving to everyone that money isn't everything. He raced with passion and fulfillment. Frank Pedregon loved his family, he loved his friends, and he earned the love of his competitors. Frank had a sense of humor, an image of piquancy in life, and an aura of well-being. His competitors called him "Flaming Frank" because he would actually set his rear tires on fire by spinning them so hard, and he called himself "The World's Fastest Mexican."

Frank never had the best equipment; he had to make do with what he could afford. He raced through hard times, dangers, and endless prejudice. Somehow Frank managed to keep his head high and his spirit soaring. Frank, Sr., is gone now, but his family honors his memory. The Pedregon racing spirit lives on today as his three sons, Cruz, Tony, and Frank, Jr., can be found blasting down the quarter mile in 300-mile-per-hour Funny Cars. The boys race in the rarefied air of big-budget, sponsor-driven NHRA World Championship professional drag racing. They race the finest equipment, and will never face the scorn of prejudice. Frank, Sr., would never have understood what money can buy, he never had that luxury.

In an interview conducted in July, 2006, Tony Pedregon talked about his dad and what he meant to his family and to the sport. It is truly a story of the power of self.

TONY PEDREGON

Most people only think of the Pedregon boys, but I have two sisters: Barbara and Dora. There were five of us hanging around when my dad was racing. We were all raised in Southern California. Although my dad was born in Texas, he came to the coast as a young kid.

In the late 50s, early 60s, my dad was working as a mechanic for a garage run by a friend of his. When the racing bug hit, he jumped into the sport with both feet. He built a dragster with a fellow named Dugan and they ran as a team for a while, then my dad decided to build his own car. He also decided that if he was going to drag race it may as well be at the top of the heap, so his first solo effort was what was considered a Top Fuel car.

My dad was a clever man with a sense of knowing how to get things accomplished. It didn't take him long to understand that although drag racing was still considered the sport for rebellious youth he also knew that the fans were looking for entertainment, because to the young fans drag racing was the coolest thing they had ever seen. With that in mind, my dad decided to be different than the pack. He built a conventional dragster, then adapted a 1938 Fiat coupe body that was chopped and cut down to fit. He did everything himself, from the chassis and body to the engine. He used to tell other racers his car was powered by genuine Mexican horsepower.

At the time, most of the Top Fuel dragster teams barely had enough money to run every week. Budgets were tight and there was no sponsor money. My dad had even less than a tight budget. So, the reason for the body was to promote the car and himself to track owners as something different and hope they would slip him a few bucks to show up.

There are a few things about my dad that not everyone knows. He came from a tough childhood and that made him a very rugged and tough man. He wasn't afraid of anyone. Secondly, his family always came first. He would haul us all to the races and let us run around having fun. He was always there for us with a hug and kiss. Racing came second to my mom and us kids.

I can't speak for Frankie or Cruz, but I can tell you that I remember, very vividly, back when I was about five years old, I remember three things that have stuck in my head: the smell of nitro, the sounds made when my dad pushed down the strip to fire up the car, and the taste of burning drag slicks when the car left the starting line.

As for money, we didn't have much. The stories are all true about my dad pulling used parts out of the trash can or getting used stuff from other teams that they were going to discard. But, the kicker was he made them work. He once got some used pistons from Dale Armstrong and rebuilt them, then went out and ran faster than Dale.

Our dad was a character. He liked putting on a show as well as racing hard. When Dave Wallace, Sr., gave his car the name "Taco Taster," he painted it on the car. He also painted "Adios Gringo" on the back of the car. The racing papers called him "The World's Fastest Mexican," prompting Bobby Tapia, another Mexican driver who was really fast, to say, "What, I'm Irish?" Nobody was politically correct, and all that name dropping worked and he got appearance money.

It was a time for characters. Guys like Big Daddy, "Rat Fink" Roth, Von Dutch, Wildman Gary Gabelich, Eddie Potter, Neil Leffler, Zane Schubert, and Bill Coburn were all very colorful and hard racers and my dad loved to hang out with a crowd like that. There were two sides to his racing. He would match race with the body on the car and get a few bucks. But, when a really good pay day was available, he would yank the body off and run as a conventional Top Fuel car. That's the way it was back in the '60s, not much money, just hard racing and good friends.

It's not fair to say my dad didn't get any help, because he picked up support from Clay Smith Cams, Horsepower Engineering, Coburn Glaze (Bill Coburn), and a few others, but never any real money. Usually just machine work or parts.

Although our dad loved racing, he wanted to be a father first. So, to us kids it didn't matter to us how fast his car was, it only mattered that he was Dad. Cruz, Frankie, and I played racing as far back as I can remember. We made noises like Top Fuel cars and raced each other on foot, on bikes, and finally motorcycles. We wanted to race, but our dad never really encouraged us. He would tell us stories about the dangers and how some of his friends died. He would show us his burn scars on his legs and tell us how he got his mustache burned off. He was really worried about the hazards of front-engine Top Fuel cars. He didn't want his boys getting hurt.

But it never worked, we thought it was all very exciting and Top Fuel was the only way to go. In the mind of an eight-year-old, any other form of drag racing was for pussies. Our heroes had to be bad-ass or we didn't like them. We liked Harry Hibler, Gary Gabelich, Tony Nancy, Bill Coburn, and Don Prudhomme. Those were the guys my dad raced with. What could be better than header flames four foot high, blowing the tires off and running 90 percent? That's what mattered to us, lighting the fuse and smelling the nitro. You know, when the big sponsor money hit Top Fuel, racing changed and the little guys were gone. It reminds me of the movie "The Right Stuff" when Chuck Yeager said he didn't want to be an astronaut, he wanted to be a test pilot. That was my dad, he just wanted to race, not become a superstar.

By the 1970s, my dad had a trucking business that had become a truck dealership and he started devoting more time to the business and less to racing. The business kept growing and, finally, he became a full-time businessman. In December of 1981, my dad was flying his own plane in Mexico when he encountered bad weather and low ceiling with poor visibility. He crashed and died, but not without a fight. The crash amputated his arm but he still managed to crawl out of the wreckage and walk about three miles for help. Unfortunately, he walked in the wrong direction. My dad never really left us. I think of him every time I light the fuse of a nitro-burning engine.

Tony, Cruz, and Frankie Pedregon all went on to become superstars in their own right driving Fuel Funny Cars. But, when they talk about racing, their dad is always first in their thoughts.

CHAPTER EIGHT

DUEL IN THE DEW

The late Mickey Thompson was a visionary, and he realized quickly that Funny Cars were the wave of the future. Mickey also knew that Funny Cars could be popular with sponsors. He joined forces with the Ford Motor Company to produce this Ford Mustang 429 Funny Car. Here, "Mighty" Mike Van Sant is shown driving it. *Tom Madigan*

"He called me a Mick son of a bitch and then hit me in the head with a wrench," Mickey Thompson said, explaining his first days running Lions Associated Drag Strip in Long Beach.

By the mid-1950s, drag strips in California had become common up and down the state, with each building its own unique reputation. Some were good and some were bad. There were short strips, long strips, narrow strips, and wide strips. Pit areas alternated between oil-covered dirt and gravel to honest-to-god smooth pavement. Goleta, the place in

California where drag racing got its start, was gone. The Father of Drag Racing, C.J. Hart, would see his dream, the strip at Santa Ana, close in 1959. However, replacing those two pieces of hallowed ground came a second generation of quarter-mile tracks to take the sport into its future.

From Fremont, Kingdon, and Half Moon Bay in the north to Paradise Mesa in the south, strips became popular. Big names included Bakersfield, Pomona, Fontana, Saugus, Colton, Riverside, and

San Fernando. Each track carried its own image and, no doubt, most Top Fuel drivers had their personal favorite. There was, however, one strip everyone knew was different.

It didn't look dissimilar from other tracks. It had all the basics: timing lights, grandstands, a pit area, a tower, and places to buy food and use a restroom. Still, there was something intangible that made the palms of your hands wet as your senses became more aware. It had its own smell—oil

Above and opposite page: Two things about Top Fuel racing in California from the '50s to the '70s are gone forever: front-engine killer cars and the great days at Long Beach (Lions) Drag Strip when Top Fuel was king and the mood was laid back and cool. *Tom Madigan*

refinery stench mixed with smog, gear oil, nitro, and ocean dew.

The instant you rolled through the gate, a strange feeling came calling. Here was a place where you were tested. Everyone who came to the place knew the score, no bullshit allowed. You would be tested, and either you showed some balls or you stayed in the push truck.

When a driver ran Long Beach, it was for pride. You had to run the brave guys, who would send the weak home with their tails between their legs. It was a tough place. It could be a very mean place and, if a driver lost respect, it was a place to die.

Nothing mattered more to a Top Fuel driver in the 1960s than winning at Long Beach. The spell it cast on a driver was something held inside, in a place nobody was allowed to view. Long Beach was the place where the Top Fuel code meant the most: never blink, and never lift.

On the morning of April 13, 2006, my wife, Darlene, and I found ourselves on the Interstate 5 Freeway. We were headed to the NHRA Museum for a memorial service in honor of Barbara Parks, who had recently passed away after a long illness. Barbara Parks was the wife of NHRA founder Wally Parks. The freeway was jammed with cars, all moving with reckless abandon, playing bumper tag with an army of 18-wheelers.

It had been many years since our last visit to this part of Los Angeles County and I had forgotten how psychopathic a morning commute could become. To avoid being late, we had departed from our base in Torrance two hours early, just in case traffic became really unbalanced. It turned out I had overcompensated, and we found ourselves prematurely closing in on the Pomona Fairgrounds and the Museum with over an hour to spare.

Suddenly a sign came into view indicating the off-ramp for Rose Hills Memorial Cemetery and a bolt of shock pierced my chest. It had been 18 years since I had taken that off-ramp.

Quickly, I broke ranks from the mad crowd and darted for the exit lane. After some initial confusion, we found the side road leading to the elegant and dignified entrance to Rose Hills. Once through the gate, a feeling of peacefulness replaced the hammer-and-tongs anxiety of the freeway.

Memory cut in sharply as we drove up a hill to a long, sloping field of grass. Truly, the last visit to this place was a sad day. Fifteen rows down from the paved roadway lay the flat marble stones identifying the final resting place of Trudy and Mickey

Thompson. Mickey and Trudy had been murdered in the driveway of their home on Woodlyn Lane in Bradbury, a suburb of Los Angeles, on March 16, 1988. To this day, I will never forget the telephone ringing that morning and a friend informing me they were gone.

I had known Mickey since the early days, and his beloved Trudy since she came to California from New York. Mickey and I had crossed paths many times over the years, at places from Baja to Bonneville, and all the drag strips in between. But, it was not until the mid-1970s that Mickey and I grew close as friends.

In 1976, Long Beach, California, transformed itself from a place once noted only for its naval yard and oil refineries into a world-class venue for auto racing. The Formula One circuit now included the streets of Long Beach, thanks to the incredible vision of a man named Chris Pook. Just prior to the 1976 race, a public relations man for Ford Motor Company offered my wife and I the privilege of being guests at the race, supplying us passes to both the pits and the garage area.

As an enhancement to an already exciting prospect, Mickey Thompson, who lived in a condominium located directly above the track, invited us to watch the action from his balcony. He promised that, after the race, Trudy would put together a large helping of her delicious tacos.

At the time, Mickey was in the early stages of creating SCORE (Short Course Off-Road Events) to run off-road races in both Baja, Mexico, and the United States. More pertinent to our story is that, in 1955, Mickey Thompson created Lions drag strip, turning a parcel of discarded commercial property into sacred ground within the halls of drag racing. The track found its most celebrated period to be those years between the late 1950s and 1970.

As we ate Trudy's tacos, at a table with a view overlooking the departing crowd of Formula One race fans, Mickey asked if I would be willing to compile a manuscript of his life from his childhood to present.

I agreed and, one week later, we sat again at his kitchen table as Mickey began recounting the story. The following is the tale of Long Beach, or simply The Beach, taken from the actual tape recorded history we made in 1976.

MICKEY THOMPSON

Lions was one of the first commercially built drag strips not part of an airport complex. San Fernando was a purpose-built strip, but it was still adjacent to an airport runway. Long Beach was a drag strip from day one.

It all started as a way to get the kids off the streets and cut down on the street racing going on. Kids were killing themselves at an alarming rate.

Actually, eleven Lions Clubs from Long Beach, Wilmington, and San Pedro got together and sold bonds to Lions Club members to finance the building of a drag strip under the banner of LADS, Lions Associated Drag Strip, Inc. The Lions Club had the backing of all of the local police departments, and the land was originally leased from the Los Angeles Harbor Department.

The clubs put up something like $5,000 each to pay for the project. In turn, they hired me to manage the construction and the overall running of the place for $75 a week. Problems started right away,

because some of the clubs had trouble coming up with their share of the money. Everyone was way too optimistic about costs. Board members even talked about taking leftover funds and using them for Lions Club charities.

I went to one of the board members, named Eddie Baker, and told him that there would not be enough capital to finish the project. He told me to do my best to finish it any way I could. So, when we ran out of money, I kept on building the strip. As the money depleted, I started to improvise. I took a couple of local guys and my pickup truck to the

Fans at Long Beach got up close and personal with the fuel burning dragsters. In this photo the Glenn & Schultz Top Fuel car is doing a burn-out as spectators cover their ears. The essence of Top Fuel racing in the 1960s was smoke, noise, and large quantities of eye-burning Nitro. *Ed Justice Jr.*

Standard Oil Refinery and begged them for old pipe they used on steam boilers. They said help yourself. We took the pipe and cut them up to make fence posts. Then we got old telephone poles from PG&E and used them to mount lights and speakers.

I kept right on charging what we needed. When the paving company came in, I told them to do the job and when they finished, I said I didn't have the funds to pay. I knew that they were not about to tear up all of the asphalt (60 feet wide and 3,500 feet long) they just laid without trying to get paid. We ended up owing about $5,000 or so in paving costs. The company agreed to give me a chance.

With the help of some local car clubs, we managed to build a small tower with glass windows at the starting line area. There were even some grandstands. We then made a deal for a complete Chrondek timing system and Fairbanks Morse scales for weighing the cars. Wally Parks and the NHRA provided sanctioning so we could get insurance.

Once everything was finished, I had a bunch of people, including the board members, bitching and moaning about money. So, I sat everyone down and told them that, if they wanted to get paid, here is how I'll do it. I made up a payment plan, and each person or company got a fair share. Everyone was paid in full within two and a half years of our opening. We had plenty of innovations too—we were first to have real staging lanes and the first to use signal lights for starting cars, along with the traditional flag starter.

The crew we had when we began racing was an awesome bunch. Several of the local car clubs provided us with free labor for all the odd jobs we needed to run an event. I remember that Eddie Baker's wife, Edna, ran the pit gate, and Eddie Davis and Roy Blakenship were my technical inspectors. My first wife, Judy; John Rucker; and Martha Blaneney ran the timing tower. Our starter was a fellow named Danny Laris, who put on a show for each pair of cars that raced. He would do a ballet with the flag, then jump high in the air as two cars would take off.

The track opened in October of 1955, running Sundays at first, then switching to a Saturday-night format. In the beginning, things did not get off to a smooth start. The area where the track was located was a rough part of town. There were a lot of gangs, and street racing was a big problem. I set the rules of behavior, and some of the first racers who came to the track did not like rules. For the first couple of months, there wasn't a Sunday afternoon or

Saturday night that went by when I didn't get in a fist fight, sometimes five or six.

The gangs would show up, maybe 20 to 30 guys with girlfriends, and want to run their cars. Most of the gangs had leaders who wanted to prove something, so they would get tough when I told them the rules. There were also a bunch of just plain troublemakers wanting to cause problems. I didn't allow any drinking alcohol whatsoever, and most of the fights were over drinking. If I caught someone drinking, I tossed them out. The only problem was that their buddies had an issue with my actions and, when I came by, they would jump me and start swinging.

We had a few security guards we hired from a rent-a-cop agency, but I never believed in calling someone to help me fight my fight, so I would just start swinging and hope for the best. Besides fists, there was always a monkey wrench, a bottle, or a hammer involved. I can't count the number of times I got hit with some type of object. A lot of the gangs were Mexican-American, and they didn't like the idea of some Irish guy kicking the crap out of one of their own. One time this guy comes up and without warning says, "You Mick son of bitch," and hit me in the head with a wrench.

If I kicked the shit out of someone, they would always threaten to sue me. I would say, "Get in line."

The trouble started tapering off after a few months, after I had fought just about every gang in the neighborhood. I guess I gained respect because some of the toughest gang members turned out to be very helpful in keeping down the trouble. Once things cooled off, the racing programs grew and spectators began filling the place. Soon, the hot fuel dragster teams showed up on a regular basis. Art Chrisman, Jazzy Nelson, Fritz Voight, Calvin Rice, Manuel Coelho, the Bean Bandits, Ed Losinski, Don Yates, Cook & Bedwell, and many more hotshoes came to the Beach.

When we opened the track, the use of fuel was never questioned. Most of the dragsters ran nitro, and many of the roadsters and coupes did the same. But, within a couple of years, speeds started to increase and it became clear to me that safety was becoming an issue. The chassis had not developed to handle the speeds we were turning and we began to have trouble with drivers crashing, and I worried that it was only going to get worse.

At the time, I was running my own car so I could talk from experience. In 1957, I banned fuel and went to gasoline only. The NHRA and several other independent tracks followed. Needless to say, I was

TOP FUEL OUTLAWS— WHO BANNED THE CAN?

Everyone knows that you can't have Top Fuel without nitro. The story of Top Fuel in California 1950-1970 had one serious glitch—the use of nitro was banned from 1957 until sometime in 1962. Over the years, many drag racers blamed NHRA founder Wally Parks as the culprit who instituted the ban. That story is not true. Greg Sharp, Curator of the Wally Parks Motorsports Museum, helped put to rest all of the old wives' tales told over the years with information as to what really went on between 1957 and 1962. What follows is the real story.

By the late 1950s, dragsters had reached speeds unheard of only a few years back. The use of nitromethane fuels had begun in the days of the dry lakes, and carried over into dirt track racing and the drag strip. With the increased speeds, safety became an issue. Drivers were still using cotton jackets, open-face helmets, plastic goggles, and Levis as driving uniforms. There were no fire suits, face masks, or drag chutes. Fire, explosion, and mechanical failure became more common.

Mickey Thompson, then manager of Lions Drag Strip in Long Beach decided that he had seen enough, and decided to ban the use of fuel at his track. Mickey once said, "As long as the cars were using carburetors and running under 150 mph the danger wasn't so bad. But when superchargers were introduced, things changed and the cars were not safe. It would take a while for the technology to catch up, so I decided to go with gasoline. The hardcore racers didn't like it one bit, and they told me so."

Other track managers joined in and began to ban the use of nitromethane. Finally, according to Greg Sharp, a meeting of track owners was held in Los Angeles

not the most popular guy in the world with the racers who liked running fuel—they had to build new engines in order to run gas. Many didn't, and they went to what were called outlaw strips because they allowed nitro. The fuel ban lasted at Long Beach until early 1962. By then, chassis design and safety equipment caught up to the speeds. I felt if we stayed on top of our technical inspections, the fast teams could run.

It may sound funny, but back in the late '50s, running 150 miles per hour was more dangerous than running 250 miles per hour or faster in a modern dragster.

Those early days produced several really tragic events. It was very difficult for me to deal with serious crashes because I raced myself and was close friends with most of the drivers. When anything happened, I would have a very rough time emotionally. I had to always keep my real feelings in check because I was in charge of the track and had to deal with whatever happened. I had a reputation for being a hardnosed guy, but nothing was further from the truth. Many times I would go home after we had experienced a major problem and lie in bed, staring at the ceiling wondering how much of this I could take.

Like the night Mickey Brown died. He was a fun-loving kid, kind of wild, but it was hard not to like him. I had told him that he had to calm down, or I wouldn't let him drive. On this night he got into someone's car without letting me know. When I found out, I ran down to try and stop him. I wanted to check out the car and put a lid on his enthusiasm, and, because many of the tracks actually held NHRA events, Wally Parks and his staff were invited to take part. Wally Parks has always been a staunch advocate of safety, going way back to the very first issues of *Hot Rod* magazine when he was the editor. After much discussion, Wally and the NHRA joined the ban and urged the tracks running NHRA events to do the same. Beginning with the Winternationals at Pomona, a ban on nitromethane and methanol-based fuels was put into place.

Now for the controversy. Many racers who were running strong and winning races on nitro hated the ban. Don Garlits was openly opposed to the ban. Racers blamed Wally and the NHRA for taking away their nitro. A pissing contest ensued as some outlaw tracks allowed fuel. The AHRA, the fierce competitor of the NHRA, allowed fuel, and some tracks started out by banning fuel but then turned their head and winked as the smell of nitro filled the air. Harry Hibler, manager of the San Fernando strip said, "Hey, if guys wanted to run nitro they ran it. We didn't push the ban hard."

Some accused Wally of making a deal with Mobil Oil Company to run only gasoline because they had been an official sponsor of the NHRA Safety Safari at one time. Parks said that was not true, and pointed out that the Safari had been discontinued before the ban was put in place.

The biggest challenge to the gasoline-only rule came in 1959 when the Smokers Car Club of Bakersfield held the first U.S. Fuel & Gas Championships. All the fuel-burning racers showed up and the crowd was over the top. It was clear that fans loved the Top Fuel cars, and the track owners knew it. The fight went on until late 1962, when the fuel ban was lifted and Top Fuel could give up the outlaw life. The ban was a hitch in the history of Top Fuel in California, but it did make the racers and track promoters aware that with high speeds came increased danger levels. Wally Parks, Mickey Thompson, and the NHRA exposed that increased danger. From their efforts came better and safer racing.

but it was too late. Mickey was leaving the starting line when I got there. He wasn't 100 feet down the strip when the car got off the track surface and rolled over. Somehow Mickey's head got outside the roll bar and he was dead. He was a great young kid and in today's dragster he would have survived, no problem. We just didn't have the safety equipment back then.

Sometimes things happened and to this day I will never understand. The night Leonard Harris died I was so stunned that I didn't think I would get through the night. In my mind, Leonard Harris would have been one of the greatest drivers to ever run the quarter mile.

He had won the 1960 NHRA Nationals. He drove the Albertson Olds dragster, one of the best-running cars in the country. Albertson Olds had become one of the first superstar teams, with a Gene Adams Oldsmobile engine and Ronnie Scrima (another superstar in drag racing) in the crew. Harris himself had taken on rock star status. He was noted for his reaction times and his physical conditioning. Leonard, at one time, was a gymnast and he trained for driving a dragster the way a fighter trains to do battle in the ring.

This night, the Albertson Olds broke something or had some kind of problem, I don't remember, but Leonard agreed to jump into another car and make a pass. Something broke, and he went off the track and rolled. He was gone before anyone could help. I could not believe that Leonard wasn't around anymore.

The faces of 1960s Top Fuel drivers needed protection from the deadly enemy Fire. Bill Simpson and Jim Deist, both life-saving pioneers in creating safety equipment, were responsible for these fashion styles. Shown are Dwight "Hey" Bale, (left) and Rich "The Hippie" Bruckman (right). *Steve Reyes*

The one thing that haunted me for years after I gave up managing Long Beach was the question: how good would these young men have been if they had lived? Leonard Harris, Mickey Brown, and Bruce Woodcock all had the same things in common: talent, courage, and personality.

Safety was always an issue with me. In the beginning, we all drove in T-shirts and football helmets. Later, we upgraded to cotton jackets and bandanas and early-style racing helmets. But, when we opened Long Beach, I was determined to keep the drivers as safe as possible.

I couldn't get some of the guys to wear a decent helmet. So I went to Cragar Auto Parts and had the manager give me 30 Bell 500 helmets for 10 dollars apiece. At the time, Bell Helmets were state-of-the-art. I took them to the track and drivers would leave their driver's license so they could use a helmet for the night.

The whole safety issue became more precarious when we went back to fuel in the early 1960s. Remember, in the old days, most of the cars ran carburetors and fuel pressure systems that used a hand pump. Even using fuel, these systems were reasonably safe. Then the use of 6-71 superchargers, fuel injectors, and crankshaft-driven fuel pumps replaced the carburetor and hand pump. More fuel and more pressure from the blower produced horsepower and explosions. If a driver blew a supercharger and didn't hit the fuel shut off and ignition kill switch fast enough, there would be a horrendous fire.

I believe that God put Jim Deist and Bill Simpson on earth to save lives. When we ran the Challenger at Bonneville, I worked with Jim Deist on the safety belts and drag chutes. At that time, he was developing a driver's fire suit made from aluminized material. Although a little bulky, the Deist fire suit saved lives. Bill Simpson followed with his version of a fire suit, and Simpson also developed seat belts and drag chutes. There were others, but Deist and Simpson became leaders in protecting the drivers from fire.

You would think that, with all of the new safety features like clutch cans, developments in chassis design, and engines with better parts and less chance for problems, drivers and crews would be jumping up and down to follow the rules. But it was the same old story. Every Saturday night I would find cars without adequate safety features and I would send them home.

It ended up that I was so hardnosed about the rules that I wouldn't bend them for anyone. In fact, one time, when Jack Chrisman was driving my dragster and the crew brought the car up to staging a minute after the final call, I shut the gate on my own car and wouldn't let it run. Chrisman thought I was nuts. When I made a rule, it didn't matter if it was the littlest team or the biggest name—everyone got treated the same.

In fact, you can ask anybody, I once banned Tom McEwen, when he was a young kid, from coming to the track because he caused so much trouble by complaining about everything. Finally, I let him back in provided he worked the technical inspection line for a few weeks to learn how to behave. After he came back, Tom became one of the best drivers I ever saw. He just needed to settle down. All the young guys were the same. They wanted to race and beat each other, and sometimes egos got in the way.

Long Beach started making money after the third year and we just kept getting bigger and better. We built more grandstands and the crowds increased so fast we had to build more. Everyone called the place The Beach. The strip got a reputation for having a good bite and all the top cars wanted to run.

It didn't hurt to have the ocean mist and fog roll in every Saturday night. Fuel-burning engines loved the place. Guys would run the motors rich at the start so they would pull hard at the top end. The fans would go crazy when two Top Fuel cars would stage

When things go bad, throw out the laundry. Rich Bruckman, the World's Fastest Hippie, blows an engine in the Cow Palace Shell Top Fuel car at Fremont. Note the drag chute behind, getting ready to blossom. *Steve Reyes*

Throughout the 1960s, many Top Fuel teams tried streamliner body designs to help cut through the air and offer some type of downforce. Shown here is Ron Scrima and the Scrima-liner. *Don Brown*

and have flames shooting out of the headers four feet in the air.

The fog would be twenty feet off the ground and the nitro would burn your eyes so bad you couldn't even think straight. Ralph Guladahl, Jr., the guys called him Digger Ralph because he loved the Top Fuel cars and used to work as a journalist writing about dragsters, once called racing at Long Beach "a duel in the dew," and that was very appropriate.

We produced a lot of innovations at the Beach, like being the first to use a real traffic signal to start the cars. The starter would hold down a photo cell button with his flag and then point to each driver and ask if they were ready. He would then jump high in the air and wave the flag. If either driver jumped before the flag came off the button, the red light on the signal would come on.

Another first came about because guys were complaining about picking a winner. We didn't have win lights like they have today. So, I stationed a volunteer at the end of the 1,320-foot mark and he or she would raise a flag and point to the lane in

which the winner ran. It didn't last because I found guys paying the spotters to call them a winner. So, we actually created a win-light system that would light up when the first car crossed the finish line.

As the track got more popular, the crowds wanted more and more action. We were the first drag strip to ever have a local TV crew film an event. Sometimes, the action would get so fierce that I would get caught up in the drama and try to make everything more exciting. This was especially true after I gave up managing the track and acted as a consultant for C.J. Hart. I'll get to that story later.

On several occasions, we would have 40 or more Top Fuel cars for a Saturday night, and teams would try and blow off the big names just to build their own reputation. So, the lesser-known drivers would have their engines on kill when they came to the starting line. It was win or blow for some teams.

It got even better when the cars from back East would show up. In the Top Fuel wars, it has always been California against the rest of the country. Cars from the East wanted to beat the big names in California. Garlits, Schubeck, Robinson, Kalitta, The Greek, they all wanted a piece of some California car, it didn't matter who.

There were a couple of times when I did go over the top and do things on impulse. I remember watching drivers battling for the Top Eliminator spot and thinking maybe I could give them more incentive. I would call the final eight or so drivers around, reach in my pocket, and pull out a thousand bucks. I'd tell them it was a bonus for the winner. It would really pick up the pace. A thousand dollars to a Top Fuel driver in the early days was a ton of money.

By the early 1960s, I was totally overworked and running myself and my wife Judy into the ground. We were running Bonneville with the Challenger record car. I was designing and getting ready to build cars for the Indy 500. I had a drive-in hamburger stand called Mick's, selling 18-cent burgers and 10-cent fries. I had started my own speed equipment business, and I still had a garage called Mick's Service Center in El Monte with 11 mechanics.

It all started to stack up. By 1960, Lions had reached national prominence. Every drag racing magazine had featured it as the place to race. It had grossed over a half-million dollars for Lions Club Charities. I was getting a fantastic salary with a percentage of the gate receipts and we had made many improvements to the overall condition of the track. But, aside from all the businesses I owned, the racing I did, and working 24/7, two things were playing on my mind and it was time to leave.

First, I was always in conflict with the Lions Board of Directors about money and how to spend it and on what. But, something that had happened a few years earlier now haunted me day and night.

One Sunday afternoon, we were running a rare daytime event, and a close friend of mine named Dave Genion brought his car out to run. Dave had two sets of wheels for the car, one set was standard steel wheels and the other set a brand-new style made from a magnesium casting. The problem was each set of wheels took a different kind of lug nut. Dave ran the

Rich Bruckman, known as The World's Fastest Hippie, got the front wheels of his Cow Palace Shell Top Fuel car a little too high one day. *Steve Reyes*

magnesium wheels, but somehow the lug nuts for the steel wheels were used. Halfway down the strip, a wheel broke off and Dave was killed instantly.

About three years after Dave died, I was sitting in an A&W Root Beer stand in Parker, Arizona, with my first wife, Judy, and our kids. Without warning, a middle-aged man wearing western-style clothing and a hat pulled down over his eyes walked out of the shadows and stuck his head inside the open car window. He looked into my eyes as I stared back. He said, "Do you know who I am?" The tone in his voice caught me off guard. I just answered, "No." The man said, "Well, you should. You killed my son."

His voice cracked as a tear was choked off deep in his throat. I tried in vain to convince the man that I had nothing to do with his son's death; if anything, it had pained me as much as it had my accuser. Finally, with my family in a state of shock, I jerked the car in gear and drove off. I never really got over that scene. Every time anyone got hurt or killed, I inevitably felt it was partially my fault.

I just couldn't bare the thought of staring down at another limp, lifeless figure being carted away like so much cold beef. I needed a rest. I resigned my position as manager of Long Beach in late 1960 but, before I did, I picked the greatest replacement I could have ever chosen. Old Pappy, C.J. Hart, agreed to take my position. After Hart took over, I acted as a consultant for a while, and that is when the story about an extra thousand bucks in the winner's pot took place.

Four years after my retirement from Long Beach, I had recuperated from my period of overextending myself and decided to return to supervising a drag strip. So, I bought an option on the property on which Fontana Drag Strip was located. The strip had been around for a while (since 1952) and was not doing all that well. Within thirteen weeks, I had increased attendance from an average of 800 paying customers on a Saturday night to over 13,000. In fact, we were pulling about 30 percent of our crowd from Long Beach. I just wanted to prove a point: I could still bring in the crowds.

I became disenchanted with the operation after a few months, and then on July 4th we had a major incident. I hired a professional fireworks crew to put on a show for the fans. As the show was about to start, the crewman for the company accidentally set off the entire display in what amounted to a huge explosion. The guy was badly burned and he sued us. As if that wasn't bad enough, I sold the option

on the track to a group of businessmen. That sale ended up in a nine-year legal battle because, when they took over, the track started losing money and they blamed me. I made up my mind that I was out of the drag strip business.

Looking back, my experience at Long Beach was a major factor in how my life worked out. I love drag racing and I got to run my own car plus race with all of the great drivers of the period. During the 1960s, Top Fuel racing in California was unreal. We had great cars and good tracks, plus every top driver in the country wanted to come to California and race.

There has been a lot written about how the east drivers hated the California drivers. Well, I'm here to tell you all the rumors are wrong. The Eastern, Midwestern, and Southern Top Fuel drivers were all super people and the California drivers loved the idea of racing them. If it wasn't for the cars coming out to California on tour, drag racing would have never grown like it did.

Jim "The Lizard" Herbert, protected by the best Bill Simpson had to offer at the time. Had his blower erupted in flame, a not at all uncommon occurrence, Herbert would have at least had a fighting chance. *Steve Reyes*

During the process of putting together the story of Mickey Thompson and Lions Drag Strip in Long Beach, I was put in touch with Mickey's first wife, Judy Thompson Creach. She consented to offer up a few remarks about her time with Mickey and tell a couple of tales regarding Long Beach and its formative years.

The following is her view of the story.

JUDY THOMPSON CREACH

At the time when Mickey began to think about getting involved in building a drag strip, he was driving a dragster, the first slingshot style if I remember correctly, and we were racing all over California. Mickey had also run in the Pan-American Road Race in Mexico and he was getting a lot of attention. He wanted to use his influence to help kids become more responsible when it came to racing on the streets.

We had also become close friends with C.J. Hart while he was running Santa Ana, and I'm not sure how much that relationship contributed to Mickey's decision when it came to Long Beach.

Mickey had always wanted to get the kids off the streets and, at the same time, give the real racers a great track on which to run. During the '50s, street racing in and around Long Beach was as big a problem as it was in Los Angeles. The newspapers and the police departments were at war with the kids in car clubs, and with hot rodders in general.

In an effort to solve some of the problems, a local Long Beach car club and certain police officers agreed that the hot rodders needed somewhere to race without fear of getting hassled. About that time, Mickey became involved with the Lions Clubs and the Long Beach car club to begin planning for a drag strip.

I don't remember the details of the agreements and arrangements Mickey made with the Lions

Early in his career, McEwen drove for Gene Adams. Adams was the king of Oldsmobile-powered dragsters, but had to be persuaded to run fuel. McEwen talked Gene into running 25 percent nitro when they took the car to Bakersfield in the mid-1960s. *Jim White/ Tom McEwen collection*

Above, right, and opposite page: North vs South! Mongoose vs Snake! One way Lions Associated Drag Strip got crowds to the track was by creating blood feuds, then advertising them on posters and in magazines and newspapers. The ploy worked. Fans flocked to The Beach, and any Saturday night bore witness to the greatest Top Fuel show on earth. *Steve Reyes*

Clubs, but I understand that Mickey has told all that in interviews over the years. The one thing I do remember is our first opening day race. We had spread the word through the car clubs and by advertising in local newspapers, but we had no idea how many people were going to show up.

The opening day was a Sunday and we figured that the crowd would be slow to show up. We could not have been more wrong. Long before we opened the front gate, it looked like a mass evacuation. Cars were lined up from our front gate all the way down the street on both sides and extending about a mile down 223rd Street. It was a mob scene. We thought we had planned for every eventuality, but we didn't have a clue.

Once the track got running with some semblance of order, Mickey had me working the tower with two other staff members recording the times of each car. Mickey built the tower and, of course, it was in his

SAN FRANCISCO AND L. A. CONTINUE BATTLE FOR CULTURAL SUPREMACY.....
FEUD BETWEEN CITIES SPREADS TO DRAG RACING!

SO. SAN FRANCISCO SENDS:
THE GOTELLI SPEED SHOP SPL.
211 MPH!

★★★★★★★★★★★★★★★

SO. CALIFORNIA SENDS:
THE YEAKEL PLYMOUTH SPL.
211 MPH!

MONGOOSE  **WOLVERINE**
(TOM McEWEN) RACES (DENNY MILANI)

LIONS

A.H.R.A SANCTIONED
223rd & ALAMEDA, WILMINGTON
PHONE 424-0961

JUNE 12th SATURDAY NITE

THE "JUNGLE 4" WILL ACT AS BACK UP CAR IN CASE SOMEONE BREAKS.
....
ALSO: TOP FUEL CARS LIKE SCHUBERT AND SWINGLE—HERBERT, R & R ENGINES, MANY MORE
....
SUNDAY—GUY MARTIN OLDS RACING TEAM IN OPEN CHALLENGE TO ALL 4-4-2's AND BUICK GRAND SPORTS! B—O—P DAY AT LIONS

Shown here in his Chizler Top Fuel car, Chris "The Greek" Karamesines has remained one of the most respected and well-liked back-east racers ever to come to California. Ken Fuller built several of his cars, and he even had teams like Beebe & Mulligan carrying "Member of the Greek Fleet" decals on their cars. In 2006, at age 70-something, Karamesines ran a Top Fuel dragster over 300 mph. *Don Brown*

own style which was functional with no frills. To get into the working area, you had to climb a ladder nailed to the side of the building; it was straight up and no hand rails. Once we were up there, the only way to get the timing slips down to the return road so the drivers could pick them up was to clip the slips on a rope with a clothespin and send them down by pulling the rope.

Within a few months, we built more grand-stands. Mickey didn't fight as much with rowdy guys in the pit area, so he could spend more time running the races. The racers had found out real quick that Mickey wasn't fooling around, and he wanted a good and safe place to race. They also found out he was serious about his rules.

It was such a long time ago that most of the day-to-day happenings of my days running Long Beach have fallen through the cracks of faded memories. What I do remember are the good times and all of the fun we had in those days. Every year, at the California Hot Rod Reunion in Bakersfield, those of us who were there relate the same stories over again and laugh just as hard as we did when they actually happened.

A FEW RANDOM MEMORIES

My contribution as a participator in this project can be shaped by a few stories told about a time dear to my heart, but hidden from view by the passing years.

Mickey hated drinking and he would never allow any booze in the pits. One night he calls the staff into a meeting and wants to know why all of the fire extinguishers are empty when there was not a single fire during the entire race. The crew starts laughing and it pissed Mickey off. Finally, the crew tells Mickey that the extinguishers are empty because that's how the guys keep their beer cold. Mickey got really mad and threatened the crew that they might lose their jobs. They told Mickey he wasn't paying them anyway, so what difference would it make?

One of the big rivalries in the early days was Fritz Voight against Jim "Jazzy" Nelson. They raced about every week for the top spot. Their cars ran so close their times and speeds were almost identical. So Fritz built two different nose cones for the front of his car. When he went up against Jazzy, Fritz would install the long nose cone. If he beat Jazzy, then Nelson would go around the pits saying Fritz beat him by a nose. Everyone wanted to win, but it was all fun. If somebody needed help, everyone would pitch in, even if the person you were helping was your biggest competitor.

The reason Long Beach grew in reputation so quickly had to do with the fact that Mickey treated the racers fair and square. At first, we didn't have much to pay in prize money, so Mickey would give the winners a case of oil, or a set of tires, maybe a few tools, things that the racers could use.

Money was tight for the staff, too. Mickey couldn't pay wages to the workers every week, but he did make sure that, if a worker needed a babysitter, he would always give that worker five bucks to pay for the sitter. Our technical inspectors, Ed Davis and Roy Blakeney; our starter, Danny Laris; and even my close friend Edna Baker, who worked the pit gate, told me many times that they were thrilled to be part of the project and that money would come at some point.

Mickey got a big kick out of setting examples for those who broke his rules. He also had an uncanny instinct for detecting anyone breaking his rules. One night, Mickey was down at the entry gate when this carload of kids drove up. Mickey had a hunch something wasn't right, so he walks up to the car and tells the driver, "I notice you guys are here all the time, so tonight we are letting you in free of charge. In fact, I want the whole crowd to meet you." Mickey jumps in the car and tells the driver to go up to the starting line. When the car gets there, Mickey pops the trunk and it's full of the driver's buddies trying to sneak in. Mickey then tells the crowd that he is having a couple of cops throw these guys out for not paying.

Mickey was adamant about keeping the Long Beach drag strip a family-friendly place. He always wanted the fans to be involved. For example, during intermission, when the cars are quiet and fans are bored, he instituted the foot race. He invited all of the Top Fuel drivers and other racers with their crew members to come down to the starting line and then he got fans to come out of the stands, all to have a foot race the entire 1,320 feet of the quarter-mile strip.

Not classified as a fuel burning dragster, the Fiat Coupe built and driven by Jim "Jazzy" Nelson became one of the most infamous cars in California drag racing history. Powered by a Mercury flathead, the tiny car blew off the hottest dragsters of the day. Jazzy had secrets he took to his grave, never telling anyone how the car could run so quickly. Nelson was a master of running nitro and worked closely with Vic Edelbrock Sr. and Ed Iskenderian. Shown here, Jazzy races another coupe and is seen blowing the doors off his archrival Fritz Voight (driving the dragster). *Author's collection/Courtesy of the Edelbrock Corporation*

The winner would get some kind of prize. The fans loved the idea of beating the Top Fuel drivers on their own track.

We can't forget Mickey's temper, which created some interesting circumstances over the years. One situation in particular, although serious, made me laugh until I cried. One night, a Top Fuel car was getting ready to make a run when one of the crew members from another team came running up to Mickey and told him that the driver had been drinking in the pits and was in no condition to drive. Mickey went running to the starting line and reached in the cockpit of the car and started taking off the guy's helmet. When he got it loose, he threw it into the dirt next to the track

and then yanked the driver out of the car by his hair. He had a handful of hair when he finally got the guy out. Then he tossed him out of the track.

Throughout all of the memories I have of Mickey and our days running The Beach, the most vivid reminiscence, the keepsake memento I hold the dearest, is the feeling of innocence that prevailed over all that went on. It may sound corny when compared to our modern, sophisticated, fast-paced lifestyle, but that was a different time. Everything wasn't so fast, and people genuinely liked being around one another.

Mickey and I became close to most of the drivers, although we did have our challenges and issues. Tom McEwen was a brat when he first

Throughout the early '60s, Tom McEwen drove for a number of well-known teams, including Don "The Beachcomber" Johnson, Kenny Lindley, Bivens and Fisher, and Broussard, Davis, and Percell. *Jim White/Tom McEwen collection*

From its first days, Long Beach's Lion's Drag Strip had always been cutting edge, and when Funny Cars became popular The Beach was ready. Here, Gary Afdahl and the Mako Shark Corvette give the fans a thrill. *Ed Justice Jr.*

showed up, and Mickey had to straighten him out. After he banned Tom from the track, he made him work his way back by helping the technical crew inspect cars. I remember Tommy (Tommy Ivo) as being very polite and friendly. He was doing a lot of movie and TV work, but he never acted like a star. As for Donald (Don Prudhomme), he was just a kid trying to get a ride. He was painting cars and racing at the same time. We all know where he went.

As for the rest of the regulars, we loved them, and many of the drivers who came to Long Beach when we started went on to become big names in the sport. Nearly every weekend, Mickey and I would hang out with the drivers. We became friends with many of the regulars; you couldn't help loving these guys, they were all great characters.

Some of the names that pop into my mind are Joaquin Arnett and the Bean Bandits, Art Chrisman, his uncle Jack Chrisman, Gary Cagle, Lou Baney, Emery Cook, Lefty Mudersbach, Howard Johansen, and so many more I can't remember. Of course, all the girls loved Bobby Muravez (a.k.a. Floyd Lippencotte, Jr.). If we girls were working the tower when Bobby came down to fire up his dragster, I would grab a record someone had bought and put it

on the record player we used for the National Anthem and play "I want to be Bobby's Girl," a popular song of the day. It was all fun.

Most of my life has passed and it seems more difficult to hold on to the early days, but sometimes when I just relax and let myself go those days at the Beach will roll in like the fog that used to appear late in the evening, when the racing was so hot it needed cooling. And, I remember certain nights, not every night, but once in a while, when the night would be electrified and you just couldn't get enough of the feeling. Nobody really wanted to go home.

On those nights, after the races were over and the crowd had left, Mickey and I and the crew would gather up the timing lights and the speakers, put everything away, and get ready to leave. Only a funny thing would happen. Many of the Top Fuel drivers and crews would still be hanging around and Mickey would give me a wad of money and I would go to an all-night local grocery store and buy lunch meat, bread, chips, soda, and beer (it was ok after the races), and we would all gather at the starting line and eat. We would laugh and bench race for a couple of hours, not wanting the night to end. For me, racing will never be that way again.

CHAPTER NINE

WHAT IS IT ABOUT FLOYD?

Floyd Lippencotte Jr. won his share of Top Fuel races, but "made his name" behind the wheel of the John Peters-owned Freight Train, a Top Gas dragster running two blown Chevy engines. *Bob Muravez Collection*

Every chapter in history has at least one participant who becomes such an integral part of the effectuation that his or her name becomes synonymous with the time. Babe Ruth, Jesse James, Muhammad Ali, and Andy Warhol are all names with instant recognition. In the history of Southern California drag racing, circa 1950-1970, one name jumps out to represent the essence of that time and its spirit. Actually, the one name posed for this honor is really two.

Bob Muravez and his alter ego, Floyd Lippencotte, Jr., created the stereotype by which all Top Fuel dragster drivers are judged—tall, thin, handsome, and braver than Dick Tracy. What separates Floyd from Bob and most others is the fact that he made his name not in Top Fuel, but in Top Gas dragsters. One might ask why, therefore, is Floyd so important to a story ostensibly concerning itself primarily with those who drove Top Fuel dragsters. The answer is a bit complicated.

Bob Muravez crossed over from fuel- to gas-burning cars as a driver. But his switch created Floyd. Muravez was the link between the gas dragsters and the fuel dragsters and he proved that they were brothers under a communal banner. Dragsters were the life's blood of the sport and they fed off of each other as they grew in technology. Between 1950 and 1970, there was a bond between drivers whose cars ran gas and those who went to the ultimate propellant.

Where's Floyd? Bob Muravez and his dog Prince pose in the fabulous Freight Train dragster. Muravez had to keep his identity secret from his parents, so his alter ego, Floyd, got all the glory. *Bob Muravez Collection*

It is this bonding that allowed Floyd and Bob to act as one. However, for obvious reasons, Bob will relate the story of their relationship.

I have known Muravez since the late 1960s, when we were thrown together as part of a pickup league basketball game between dragster drivers and automotive journalists. Today, at an age when most men his generation are rocking on the porch, Muravez is rocking at the drag strip, making 250-mile-per-hour blasts behind the wheel of vintage dragsters. It is hard to distinguish between Bob and his alter ego Floyd as to who is having the most fun, but both jumped at the chance to record their thoughts and memories in those decades spanning our story.

BOB MURAVEZ A.K.A. FLOYD LIPPENCOTTE, JR.

I was born in hot rodder heaven, commonly known as Southern California. I grew up in the San Fernando Valley, the place where hot rodding and race cars were everywhere and kids like me dreamed of the day when we would be driving. For kids my age at the time, our big deal was going to a drag strip with the older guys or cruising by a drive-in to see all of the street rods. We used to go to local speed shops just to look around at all the cool parts hanging on the walls and pick up on what the hot rod guys were talking about, then repeat what we heard to our friends.

In 1955, all of the wishing and hoping reached a mighty crescendo when I became the owner of a 1954 Corvette with a six-cylinder, 150-horsepower, Blue Flame engine with three Carter YH carburetors. The car had some history as well—it once belonged to the very famous movie actress Betty Grable. The first thing I did was head for the drag strip. It took two runs before the Powerglide automatic puked itself all over the strip, leading me to discover that running your street transportation at the drags was not very smart.

I decided to keep the Corvette for cruising Bob's Drive In and find another way to express my desire to race. Very fortunate for me was the fact that the city of Burbank was home to one of the most famous car clubs in Southern California, called the Road Kings. I joined as a junior member and somehow found my way to TV Tommy Ivo's garage.

Ivo was a senior member of the club and had just begun his drag racing career. He needed a grunt and I was just the guy for the job. Ivo was running a gasoline-burning dragster at the time. The car was built by Ken Fuller and was powered by an injected Buick V8. This particular car was an extreme example of what was happening in drag racing at the time. Dragsters were becoming more sophisticated and Ivo had a decent racing budget, so he was in the forefront of this dragster revolution.

In true California fashion, the Dragmaster team went to Hollywood. One of their cars was used in the Universal Studios production of "The Lively Set," starring Doug McClure (left) and James Darren (right). *Dode Martin Collection*

My primary jobs were cleaning and waxing and chasing after parts. If I worked hard, I got to go to the races as a crew member.

The very first time we ran the car at San Fernando, I fell in love with the idea of driving a dragster. Ivo had this cool leather jacket and Tony Nancy leather face mask attached to aviator goggles. The whole outfit gave him an image of a real racer.

I really have to take pause and offer up some memories of the atmosphere and lifestyle prevailing in Burbank during the mid-1950s. Burbank was still a small town, located in the heart of the San Fernando Valley, surrounded by orange groves, palm trees, and quiet neighborhoods where families lived in Spanish-style homes with tile roofs and stucco

THE CAR CLUB OF CHAMPIONS

Car clubs and California have always been synonymous in the world of hot rods. Going back to the late 1920s and the dry lakes of the Mojave Desert, groups of racers joined forces to compile knowledge and find comradeship. Colorful names identified one club from the other. Roaring across the sands of Muroc Lake would be members of the Gophers, Mobilers, Road Runners, Bungholers, Throttlers, Albata, Sidewinders, 90 mph Club, and Idlers. Most, if not all, California hot rod pioneers were in clubs and ran the lakes, Vic Edelbrock, Sr., Stu Hilborn, Ak Miller, Jack McGrath, Manny Ayulo, NHRA Founder Wally Parks, Jack Engle, Phil Remington, movie star Robert Stack, the Spalding Brothers, and Ray Brown, to name a few. When talking about car clubs and Top Fuel drag racing in California, there is only one name that stands at the top: the Road Kings of Burbank.

The Road Kings club was founded in 1952 by a hot rodder named Ralph Marshall. Marshall was joined by his wife, Margaret; Dave Osterkamp; Al Totlenno; and an additional 17 members, all from the city of Burbank, and all younger than 21 years old.

By the mid-1950s, the Road Kings had grown into a group of dedicated racers. Unlike many of the early car clubs, which spent their efforts racing the dry lakes and the streets of Southern California, the Road Kings turned to the newest form of auto racing and the drag strip. They even built a dragster to prove they were serious racers. Before long, membership grew to around 35 or 40, and, although Road Kings could be found in all classes of drag racing, it was fuel-burning machines that became the club's tradition.

From the earliest years, the Road Kings drew the interest of serious racers. Tommy Ivo, Tom McCurry, Kenny Safford, Don the Beachcomber Johnson, and chassis builders Roy Fjastad, Rod Pepmuller, Don Gaide, and Jim Miles all were hardcore racers. The second generation of Road Kings produced the likes of Don Prudhomme (who actually drove the club's Fuel Dragster), Bob Muravez, the Cedarquist Brothers, Gary Cassidy, and also the formation of the Don Gaide, Kenny Stafford, and Don Ratican team run-

walls. People were safe and secure, and the thought of super-sized shopping malls and freeways remained distant fantasies.

The one thing Burbank did have was a flourishing devotion to creating hot cars. This captivation for the automobile was a byproduct of World War II and the aircraft industry. Burbank was a strategic aircraft industry center during the war. Large plants and small shops produced untold numbers of aircraft components for the war effort. After the conflict, Burbank became home to aircraft surplus stores filled with a bountiful supply of exotic metals, tubing, fuel lines, fittings, aircraft-quality nuts, bolts and fasteners of every description, and all for pennies on the dollar. It was a treasure chest of technology waiting to be discovered by the race car builder.

Burbank also sported the movie industry. Warner Brothers and other studios dotted the landscape and in the back lots of movie making were the great stars of the time, many of whom were car enthusiasts.

This combination of movie star glamour, money, and surplus stores filled with cheap, high-tech innovations, all in a place where the sun shines 350 days a year—well, it was little wonder that the hot rod movement exploded. It was not just Burbank, but the entire San Fernando Valley in which the performance industry was blooming.

ning what would become a truly famous Oldsmobile Top Fuel car. Not only did the club produce Top Fuel champions, but other members achieved success in Fuel Coupes, Gas Dragsters, Fuel Boats, the Bonneville Salt Flats, circle track racing, sports cars, and motorcycles.

In 1967 another San Fernando Car Club called the Road Rumblers joined forces with the Road Kings to form a larger and more diverse group of racers.

All of the Road Kings interviewed for this project, including Ivo, Prudhomme, Stafford, and Muravez, agreed that their membership changed their lives and went a long way to help create a career in drag racing.

As Kenny Safford put it, "The Road Kings were more than just a bunch of hot rodders hanging around Bob's Big Boy drive-in. We were all serious racers, and we all helped each other to learn the ropes."

Prudhomme adds, "I leaned a lot from being a member of the Road Kings. They changed me from being a street racer to being a real racer."

Bob Muravez says, "One thing about the Road Kings, if they caught you screwing around on the street you got an ass-chewing at the next meeting and sometimes they would hit you with a fine."

Ivo says, "When I built my first modified Model T roadster with a Buick engine, being a member of the Road Kings was a big deal, and there was a lot of tradition built around the image of hot rodding, the city of Burbank, and Southern California being the capital of drag racing."

Today, the Road Kings still claim more than 100 members, but they limit their racing to Vintage cars and cruising street rods. According to their own press clippings, the Road Kings have become more of a hot rod club than a race car club. They put a tremendous emphasis on charity work, raising money through putting on excellent car shows.

However, when you gather the oldest member for some bench racing, the subject always turns to the days of cruising Bob's Big Boy, drag racing at "The Pond" (San Fernando drag strip), and bragging about the once-young kids who became superstars in the sport of Top Fuel racing.

Frank Kurtis had his facility, located in Glendale, building Indianapolis 500 roadsters and midgets for drivers like Bill Vukovich, Jack McGrath, and many of their friends. Manufacturers like Venolia Pistons, Barney Navarro Racing Equipment, Phil Weiand, and speed shops like So-Cal Speed Shop offered the latest in parts and pieces. There were even places a racer could go for a complete ready-to-run race car. Famed upholsterer Tony Nancy opened a complex in Woodland Hills where chassis builder Ken Fuller would weld up a chassis, engine builder Ed Pink could install the power, and Tony would have one of his pals pound out a body and then finish the job with one of his hand-stitched leather seats. The city of Burbank even had a Bonneville Streamliner bearing its name, built and driven by a local garage owner named George Hill. The valley was the place.

As I became more involved in drag racing, I realized that being a member of the Road Kings was not like other car clubs of the time. The Road Kings club was made up entirely of real racers like Ivo. If you were caught squirreling around in your street car, you were in line to get a public admonishment at the next meeting.

As a side note to my joining the Road Kings, I was initiated into the club with the world-famous Don "the Snake" Prudhomme. Only he wasn't famous yet, so both of us had to face the wrath of the established members. It was not a pretty sight. As the story goes, I was dressed in drag, girl's clothes, and given an assignment.

My job was to sit in a rickshaw, owned by the father of a Road King member who had bought it in China. Donald was wearing a baby diaper made from an old bed sheet. Donald's job was to haul me through the drive-in area of the Bob's Big Boy hamburger stand in Burbank. However, the club members discovered that Prudhomme was not known that well in Burbank because he was a Van Nuys guy. So, we had to reenact the same scene at the Bob's in Van Nuys. This time The Snake got really red, but it was all in good fun.

Working for Ivo turned me into a hardcore drag racer and I was not satisfied with grunt chores anymore. I wanted to drive dragsters. By the late '50s, early '60s, California became the focal point for the country's drag racers. Big names from the East came west to check out the competition, and I wanted to get in on the action.

In my mind, the only chance to become part of the dragster class was to build an engine. I couldn't afford both an engine and a chassis, so a common practice back then was to partner up with someone and form a team. As luck would have it, a fellow Road King, named Don Gaide, had bought a used chassis built by a well-known racer and chassis builder named Rod Pepmuller. When Don went looking for an engine, I was ready to install my blown Chevy and go racing.

It was agreed that I would do the driving, and we began to run a couple of the local tracks, the Pond and the Beach, gaining experience and just having fun.

Fuel-burning dragsters had the top spot in the drag racing pecking order. But, in the late '50s and early '60s, nitro became an issue with both the NHRA and Mickey Thompson. Fuel was banned at NHRA meets and Mickey did the same at Long Beach. Banning fuel caused some bitter feelings, and many of the dragster teams decided to kiss off the NHRA and Long Beach in favor of running what they called outlaw tracks. There was no way some of the hardcore guys were going to give up nitro.

By 1962, the ban was lifted. Mickey Thompson told me that he felt the safety of the cars had been improved and running fuel was okay. The NHRA, in my opinion, lifted the ban because the outlaw tracks were getting bigger crowds because the fans wanted to see the Top Fuel cars.

When the '60s hit, drag racing started to grow into a youth culture thing like rock & roll music, drugs, and the sexual revolution. California was still king of the hill. In fact, I have a theory about this very fact.

The reason why California was the leader in Top Fuel and Top Gas dragsters was simple: we had more cars. Sure, Florida had Don Garlits, Ohio had Joe Schubeck. The state of Texas produced stars like Eddie Hill and Vance Hunt. Chris Karamesines was a huge name in the Midwest and the same goes for Jimmy Nix. In the early days, racers like Setto Postoian, Melvin Heath, Art Arfons, and Neil Leffler came west with established reputations.

But, for every hard-running dragster based east of Phoenix, there were 10 cars in California. There were two reasons for this out-of-balance ratio: the weather was one contributing issue, but the major factor was that most of the speed equipment manufacturers and Top Fuel engine builders were in California.

The drivers and crews would hang out at various speed shops around Southern California, depending on their location and their loyalty to certain manufacturers. For example, Joe Reath would host racers from Long Beach, Los Angeles, and Orange County, and a completely different group would frequent Ansen Automotive, owned by Louie Senter.

The relationship between racers and manufacturers became even more critical when fuel became the big issue. The teams didn't have engineers and computers or on-board data acquisition systems. They just used a simple hydrometer to determine fuel percentages. The idea was to put in more nitro and get more power. The problem was, the more the nitro percentage, the greater the damage when things went bad.

The manufacturers quickly realized that if they made a better part, all the racers would buy from them. One company developed a stronger rod, another a better piston, and the process continued for crankshafts, cams, blowers, clutches, tires, even down to the smallest pieces. Everything being created for the fuel-burning dragsters was predicated on how much power nitro produced. Those of us who couldn't afford nitro were forced to run gasoline, but there was a trickle-down effect, and better, stronger parts found their way into the Top Gas dragster ranks.

For a period of time, the gas dragsters and the fuel burners were related in many ways. But, by the mid-1960s, Top Fuel was king. There seems to be a conflict about why gas dragsters and fuel dragsters became so distant. I think that drag racing historians make too much of the so-called fuel ban from '57 to '62. It was only a small part of the history related to California drag racing. Granted, in NHRA competition Top Gas was a big deal, but many racers never stopped using fuel. They just moved on to outlaw strips that allowed its use.

The real truth of the matter is that the gas and fuel dragster teams went in different directions because of escalating costs and, in some cases, it was the safety issue. In the mid '60s, Top Fuel drivers paid an inordinately high price for going fast—engine fires, blower explosions, clutch failures, a lot of stuff that didn't happen to Top Gas dragsters. It didn't mean that gas dragsters were second rate; it just meant different ideas and goals.

As things worked out, I ended up in the Top Gas dragster ranks, at least during the time covered by this story. In my opinion, we stood side by side with the Top Fuel drivers as the sport moved forward.

By 1962, I had progressed to the point of having an excellent ride in the Top Gas class. I was driving the Qunicy Automotive Special, a twin-engine Chevy-powered car built by John Peters and Nye Frank. This car would become the Freight Train. We

went to the Smokers U.S. Fuel & Gas Championships in Bakersfield with high hopes.

Remember that, in 1961, Lefty Mudersbach won the final round driving an unblown twin-engine Chevy running gas, beating Jack Ewell. Ewell was driving a Top Fuel car, so Ewell was declared the Top Fuel Champion of the meet. Talk about parity—that was an accomplishment that we looked at as a possibility.

We didn't beat any Top Fuel cars, but we won the Top Gas Eliminator title. My fellow Road King buddy, Donald Prudhomme, won Top Fuel driving the Dave Zeuschel/Ken Fuller car. I was on top of the world.

When I came home from the race, my dad gave me a choice to make. He told me what I had done was a great accomplishment and not many drivers would ever win as big a race as Bakersfield, so I should consider my blessings. Then he gave me an ultimatum of either going racing full time or coming into the family appliance business. I said, "Hey, I'll come into the business. You can't make a living driving dragsters."

A very rare shot of Bob Muravez driving the famed Nye Frank Pulsator twin-engine Chevy Fuel Dragster without the streamliner body. The car was one of a very few 1960s dragsters running a fully-enclosed body. *Bob Muravez Collection*

Not all early dragster champions came from California. Melvin Heath was based in Oklahoma and beat the boys from the west coast at the 1956 NHRA Nationals. Heath did, however, use speed equipment manufactured in California. Hot Rod/Motor Trend *Archives*

I officially retired in June of 1962—never to drive a dragster again.

Wrong! Nye and John had put Land Speed Record holder Craig Breedlove in the car, and he had a terrible time controlling the trajectory of the car. Next came Tom McEwen, he had the same problem. In this first version of the car, Nye had built the front end with coil-over shocks. The idea was that, as the car left the starting line, the front end would rise up about 10 inches, transferring the weight to the rear wheels. The trick to keeping the car straight was timing.

The car was equipped with rack-and-pinion steering. When you would leave the starting line, the car would take a sharp right turn. The driver had to have perfect timing in turning the wheel a quarter turn to the left. If you didn't have the touch, the car was all over the track. At the top end, running about 180 miles per hour, the process was done in reverse, and you had to turn right when you rolled back the throttle. In

between the starting line and the finish, every time you got off and on the throttle, you had to correct the steering.

The drivers were just not used to that type of handling. The real problem was that it had taken me a long time and many runs to get the technique down, and the new drivers wanted to go fast right away. They had no patience. Even the great Leonard Harris tried and he didn't like the car at all. Finally, Nye and John put Bill Alexander in the car and he stayed with it the longest and he began to understand the principle and the car began to run hard again. But, Bill got the chance to drive a Ken Fuller-built car for Ernie Alverado. Ernie owned a camera store and the car was called the "Shudderbug." In my opinion, it was one of the most beautiful full-bodied cars ever built.

About four months into my retirement, I was still crewing on the car, and one night at The Beach, Alexander says to me, "Bobby, we have made so

Floyd Lippencotte, Jr., driving newly-christened Freight Train at Fontana in 1963. *Bob Muravez Collection*

many changes to this car that even you couldn't get it down the track." So, I slipped into Bill's fire suit and helmet, and had a pass in the car. I turned 185 miles per hour, and as straight as an arrow. It was decided right then and there that I would get back into the car.

Only we had a big problem: I didn't want anyone to know it was me. So, I went to Doris Herbert, who owned *Drag News* newspaper at the time, and asked her not to show my face in the paper. I also went around to the starting line photographers and asked them to do the same. I assured everyone that I would never take my facemask off when I was in the car. I started driving under the car owner's name, John Peters. Two months later, we win the NHRA Winternationals in Pomona. To avoid being discovered, I had a friend of mine named Rex put on my leather jacket and driving gear and kiss the race queen and get my trophy.

After the Winternationals, my situation got a little sticky. At the time, *Drag News* had a promotion going called Mr. Eliminator, a top-ten list for both Top Fuel and Top Gas cars. The idea was that any-

one on the list could challenge the number one spot in a match race format. We ended up Number One and, at the end of 1963, got challenged by Sneaky Pete Robinson for our position. San Gabriel drag strip offered us a thousand dollars to race Robinson. Imagine that: a thousand bucks for a gas car to race. Unheard of in 1963.

By the time the race came around, my hidden identity was really causing problems and I needed to find a new way to hide. Two friends of mine, Steve Gibbs and Mel Reck, decided that what I needed was a new name. Gibbs was writing stories for Mickey and Judy Thompson, who owned Fontana drag strip and Reck was the announcer at the same track. Gibbs had a college professor named Lippencotte, so he came up with Erwin Lippencotte III. We kicked that around and eventually changed it to Floyd Lippencotte, Jr. And, so, I became an alias.

Name changing was not limited to just Floyd. The relationship between Nye Frank, John Peters, and Quincy Automotive wore thin, and Nye and John began running on their own. This move meant that the team needed a new image.

Awesome, beautiful and winner of "Best Engineered Car" at the 1965 NHRA Winternationals was the "Pulsator," created by Nye Frank and driven by Floyd Lippencott Jr. (aka Bob Muravez). The car featured two unblown Chevy engines, and a total body package. Muravez says, "The car was very quiet because the driver was totally enclosed with a canopy. It was sort of peaceful going 200 mph." *Don Brown*

Long before streamlining and aerodynamics, Flaming Frank covered his home-built fuel digger with a Fiat coupe body and called it "Show Time." Pedregon proved that drag racing was more than just speed; it was smoke and fire, noise and image. *Jere Alhadeff*

One Saturday, we ran Fontana Raceway, then owned by Mickey Thompson. Mickey's first wife, Judy, worked the tower, and we all had been close friends since the early days at The Beach. The track had several bumps at the far end and, when you ran really fast, the rear wheels would bounce slightly and get airborne. This day, I made a strong run and, when I hit the bumps, the rear wheels unloaded and the tires spun, causing the two engines to rev high. This process created a blast of black smoke to come out of the headers. Judy was on the PA system and she exclaimed, "Hey, that car looks like a train!" From that point on, we ran the Freight Train.

We were very lucky, because the Train became popular with the kids and they created a following, dragging along their parents. Kids love trains, and we would dress up like railroad workers, wearing bib overalls, red neckerchief, and engineer hats. The Train was one of the first theme cars in drag racing.

No matter what people say, I believe that the fuel ban during the early '60s put a wedge between some of the drivers.

During the ban, the Top Gas dragsters got a lot of the glory, and that pissed off the fuel racers because their spotlight was taken away. Gas drivers would say that anybody can go fast on nitro, but it takes brains to make a gas car go fast. I felt torn because I had driven both gas and fuel cars. The fuel cars had to run outlaw in order to make any money. The fans lost out because they didn't always get to see the big speeds. The gas cars were quiet by comparison to the ground-shaking fuel cars. Fans loved getting their ears blown out and their eyes and noses filled with fumes.

For a time, things were confusing. Money played a big role in the gas vs. fuel wars. The outlaw tracks paid cash money to the fuel cars and the gas cars would get a Savings Bond. Top Fuel paid $500 at some tracks and Top Gas would get a $50 bond worth $37.50. We even ran the Train on fuel several times. If you see a photo of the Train with two fuel tanks in the front, we are running nitro. Once the ban of fuel was lifted, even the Village Idiot knew there was no money in Top Gas dragsters.

Once Top Fuel was reinstated, the Top Gas cars changed direction. Many of the teams went to two engines, both blown and unblown. For us, the Freight Train had something going: it had promotion appeal. In the 1960s, track promoters got a message, and that was the fact that, in order to get the fans in the gate, they had to have a gimmick, a promotion, and name identification became the way to start.

Above and top: Bob Muravez, sans Floyd, was an awesome Top Fuel driver and did his share of winning big events. In 1965, Muravez, driving the Don "the Beachcomber" Johnson's Roy Fjastad-chassis fuel digger, won the Mickey Thompson 200 mph Invitational race at Long Beach. Cars had to have previously run over 200 mph to qualify. Note Beachcomber Don standing with arms folded as Bob poses in the winner's circle. *Bob Muravez Collection*

The idea was to give racers names and then promote them on radio, in magazines, and in the newspaper. It started slow, but soon it seemed everybody and every car had a name. We had the Train and there was the Snake, the Mongoose, the Loner, TV Tommy, the Zookeeper, the Surfers, Flaming Frank Pedregon, the Frantic Four, and Don the Beachcomber.

Above and opposite page: Even the most diehard Top Fuel racer conceded that by the early '70s, California drag racing was going through an evolution—the Funny Car would soon become a fixture, and the front-engine Top Fuel car would soon become history. *Tom Madigan*

The racers from back East caught onto the idea quick enough. The Swamp Rat had been around for a while, but soon invaders like The Greek, the Bounty Hunter, Sneaky Pete Robinson, Gentleman Joe, and the Green Kid (Art Malone) headed west to join in the fun. The radio air waves were then filled with high-pitched announcers challenging fans to come out and witness struggles between drivers with strange-sounding monikers.

With the promotion frenzy came an increase in costs to the teams, who now had to live up to their billings and put on a show. Although it was a subtle transformation, money began to play into the world of Top Fuel dragsters. The cars from the East got tow money or appearance money from track owners to venture west. Many teams would spend the winter racing in California. They could earn enough to build a new car, maybe even a car built by a California chassis builder. Staying the winter also allowed time for research and development sessions with local California manufacturers.

Big-name California cars wanted their piece of the pie and started asking for appearance money. Match racing became another moneymaker. East cars could run West Coast cars in grudge races, getting paid cash money for the winner. Even the losers got paid.

Like any business venture, supply and demand dictates outcome. At first, Top Fuel teams multiplied and tracks would get 100 cars to an event. Then costs went up in relation to speeds, and soon money was the culprit. Name cars got the first-in-line treatment and small, local teams sucked hind tit. Suddenly, if you were just a weekend racer and didn't win round money or top eliminator money, there was no way to keep going. Many of the local hardcore Top Fuel teams ignored the changes and went on racing for the pure love of the sport. They would hang on for a while, but it wouldn't be easy.

For me, I could see the money train coming and I knew that corporate racing was just around the corner.

This whole mindset of change reached a climax in the late '60s.

Teams were divided into two camps: those with budgets, and those who were living on a shoestring. The bad side of this situation was the low-budget teams had to win no matter what. Just dump the can (nitro) and hope for the best. This thinking could end badly—the 1,000-foot bomb became the offspring of too much nitro. For the other teams, those with some reserve in their budgets, they knew that, in order to make a profit and stay alive during an event, you had to build in reliability and safety. In order to win an event, a car had to survive through many rounds of racing.

An example of this scenario happened to me in the mid-1960s. There was a money meet at Long

Beach and nearly 100 Top Fuel cars showed up. I was driving for Don Johnson at the time, and he always had a very well-prepared car.

The race had so many cars that an exception was made for anyone who had run 200 miles per hour in the past. You did not have to qualify for the race if you were a 200-mile-per-hour car. They simply made a list of cars and paired them on a random basis. Each round paid money, so the more rounds you went, the better the payday. I can't remember how much you got for winning, but it was a couple grand at least. We won the event, but had to go seven rounds of eliminations. It became very evident that in order to make money, you had to last.

When engine builders like Ed Pink, Keith Black, Sid Waterman, and Dave Zeuschel began building horsepower motors for those who could afford the price tag, the only hope for the budget teams was to load up on nitro and try to pick off one of the big teams in hopes of earning a few bucks and bragging rights to shooting down a name.

The same mindset created by the racers carried over onto the product manufacturers and their way of thinking.

To make real money, manufacturers needed their products to be used by the masses, the amateur racers, and street rodders. They had to have winning cars for ads to be placed in national magazines. If a manufacturer was going to put sponsor money into a Top Fuel dragster, that car had to win. Money talked and bullshit walked. The Marketing Man could care less about the purity of the sport, the true meaning of racing Top Fuel. He wanted ink, baby....

When corporate racing took over, I couldn't stay with the program. I had too many business and family commitments. I retired Floyd Lippencotte, Jr., and returned to being just Bob Muravez. I consider myself a very lucky person to have been able to compete in drag racing during its most meaningful time period.

When someone asks me to tell a story about the old days, I always relate my favorite. We went to Taft, California, a farming town southwest of Bakersfield, to run a local track. It was a night race, and the promoter's idea of lighting the track was to have a single searchlight mounted at the starting line facing down the track. You would leave the starting line and head down the track into a black hole. We did it because that was the way it was. Racing was racing, and you adjusted.

Many years after Floyd and I retired, I was paid the greatest compliment I could have ever expected. John Force was asked who was his hero when he started racing, and he said he couldn't remember the guys' last name because it was real long, but he remembered that the car he drove had two engines and when it came to the starting line, he would run to the fence to watch.

Force went on to comment that he thought the driver's first name was Floyd.

CHAPTER TEN

GETTING HIP

Not only did Tommy Ivo prove to be a tremendous driver, he also built his own cars. He loved the mechanical side of racing as much as he did the driving. *Tommy Ivo Collection*

It would be ludicrous to try to convince anyone that Top Fuel drag racers in California were not influenced by the Swinging Sixties. This time period was a turning point in the whole country's Cultural Revolution. It was the changing of the guard—new rules with new attitudes. The hip generation came into being.

California could no longer claim its isolationism as the Mecca for Top Fuel warriors. Now, cars from every state in the union came calling on the West Coast hotshoes to do battle.

The 1960s, of course, were more than the story of drag racing. During the decade, the United States experienced some of its most turbulent times. The country fought an unpopular war in a land few had ever heard of. At home, Civil Rights tore out the hearts of millions, pitting black against white in a struggle as fierce as in the years of slavery. A beloved president, a fervent voice for Civil Rights, then the brother of the aforementioned beloved president would all die by the gun. Music twisted into a strange sound and teenagers idolized the likes of the Beatles, the Stones, the Kinks, and a poet named Dylan. Men went to the moon, while poverty raged in big cities.

The innocent 1950s were gone. Ozzie and Harriett had closed up the house and moved from the neighborhood. Being hip was the rage. *Father Knows Best* was replaced by the teachings of a guru named Dr. Tim, whose message was carried by three simple letters: LSD. New names became main-

A slice of 1960s cheesecake, posed on the streets of San Francisco's North Beach. This promotional shot featured Tommy Ivo's Top Fuel car and beauty Yvonne D'Angons. *Steve Reyes*

headers, and breathtaking crashes took their places in the spectacle everyone came to expect.

The 1960s were, as this story goes, the jumping-off point in the climb to the pinnacle of drag racing success. The decade provided an explosion of new ideas—everything was an experiment and every day something new appeared. Life was to be lived on the edge, even if only in the imagination.

Into this counterculture environment came the new breed of Top Fuel driver. They were cocky, aggressive, and fearless. The Top Fuel driver of the 1960s wanted image, wanted to be set apart from the others in drag racing. They wanted to make history, be it good or bad. During the 1960s, just being hip was half the battle.

POISON IVO

Of all the characters who played a part in this story, none were more surprising, complex, and revealing than TV Tommy Ivo. Quiet, lightweight, and youthful looking throughout his life, Ivo proved to be two complete personalities in one man. He was, in his youth, a fantastic entertainer, a movie actor, stage player; a person of fantasy. Then, when Tommy donned his leather race mask, he became a key player in Top Fuel history.

I first met Tommy Ivo during my incubation period as a dragster driver. The location was Long Beach drag strip. I was part of the Pfaff & Sowins team running a blown, fuel-burning Chevy small block. Dave Sowins had built the chassis and a fellow named Eddie Potter had pounded out the body. Ivo was running his dual-engine, unblown, gasoline-powered Buick dragster. At the time, it was commonplace for unblown gas dragsters sporting two engines to run against a blown, single-engine fuel car. I remember he came over and checked out our car. He was pleasant, friendly, and reserved. He made small talk, but his eyes told a different story. Ivo knew that the car he was examining had little chance against his monster.

Over the years, we crossed paths on many occasions at the shop of Tony Nancy, a friend to both of us. In 2001, we renewed our friendship while attending a party at the NHRA museum honoring Vic Edelbrock, Sr., as a hot rod pioneer. In 2006, Ivo agreed to relate his part of the California 1950-1970 drag racing story.

The interview was conducted at his home, on "Ivo time." What is Ivo time, you might ask? The product of years on the road and working long into the night, Ivo long ago discovered that his world works best when conducted from mid-afternoon to

stream: The Beach Boys, Malcolm X, James Bond, and Muhammad Ali. No one saw the dangers of smoking pot or burning draft cards. There would be no turning back—the revolution had begun.

If the 1960s seemed to be tearing the fabric of the nation apart, the opposite was being played out in the world of drag racing. During these chaotic times, Top Fuel racing in California exploded into its most dynamic period.

With raw and unabashed innovation, Top Fuel racers broke down the gates of confinement and engaged in an orgy of speed and power. The number of Top Fuel dragsters increased as fast as tubing could be welded into place. New drag strips provided new battlegrounds. Fans flocked to witness the power and satisfy their lust for speed. Nitromethane was the drug of choice and smoking tires, flame-throwing exhaust the following morning. Daylight, in his world, is for sleeping. No phone calls before 2:00 p.m.

As we began the interview, I was struck by the blending of his surroundings. Years of racing memorabilia were offset by artwork from around the world, remnants of movie sets, posters, and photos of movies now found only on Turner Classic Movies late in the night. It was obvious that some complexity was about to be exposed.

TOMMY IVO

Before we can talk about the racing aspect of my life, it would be advantageous to explore what created my career in drag racing and how things ended up the way they did.

I was born in Denver, Colorado, and lived there until I was seven years old. Very early on in my childhood, I discovered a gift. When only five years old, I discovered my voice was as strong as a much older child, carrying the tune and tone of a song. My family, being Swedish, had a tradition of throwing large parties for any occasion. When my parents brought me to a party, I would sing and, once I started, it was difficult to shut me up. I knew from my earliest recollections that singing and dancing would be my life. When World War II was raging, I had the opportunity to play in shows at military hospitals to entertain the wounded troops.

We were dirt poor, no money, and my mother had terrible arthritis not helped by winter in Denver.

Tommy Ivo (foreground) was the first California dragster driver to go on tour back east and get paid for his efforts. Ivo also maintained a huge following in California, partly because he was based out of Burbank and partly because he was a TV and movie star. Here, he competes at the 1964 NHRA Winternationals. *Don Brown*

Finally, someone told my mom that she should take me to New York or Hollywood. Her choice was Hollywood. I started doing amateur shows and one day, at what the show-business people refer to as a Cattle Call at Republic Studios, I was picked to play the son of Dennis O'Keefe (a big star at the time). My getting picked was a sign of things to come. There were about 20 little boys with blond hair standing in the line waiting to be picked. The director chose me because I had just lost my two front teeth and I had the look he wanted.

That first encounter with the business led to over 100 movies and appearances on 200 television shows. Over my career, I worked with many famous actors, including Dennis O'Keefe, Boris Karloff, William Holden, Rudy Vallee, Spencer Tracy, Irene Dunne, Myrna Loy, and Edgar Bergen. However, most of the drag racers know me from the 1961 TV show *Margie*, where I played Heywood Botts, the dorky boyfriend.

When I turned sixteen, I bought a 1952 Buick, then moved up to a 1955 Buick Century, and found a home at the drag races. Stuck on Buick V-8 engines, I decided to build a real hot rod. I built a Buick-powered T-bucket roadster fashioned after a car I had seen at Bob's Drive In. It was owned by a colorful character, and part-time movie actor, named Norm Grabowski. The car was a real racing machine and was never beaten in its class. It even won a couple of top eliminator races, beating a dragster in the process.

After the roadster, there was no going back. The next step came when Don "The Beachcomber" Johnson asked me if I would like to run my roadster engine in his Ken Fuller-built dragster. Yes! From there I wanted to build my own car, so I contacted Fuller to build a chassis fashioned after a Scotty Fenn-style car with what we called a Trapeze roll bar. The car came out awesome and, because the fuel ban was on at the time, the injected Buick engine used in the car turned it into the biggest bear in the woods. It was the first gas-powered dragster to run under 9 1/2 seconds ET.

The little car ran its course as the other competitors caught up in technology, so we began running a

The crossing of two worlds is engaged as TV Tommy Ivo explains the finer points of going 200 miles per hour in a Top Fuel car to world-famous Formula One champion Sir Sterling Moss. *Tommy Ivo collection*

The very first snap-shots taken of the Tommy Ivo four-engine Buick powered dragster. Built by Ken Fuller, Ivo brought the car to San Fernando Drag Strip for its initial testing. Track manager Harry Hibler took these photos shortly before the first run made on the car.
Harry Hibler

As early as 1956, fuel dragsters began to take on the look of real race cars. Oakland, California racer Romeo Palamides created a masterpiece of drag-racing art, powered by a fuel injected DeSoto Hemi engine. The unique roll bar was added after the car was originally completed. He would later reprise his fascination with unique powerplants, building a jet car. Hot Rod/Motor Trend *Archives*

supercharged Buick. But, after seeing the Howard Cam twin-engine car, I wanted a twin. Again, Ken Fuller was the builder and we created the twin-engine Buick. It was the car that made me famous, or infamous, as a drag racer. It was the first gas car in the eight-second bracket, the first over 170 miles per hour, and first over 180 miles per hour.

I started getting a lot of publicity and my show business background surfaced. I wanted to put on a show, so the car came to the track in perfect condition with beautiful paint and chrome. I wore leathers, mirrored goggles, and a custom-painted helmet. I started picking up nicknames like Instant Ivo, Poison Ivo, and TV Tommy. It all worked to improve my image. Magazines loved the car, and getting placed on cover shots allowed me to get known all over the country.

In 1960, track promoters back East got the idea to hire out some of the cars they saw in the magazines from California to run their tracks. Because of my movie career, I was allotted spare time between films. So, when they asked, I was ready. I think I was the first Californian to go on tour. On that first trip, I took a young kid who had painted my car along as a helper. He turned out to be a great help, and worked hard and loved the

sport. Oh, by the way, the kid's name was Don Prudhomme. We got $500 per stop, so we paid for the trip and made a few bucks to spare.

After the first tour, we stopped in Chicago. A fellow named Ron Pellegrini wanted to buy the twin car. I sold it and we headed back to California.

If two engines were good, four engines would be great, so I decided to build a four-engine Buick dragster. For the third time, Ken Fuller got the job of chassis building.

As the car was getting ready to run, two problems arose.

First, the track promoters panicked when they saw the car and would not let it run in competition because they thought it was too heavy and, if it got out of control, it could crash the guard railing and get into the crowd. They also didn't want a fleet of four-engine cars being built. So, they said we could run as an exhibition car only.

Problem number two was the fact that I had just started the *Margie* series on TV and the producers freaked out at the sight of the car. No racing for me! I actually hired Prudhomme, who had bought my single-engine Buick car and was starting his career, to drive the four-engine car for $25 a race and expenses. In 1962, just as everything settled down, the NHRA lifted

The first California driver officially to go back east on tour and get paid for his appearances, Ivo brought elements from his show-business background into the world of drag racing. He was always a showman as well as a racer, proven here by the fabulous, glass-walled display truck in which he carried his race car and a show-stopping Corvette personal car. *Tommy Ivo collection*

the fuel ban and Top Fuel was again king and gas-powered dragsters lost their number one position.

My next move would be to Top Fuel. I had a chassis built by Rod Pepmuller and partnered up with engine builder Dave Zeuschel, and we went Top Fuel racing. We beat Garlits in Seattle our first time out. The car ran in the sevens within a month; I believe it was the first on the West Coast.

Tracks began offering California cars $1,000 appearance money and I wanted to get back on the road. Zeuschel was just getting his engine-building business into high gear and he didn't want to leave, so we went our separate ways. Prudhomme, too, had begun his awesome career, so I teamed up with a fellow named John Austin, Tarzan to everyone in the racing business, as my crew chief and we began touring. My real brother had passed away only months after I started drag racing, so John Austin and I became like brothers and actually made a good team.

From 1962 to 1964, touring became my life and the car we ran became known as the Barnstormer. In '64, I took the car to England with the U.S. Drag Racing Team. Other members of the team included Don Garlits and Tony Nancy.

The transition from gas to Top Fuel was easy for me. I had made thousands of runs and the upgrade

in power had little effect. If fact, it was kind of magical because you had all that power. You had two giant pillars of flame flying out of the headers and the tires would blaze the length of the track and you could count on a faceful of oil at the thousand-foot mark. Top Fuel was addictive.

One thing I learned by touring was that it was much easier to get paid $500 in advance to race some local hero than it was to show up and wade through a 40-car Top Fuel field to win a $500 Savings Bond worth $375. So, for me to make a living, I had to get appearance money. At the time, running NHRA National events didn't pay enough to make a living.

Back in California, I found a new form of payment. I went to Jim Tice, who was running San Gabriel Valley Drag Strip, and asked if anyone in a Top Fuel dragster had ever raced a jet dragster. He said no, they only do single exhibition runs. I suggested that I would match race Romeo Palamides's jet car (Glen Leasher driving), two out of three, winner take all for $500. The track drew a huge crowd and they went nuts waiting for me to get roasted.

Tice wanted to do it again and I suggested that I race the Snake (Prudhomme) in a grudge race. We had both run in the seven-second bracket and it would be the first side-by-side, seven-second dragster

Above and below: The very first outing of the famed Tommy Ivo "Videoliner" was at Fremont Drag Strip in March of 1965. The car, designed by Steve Swaja, was revolutionary, but it didn't handle very well. The Videoliner was to have run with a full canopy covering the driver, but it got smashed on the way to the track. *Steve Reyes*

race on the West Coast. They played the race up on the radio for a couple of weeks before the event. The place was packed on the night we ran. I had brought match racing to California.

By the mid to late '60s, Top Fuel in California had gotten very big, but I stayed with the idea of touring and match racing. The only National events I would run were the Winternationals and the Nationals at Indy. Most of the time, I didn't do all that well—there were too many hot teams running all of the National events and they had better combinations.

Every year, I would build a new car and hit the road. Don Garlits and I would run about 50 or 60 times a year. Actually, Garlits is one of my heroes because he did everything himself, from building, tuning, and driving the car to booking it and taking care of all the expenses. I did the same, but never reached the status in the sport he did.

After Garlits hurt himself at Long Beach and then built a rear-engine car, I knew it was going to be a bad year for touring. I was committed to my program, which included two front-engine dragsters, a Corvette show car, and an all-glass show trailer that I was hauling all over the country. I had an idea for a rear-engine car, but couldn't just dump what I had in place.

Before going to a rear-motor car, I tried the idea of a streamliner. Full bodied, streamliner cars became a trend in the late '60s to early '70s. I had asked the very famous automobile artist Steve Swaja to produce a design. He designed a car for me and a car for Garlits. I was hot for the idea because my favorite part of drag racing, aside from driving, is the research and development of new ideas. Race Car Specialties (Frank Huszar) built the chassis and Bob Sorrel crafted the Swaja-designed body. We named the car the Videoliner and started running it in California.

The shape of the car was a reverse teardrop, and it looked like a work of art. The problem was it didn't handle and, at the top end running 190 miles per hour, it wanted to dance around and unload the rear wheels. I was struggling with the car until, one night

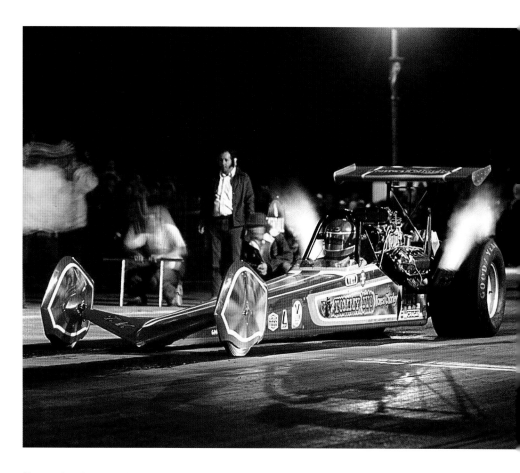

Always the showman, Ivo built some of the most beautiful Top Fuel dragsters ever conceived. This rear-engine car was awesome in its beauty, but brutal in its performance. Ivo had the worst crash of his career in this rear-engine machine. *Tommy Ivo collection*

at Long Beach, a driver in a streamliner crashed and was killed. The yellow stripe down my back got really bright and I said no more streamliners. We built an RCS conventional dragster with a Tom Hanna body and went racing.

By the early 1970s, I had my first rear-engine car. Now all my troubles were behind me—or so I thought. I had my worst crash in my rear-engine car.

I became an original member of the 5-second ET club and continued racing until the 1980s. My career included single-engine cars, twin-engine cars, a four-engine car, rear-engine car, Funny car, and a Jet car. My fingerprints are all over drag racing and its history between 1950 and 1970.

I have always felt that California influenced Top Fuel racing all over the world. I guess you could say that you didn't have to be from California to have a Top Fuel car, you just had to run like you came from California.

CHAPTER ELEVEN

THE ROCKING '60s

An extremely rare photo of Ed Garlits (Don's brother), getting ready to run at Long Beach Drag Strip in the late 1950s. Ed ran in the Top Gas dragster class and never received the recognition that his brother did. He supported Don in many ways during the early days when times were tough. *Tom Madigan*

The world of drag racing, particularly in California, has always had a bulwark against the hardship, pain, late nights, disappointments, and relentless work associated with the sport—fun and laughter.

Drag racers have always placed a high priority on practical joking, pranks, humiliation, and the telling of nasty stories. All the hard-living, tough-minded racers joined in, firmly believing that the bottom line in life was having fun. Within this story, there resides a character who epitomized the spirit of a good laugh. His name is Tom McEwen, better known to all as the Mongoose.

As he made his way to the pinnacle of drag racing immortality as a Top Fuel and Funny Car driver, he proved himself to be a fierce warrior with a long history of overcoming all obstacles in his path. At the same time, he never took life with such gravity that he did not leave space for a laugh.

His greatest success came in the late 1960s and early 1970s during the peak of Top Fuel racing in California. However, most interesting about his career is the fact that his alter ego, the Mongoose, became a hero to children all over the country. Bringing joy to a child is one of the great pleasures of being a public figure and Tom McEwen always had time for the children.

Tom McEwen and I have been friends since the mid-1960s, and never once has he turned me down when I needed a favor. With that in mind, I asked him to recall his years as a professional Top Fuel and Funny Car racer. He agreed to do his best and, in 2005, we conducted a little bench racing session. The results follow.

Above and right: Tom McEwen has always played the role of good guy in the history of California Top Fuel drag racing. He always proved to be popular with fans, and when he became the Mongoose, the kids went wild. *Jim White/Tom McEwen collection*

TOM MCEWEN

I'm as close to a California native as most people who live here. I came to Long Beach as a very young child, after my dad was killed while testing a fighter plane during World War II. For a long time, my interest was horses and not horsepower. We had some property and raised a few horses as a way to keep me home and out of trouble.

Despite the best intentions of my mom, horsepower won my attention by the time I was fifteen. In 1953, I took my mother's Oldsmobile to Santa Ana Drag Strip without the benefit of a driver's license. She was out of town at the time and I figured she would never find out, and she didn't until a few months before she passed away many years after. Once I got my license, then drag racing became a more intense hobby.

I got the first 1955 Chevy with the new small-block V-8 to be delivered in Long Beach. I put a Paxton supercharger on it, and told the technical inspectors at the drag strip that it came that way from the factory. They didn't know any better, so they let me run in a stock class. Old Hayden Proffitt, a racer who became a superstar in Pro Stock and early Funny Car racing, threatened to beat me up because he said I was cheating. I asked how did he know, and he told me he was cheating and I was beating him.

I ended up burning that car to the ground one night at Saugus drag strip. Lou Baney and Don Rackemann were running the place and they put everyone with a supercharger in the same class. I had to race some guy with a blown Oldsmobile, and I over revved the engine and *bang* it was done. During my teenage years, I had a terrible time with my mother over the cars I wrecked.

At any rate, I thought I was hot stuff and, in 1957, a friend and I towed a '57 Chevy two-door back to Oklahoma City to the NHRA Nationals. We were going to show the East boys what was happening in California.

Well, what was really happening in California was real racers like Gene Adams and his blown

One of the most famous California dragsters in the early '60s was the Albertson Olds driven by the great Leonard Harris. When Harris was killed in another car, McEwen was asked to take over the job. *Jim White/Tom McEwen collection*

Oldsmobile and Glen Ward with his blown Cadillac were going to Oklahoma. They wanted to square off with locals like Jimmy Nix and his '39 Ford Sedan with a set-back engine and four-speed transmission. We got our ass kicked in the first round and went packing back to California. On the way home, we flipped the car over on the highway with me asleep in the back seat. It was time for a change.

I hooked up with a fellow named Bud Rasner and we bought a Fiat coupe built by Ito Automotive in Los Angeles. Then I bought a used Chrysler Hemi from Frank Cannon, who was partnered with Art Chrisman in the Hustler One dragster. We blew the engine the first week we ran and had to buy another engine, this time from Joe Reath. One night at Long

Beach, Mickey Thompson, who was manager of the strip at the time, came up and said, "Hey kid, if you want to be a big name, get a dragster."

"Good idea," I thought, so I bought an old Scotty Fenn Chassis Research K-88 chassis and installed a 4-71 GMC blown Chrysler, and I started driving dragsters. Unfortunately for me, the gasoline-only ban was in effect and I had to race guys like Lefty Mudersbach, the Albertson Olds, the Howard Cams Twin Bear—all bad dudes. So we took a beating and lost a lot of races, but I learned how to leave the starting line and get the car moving without blowing the tires off. We just didn't have the power the other teams had.

Next, I teamed with Ed Peters from Long Beach and we upgraded to a bigger Hemi with a stroker crankshaft and more power. I started winning once in a while. My next upgrade came when Art Chrisman loaned me one of the Chrisman-and-Cannon 450-cubic-inch Hemi engines they were running at the time.

It was a combination of used parts and whatever they could give me. It had the water jackets filled with plastic and aluminum chips. I even think it had used pistons. But, coming from Chrisman, it was better than anything I had at the time. I again borrowed my mom's new Ford Thunderbird and put the race car on a flatbed trailer and headed back east. I ended up running second to Ed Garlits (Don's brother) in an AHRA event back in Kansas. From that point, I was on my way. Sort of on my way.

I ran my own car for a time, but still had trouble with the hard runners like the Dragmasters (Martin & Nelson), Bob Muravez, Bob Brissette, and Tommy Ivo.

In October of 1960, my good friend, Leonard Harris, driver of the famed Albertson Oldsmobile Top Gas dragster, was killed in a crash at Long Beach in a dragster he was testing for another team. Harris was a great guy and one of the best drivers in drag racing, so when he died everyone got a wake-up call that the sport was dangerous. Gene Adams and Ronnie Scrima, who ran the Albertson Oldsmobile, asked me if I wanted to drive the car as a replacement for Harris. It was a

very sad moment, but it was my step into the big-time world of drag racing.

I started driving the Albertson Oldsmobile as well as my own blown Chrysler-powered dragster. At first I had trouble driving the Albertson car, and Gene Adams was always yelling at me because I didn't leave the starting line like Harris. Leonard was like a machine. He was a trained gymnast and in near perfect physical condition with reflexes like a cat. I was slow.

The one thing that not many people knew about Harris was that he had perfected the art of sliding the clutch, using the brake and throttle— all at the same time—to prevent excessive tire spin. Back in those days, with narrow tires, short wheelbase chassis, standard clutches, and a lot of horsepower, you had to be a driver to get down the quarter mile without crashing.

After the Albertson car, Gene Adams and I stayed partners on a number of cars, including several Pontiac-powered cars involving Mickey Thompson. But Gene was an Oldsmobile man, and in the mid-1960s I talked Adams into going Top Fuel racing. Ken Fuller built us a car that we nicknamed the Shark car because of a pointed rear body panel that looked like a shark fin. We headed for Bakersfield and the Smokers U.S. Fuel & Gas Championships.

It was a big deal—I was going to be a Top Fuel driver. We decided to run the Oldsmobile on 25 per-

During the 1960s, hand-formed aluminum bodies on Top Fuel cars became the rage, and the more exotic the better. As his entry, McEwen offered up the Shark Car. It featured a very intricate rear chute treatment. *Jim White/Tom McEwen collection*

Big Daddy Garlits gets a holeshot on sleepy Tom as McEwen and the Gene Adams Olds light up the tires in an attempt to catch the old Swamp Rat. *Tom McEwen collection*

cent nitro, but Adams didn't like the idea at all. He didn't feel comfortable running nitro. First round of eliminations, we draw Garlits. I'm thinking, "Oh, shit, we're gone." But I beat him, and the idea of getting beat by an Oldsmobile really pissed him off. The next round, we blow the engine, and now Adams is pissed because I broke his engine.

Gene and I ran Bakersfield a second time, but with a Hemi instead of the Oldsmobile, and we were runner-up to Art Malone. Within a year, Gene and I decided to move in different directions, so we parted. I was now a full-time Top Fuel driver who had beaten Big Daddy Don Garlits; there was no hat size big enough for my head. My ego was deflated in a big hurry. Top Fuel racing, I found out, was a tough game.

During the 1960s, California Top Fuel drivers thought themselves at the top of the food chain when it came to innovations. Most, or at least many, of the major manufacturers of hardcore racing parts were in California. The teams from back East had to contend with the weather and, if they wanted to make a name in Top Fuel, it was a long tow to California. Some of the teams would come out for the Winternationals and stay the winter. Gather up parts, do some testing, and maybe build a complete car, then head back East in the spring.

The truth was that there were many super-running cars back East and, when they came west, they proved the point by kicking many of our butts.

Once I decided that I would stay in Top Fuel, I moved to Orange County and started driving different

You had to come to California to be tested, and Top Fuel racers from the east took up the challenge. One of the best was Art "The Green Kid" Malone. Malone raced against all the big dogs, at events like the Winternationals (shown here) and Bakersfield. Malone also proved himself as an Indy 500 driver, qualifying for the 1963 and 1964 events. Art also set a closed-course one-lap world record at Daytona in 1961, running 181.561 mph on the 2-1/2 mile track. *Don Brown*

Not only was McEwen the regular driver for many teams, he also acted as a fill-in driver if another team had a problem with their regular driver. For example, McEwen filled in for an injured Gary Gabelich in the Rapp and Rossi Top Fuel car. *Jim White/Tom McEwen collection*

cars, shopping around for a good ride. I based out of a shop that had a long list of hard racers hanging around. The Beebe & Mulligan car and Jerry Ruth were there on a permanent basis, and the door was always open for teams who needed a place to work.

During this period, I was exposed to many of the great teams from around the country. The Greek, Garlits, Joe Schubeck, Gordon Collett, Connie Kalitta, Ron and Gene Logghe, Jimmy Nix, Vance Hunt, Bob Creitz, and a bunch of other hard runners from the east would show up at various shops and tracks during the winter. I soon found out that they were really good people just trying to get a leg up on us. The advantage we had was the inside line with engine builders, manufacturers, and chassis builders. The east guys had to overcome this head start by outrunning the California cars, and then the manufacturers wanted to advertise their exploits over the locals.

I teamed up with Ed Donovan (creator of the Donovan clutch can, aluminum block, and other related racing parts) and started driving his fueler. It was Ed Donovan who gave me the name Mongoose.

During the 1960s, Top Fuel drag racing reached a fever pitch in California. Mongoose-a-mania, however, was just getting started, later reaching heights Top Fuel could only dream of. *Steve Reyes*

Prudhomme had already started his Snake thing, and I beat him several times, and Donovan says, "Hey, you beat the Snake, and the only animal that can kill a snake is a Mongoose, so you should be the Mongoose. Maybe you can get some press out of it." So, I had that ugly rodent thing painted up and I became the Mongoose.

Lou Baney was working as general manager for a huge Chrysler/Plymouth dealership in Downey, California, called Yeakel Plymouth, and he got his old high school buddy Bob Yeakel to sponsor a Top Fuel car. Baney and I had been friends for a long time and he offered me a pocketful of money to drive the car.

So, I went to Donovan and told him I had a chance to drive a high-dollar car and make some money. He glared at me when I told him I was leaving and he said, "That little fucker bought you away from me with his

California racer Gas Ronda began in the days of the FX (Factory Experimental) class, which later morphed into Funny Cars. He was a major player, but paid a heavy price when he was badly burned in a major fire. *Tom Madigan*

Tom McEwen was a key figure in the history of California Top Fuel racing between the decades of 1950 and 1970. He was fast and quick and had a tremendous sense of humor. He also drove many different cars, including the McEwen & Bivens machine shown here. *Jim White/Tom McEwen collection*

By the mid-1960s, McEwen had established himself as a top driver of Fuel dragsters. He even became President of the UDRA (United Drag Racers Association) in an effort to organize drivers into a union. *Jim White/Tom McEwen collection*

Long before carbon-fiber became popular, Top Fuel dragster bodies were pounded out of aluminum sheets and hand formed into works of art by "Tin Men" like Doug Kruse, Wayne Ewing, Bob Sorrel, Tom Hanna, Don Borth, and Lujie Lesovesky. *Tom Madigan*

money." He was not happy. But, I went anyway and took the Mongoose name with me.

The car had an Ed Pink engine with a B&M Torkmaster transmission. Ed Pink was considered one of the best engine builders in Top Fuel racing, and his engines produced a ton of horsepower and they stayed together. I had a super crew chief named

John Garrison and together we won a lot of races. It was under the Yeakel deal that we built the Hemi 'Cuda rear-engine early Funny Car and ran it for a while until it crashed at Long Beach.

Then, in the late 1960s, Baney left Yeakel Plymouth (Bob Yeakel had died) and went to Brand Ford. At the same instant, Ford Motor Company was

Top Fuel dragsters became works of art throughout the 1960s as teams tried very hard to produce their own individual image. Body work was usually hand-formed aluminum, and the results created a wide variety of styles. *Don Brown*

introducing their all-new SOHC engine, dubbed The Cammer, and Ford selected a few teams to run the engine in drag racing. I can't remember everyone, but Jack Chrisman, Don Nickelson, Mickey Thompson, Gas Ronda, Connie Kalitta, and Baney were the ones I recall.

Ed Pink got the job of building the engine for the Baney Top Fuel car and I got the driving job. At first we had problems, but Pink finally got it running strong. Then Pink and Baney fired me and put Prudhomme in the car. That created a little problem. The Snake and Mongoose thing had blossomed into a big deal, and Prudhomme jumping into my car turned a make-believe rivalry into the real thing.

The SOHC car became known as the Super Snake, and Carroll Shelby got involved. Prudhomme won the NHRA Springnationals in the car, and I ended up driving for several other owners, including Don "The Beachcomber" Johnson, Kenny Lindley, Bivens and Fisher, and Broussard, Davis, and Percell. For a time after Prudhomme replaced me, I

would track that car like a bounty hunter and try to beat him.

There was a while when we really became rivals. In 1967 to 68, I got my own Woody Gilmore car and started running on my own. I had a few friends help out and we ran on a limited budget, built our own engines, and did some match racing.

I also became President of the UDRA (United Drag Racers Association). We tried to organize the Top Fuel drivers, and that is a little bit like herding cats.

A blind man could have seen the changes from the early '60s through the late '60s in Top Fuel racing. The cars started getting better and more professional. Chassis builders like Fuller, Don Long, Woody Gilmore, and others around the country began creating cars that handled. The bodies were works of art, as aluminum beaters like Tom Hanna, Doug Kruse, Wayne Ewing, and Bob Sorrel created masterpieces in race car design. Engine builders like Ed Pink, Keith Black, Sid Waterman, and Dave Zeuschel took the engine profession to its highest level.

By 1966 to 67, the track owners began paying the Top Fuel cars more prize and appearance money so teams had a chance of breaking even. You even could make a living match racing, maybe, if you didn't break parts. And, some of the best-running cars were getting sponsor money amounting to a few thousand dollars a year, plus free parts in exchange for decal placement on the cars.

But, for most of us, you had to have a partner with money, like Tommy Greer or Lou Baney, to help pay the bills. Some guys had speed shop sponsors like Vic Hubbard or Champion Speed Shop in San Francisco. Other teams began to put deals together to form teams like the Frantic Four of Weekly-Holding-Fox and Rivero. It was tough to make a living Top Fuel racing. And, all of us Top Fuel drivers knew that the Funny Cars were coming and we would have to share the spotlight.

One thing that saved my butt was the fact that I was involved with the tire companies and did a lot of testing. I tested for M&H and for Goodyear. The deal was you got expenses, tires, and they paid for

It's very hard to explain the impact Funny Cars had on California Top Fuel but the change was sudden and permanent. Fans loved the Funny Cars; they could identify actual street machines in these wild Funny 'Vettes. *Ed Justice Jr.*

Left and below: Unlike racing in the new millennium, Funny Car teams of the 1970s didn't have 18-wheelers, million-dollar budgets, and an army of crew members. They had a few close friends and money from their own pockets. *Tom Madigan*

engine rebuilding if you broke parts. I even got into the actual design concepts of the tires. It was a great way to supplement your budget.

In 1968, seeing the handwriting on the wall, I bought a Funny Car from Candies & Hughes out of Houma, Louisiana, and started running both the Top Fuel car and the Funny. I was lucky enough to land a pharmaceutical company as a sponsor. They had a product called Tirend Activity Booster, and a breath-freshening product. They paid me a couple grand, which was a lot of money back then.

People kept making a big deal out of the Snake and Mongoose thing, so Prudhomme and I took advantage. We were friends behind the scenes, but bitter rivals at the track. It got even better when the magazines and weekly racing newspapers would play up our races.

Actually, there was a big difference in how we approached the rivalry. I played to the crowd and had fun. Prudhomme lived racing 24/7, and he wanted to win. There was nothing humorous about racing with Donald. Prudhomme and Garlits are close when it comes to intensity. That's the reason they both have been so successful. They are champions, and it takes dedication to accomplish what Prudhomme and Garlits have done.

At the time, I thought it was funny when I beat the Snake and he would get so pissed off he was ready to fight. I'd make some off-color remark about him sleeping at the light and off he would go into orbit; the guy hated losing.

The Snake and Mongoose joust continued to grow to the point where it became a nationwide deal. So, in 1969, I went to the Mattel Toy Company with the idea of creating a line of toys featuring the Snake and Mongoose. They were receptive, so I went to Prudhomme and we formed the Wildlife Racing Enterprises Corporation. Then we started the Mattel Hot Wheels toy and game program featuring the Snake and Mongoose.

This was the first real major sponsorship program on the West Coast, and it went crazy. We raced front-engine dragsters, Funny Cars, and rear-engine dragsters. The company made toy cars, games, decals, all kinds of stuff. The kids started collecting Snake and Mongoose toys and they would come to the races with their parents. It

It started as a show for the fans but, when Prudhomme took McEwen's place in the Shelby Super Snake car, the Mongoose vs. Snake Rivalry took on a whole new meaning for Tom McEwen. *Tom McEwen collection*

was a wonderful time to be in racing, and the Snake and Mongoose image launched both our careers. Prudhomme is still going strong.

The Hot Wheels program continued throughout the 1970s. When we started running both Funny Cars and Top Fuel, I bought the first rear-engine dragster Don Garlits built for an outside customer.

Above and below: Switching from Top Fuel to Funny Cars, the great battle between The Snake and The Mongoose continued unabated into the 1970s, making the Mattel Toy Company and their line of Hot Wheels toy cars very successful. *Tom Madigan*

The Mongoose logo found its way onto many cars, including front-engine Top Fuel dragsters, Funny Cars, and a rear-engine fueler with a chassis from none other than Don Garlits. *Jim White/Tom McEwen collection*

In the early 1980s, the Hot Wheels deal had cooled off and Prudhomme had gone his own way. I wanted something different, so I had a 1957 Chevy Funny Car built and toured on my own for a couple of years. Then I teamed up with Major League baseball player Jack Clark for one more shot at Top Fuel during the 1991-92 seasons. That was the end of my driving career.

Of all the times and all of the experiences I had over the years, I remember the 1960s as being the most fun. It was the best of times, the hardest racing, and Top Fuel was king. There were hundreds of Top Fuel cars and 99 percent of them ran hard.

I loved racing with Ed Pink and Ed Donovan. Lou Baney was like a father to me. Even the practical jokes I had to endure from Tommy Ivo make me laugh today. And, believe it or not, racing with and against Don Prudhomme was the most fun you could have as a driver.

CHAPTER TWELVE

RACING AT THE RAINBOW

The car that put California Top Fuel racing into the national spotlight rose like a Phoenix from the ashes of destruction. Tommy Greer bought a Ken Fuller chassis from racer Rod Stuckey after it had been badly burned by an engine fire that had also burned Stuckey. Greer had Fuller rebuild the car and, together with Keith Black and Don Proteome, formed a winning combination. With Prudhomme behind the wheel, the GBP car was unbeatable for a long period of time during the 1960s. *Don Brown*

Ask any hardcore drag racing fan to name five of the all-time Top Fuel drivers in drag racing history, and the name Don Prudhomme will be part of the mix.

Don Prudhomme is straight out of Central Casting, answering the call for the definitive dragster driver. He is tall, lean, ruggedly handsome, quiet, and projects an image that radiates attitude. Throughout his career as a driver, he was fearless, cocky, and talented. His image was that of the competitor you had to beat. So sure was he of his place in his chosen

profession, that at one time he drove a Ferrari with a personalized license plate reading, "Soo Fast." Prudhomme came up the hard way, worked for everything he got, and beat odds that were stacked against him.

Prudhomme grew up in the San Fernando Valley, and, typical of Southern California kids, became a car freak at an early age. He was a street racer, car club member, and had to work for a living painting cars. He started his life in drag racing as a

gofer for TV Tommy Ivo. He learned to drive Top Fuel cars on his own terms. In the end, he became a winner, a champion, and a legend.

I met Don Prudhomme in the early 1960s at Tony Nancy's shop in Woodland Hills, California. He was in the early stages of his driving career. He was driving an unblown Buick-powered dragster once owned by Tommy Ivo and was about to become involved with Ken Fuller and Dave Zeuschel. On a personal level, my wife, Darlene, had

Above and below: A snake can strike in many ways. One of California's most successful Top Fuel racers is Don "The Snake" Prudhomme. He made the switch from Top Fuel dragster (Wynn's Winder) to Fuel Funny Car (Hot Wheels) and for a while drove both. *Ed Justice Jr.*

The most famous Top Fuel car of the early 1960s was the Greer/Black/Prudhomme Top Fuel car. It is shown here running a front wing for down force, something added after the car was originally completed. The man with the microphone is *Hot Rod* magazine publisher, the late Ray Brock. In the center is a youthful Prudhomme, and legendary engine builder Keith Black is on the right. *Hot Rod/Motor Trend Archives*

attended the same high school as Prudhomme. Don's wife, Lynn, and a close friend of my wife had been classmates.

Due to these connections, I knew something about Prudhomme and the reputation he had as a racer. Tony Nancy once told me, "That guy is a real racer, and he would cut your nuts off in a heartbeat if it meant winning. He can't stand losing. To him, it means failure, and failing doesn't wash with his way of thinking."

Over the years, I would cross paths with Prudhomme at the races, press functions, and a few times at Tony Nancy's shop or Ken Fuller's place after work hours, just bench racing. In the early years, Tony would play host to many racers from back East. They would hang out at his shop, as would some of his Hollywood friends. Steve McQueen was a regular at the shop.

However, it was not until this project that I actually considered sitting down with Don Prudhomme to discuss his colorful career. In 2005,

From a very young age, Prudhomme wanted to be a drag racing champion. He proved he could do the job, becoming not only a World Champion, but a racing legend. *Bob Plummer*

Terrible Tempered Ted Gotelli had several top drivers in his cars throughout the 1960s. One of the best was Kenny Safford, shown here at Half Moon Bay Drag Strip in 1966. *Steve Reyes*

he consented to a recording session to be conducted at his race shop near San Diego. Limited to the boundaries of this project, namely 1950-1970 Top Fuel in California, Prudhomme offered some insight into his life and career during the period.

As the session began, the drag racing portion of the story was placed on the back burner. My wife and Donald began an impromptu recall of their teenage years as valley kids and the joys of Saturday nights at the Rainbow Roller Rink.

Located on Calvert Avenue in the city of Van Nuys, the Rainbow was the place to be on Saturday night. It was the undeclared sanctuary for teens of the 1950s to perform the ritual dance of rock & roll—to rent wooden-wheeled skates and go wild.

The Rainbow was not just another roller rink. It featured live entertainment, which included some rock & roll icons in their incubation period. For example, the incomparable Ritchie Valens belted out his version

of "La Bamba" at the Rainbow long before he made headlines as part of the terrible trio of Valens, Buddy Holly, and the Big Bopper J.P. Richardson, all killed in an airplane crash in the farmlands of Iowa.

The high school girls would skate and flirt, laugh and giggle. The boys would show off and try to be cool. Then there were the racers, who would slap on custom skates with shaved front wheels and savage the innocent. These bad boys of the rink would race over the floors at reckless speeds, squatting low for less wind resistance. If more chaos was needed, four or five racers would grab hands and do the whip, sending the last rider into orbit.

After a night of skating, the boys and girls could either go to Bob's Big Boy drive-in or head down Van Nuys Boulevard to do some cruising.

According to Prudhomme, racing at the Rainbow was his first taste of competition.

In 1962, driving a Ken Fuller chassis that once belonged to Tommy Ivo, powered by a Dave Zeuschel Hemi, future Champion Don Prudhomme (foreground) blew away all comers to take the Top Fuel title at the U.S. Fuel & Gas Championships in Bakersfield. An interesting side note: this photo is from the collection of Bob Muravez, aka Floydd Lippincott, Jr. On the back, it says, "Bakersfield, 1962. Don Prudhomme. He won top fuel. I won top gas." *Bob Muravez Collection*

Ford Motor Company got into the Top Fuel arena in the late 1960s with their 427-SOHC engine, run by several top names, including Lou Baney. Baney's engine was built by Ed Pink and, once Tom McEwen got it running right, the car was driven by Don Prudhomme. To everyone's benefit, a budding rivalry blossomed. Hot Rod/Motor Trend *Archives*

DON PRUDHOMME

Before we get too far down the road, there are a couple of misconceptions I have to clear up about myself.

Everybody thinks I was born in Louisiana and came out of the bayou. Wrong! My parents came from Louisiana, but I was born in Los Angeles. I'm a native California guy.

Second, I was not born with a gold spoon in my mouth. My parents had to work hard for everything they had. In fact, growing up in the valley after World War II was a struggle. I remember as a little kid, it was a big deal to go to Butler Brothers department store in Van Nuys and ride the elevator; that was the coolest thing in town.

My dad, his name was Newman but everyone called him Tex, worked in a body shop called Ray

Brooks Auto Body, and from my earliest memories I loved going to the shop and hanging around by the cars. When I was about ten or eleven, my parents took me to see a cousin who lived in Gardena. His name was Harold, and he had a roadster with a DeSoto Firedome Hemi V-8 engine. Harold would go out street racing at night, and I thought that was so cool.

In my early teens, I would get out of school and head straight for my dad's shop. He started teaching me the trade and, as I got older, I worked more hours. Of course, I got the dirty jobs like sanding, cleaning parts, pounding out dents, but that was the way you learned. After a time, I started painting whole cars.

Once I hit my teens, cars became more of a lifestyle. We all hung out at the Rainbow Roller

Rink. There was a real connection between that place and hot cars. All the bad boys would park outside, in front of the entrance, so the girls could catch a look. In the '50s, cars all had rakes. You know, little tires in front and big rubber in the rear. We would do the same thing with our skates.

Yeah, we were bad boys back then and we considered the Rainbow our territory.

The Rainbow is where I met a lot of car guys like Tom McCurry and Kelly Brown. My future wife, Lynn, was part of the crowd. Tom Madigan's wife, Darlene, was a regular; I think we ran her over a couple of times.

Before I got a driver's license, I would go cruising with McCurry. We drove up and down Van Nuys Boulevard, went to Bob's Big Boy drive-in, and played bad boy. You had to sit a certain way when you went cruising. We all thought we were hot, but we were punks. Then, I joined the Chancellors Car Club, did more cruising, more street racing, and more chasing girls. But I was still a punk.

Finally I wised up and joined the Road Kings.

Things changed in a big hurry and got serious. The Road Kings had a membership filled with real racers and I became friends with guys like Tommy Ivo, Roy Fjastad, Bob Muravez, Rod Pepmuller, and Kenny Safford. My buddy McCurry also became a member. The club members didn't allow you to be stupid on the street. If you were a punk, they jumped all over your ass and you stopped. I hit it off with Ivo, Muravez, and Pepmuller, and all three were hardcore racers. The club had a dragster and we would take turns driving. Once I sat in that car, I was hooked. A serious racer, game over.

When Ivo built his twin-engine Buick dragster, my life changed forever. First, he asked me if I wanted to go on tour with him as his helper. I had never been anywhere without my parents, so I jumped at the chance. Second, I bought his old single-engine Fuller car and actually started driving on my own.

But, our tour cut that short, and Ivo and I headed east. We went from California to New Jersey and every place in between. I was Ivo's gofer—cleaning the car, wiping tires, polishing chrome, and fixing broken parts. In reality, I was going to Drag Racing College, learning my trade, my craft. Ivo was a hard runner and racing was serious business. We got paid to race and he didn't want to miss any paychecks. Actually, Ivo was a great guy to learn from and he taught me a lot.

When I got home, I was convinced that drag racing would be my career. I ran the Buick from my Ivo car in the Road Kings dragster for a time, then put the engine back in my chassis and started running on my own.

From the very instant I started driving, I was as serious as a heart attack about racing. People around me thought I was a jerk, but it was just my concentration.

My next step up was nearly suicidal. I put a blown fuel Hemi in my 96-inch wheelbase chassis. The engine belonged to the Schofield brothers. It was life changing. The car had so much power that it was all over the place and I said, "So what!" It was awesome. I loved the feeling. The car would smoke the tires all the way though the lights.

Next, I was hanging out at Tony Nancy's shop, where Ken Fuller rented a stall. He (Fuller) was in the process of building his own personal chassis. Fuller's buddy, Dave Zeuschel, had just completed a Chrysler Hemi, and Fuller suggested they put the engine in his chassis and go racing. They asked me to drive. That car was unreal, it had awesome power, and the Fuller chassis handled great. We took the car to the Smokers Meet in Bakersfield and won Top Fuel. I couldn't believe it. Winning Bakersfield was like the biggest Top Fuel race in the universe and we won it! I got my name in *Drag News*.

As for my image, my hat size got a little bigger. Remember, the NHRA had banned fuel in, like, 1957 and in '62 the ban had just been lifted. Bakersfield was still considered an outlaw track and many of the drivers who ran there had been outlaws throughout the ban period. There was a group of badass racers who ran fuel. Guys like Ted Gotelli, Rod Stuckey, Don Garlits, Slamming Sammy Hale, Big Bob Haines, Chris Karamesines, and Flaming Frank Pedregon. I wanted to be part of that group.

However, things didn't look good after Bakersfield. I went back to painting cars. McEwen would come by and want to go to lunch. He would leave the door to the paint booth open and all the bugs would come in. I'd tell him I had to work and couldn't go to lunch. He got a big kick out of watching me work. He was a full-time racer.

Then, out of the blue, I got a call from Keith Black. Keith Black was a hero to us racers. He wore a white shirt and pants to the races. He had class. He was a father figure to guys like me. A guy named Tommy Greer had bought a dragster chassis and wanted Keith to build an engine. He would also need a driver, and Black called for me.

The car was originally built by Ken Fuller for Rod Stuckey. Stuckey got burned really bad in the car and sold the chassis to Greer. The car was rebuilt by Fuller, and Wayne Ewing created an all-aluminum

It seems that The Snake (in car) knows how to maintain focus on the camera as his picture is being taken, Meanwhile, his crew looks to be distracted, probably by something shiny, at the 1965 Bakersfield U.S. Fuel & Gas Championships. That's Roland Leong on the right. *Roland Leong Collection*

body for the chassis. Actually, it was Ken Fuller who suggested that Black hire me to drive the car.

Once the car was together, I learned quickly that Keith Black was way ahead of the pack.

Most of the cars I had driven were big stroker engines, but Keith ran a 392-cubic-inch Chrysler for reliability. He secret was in the tuning—the fuel system and his knowledge of setting the clutch. He and Paul Schiefer came up with a slider clutch that allowed the car to get a better bite.

The Greer, Black, and Prudhomme car started winning a ton of races and I was making a few bucks. No more painting cars. The car won so many races that teams started calling Black's engine shop to find out what track we were going to run, and they would go someplace else.

We took the car to Hawaii for a paid race, and I met Roland Leong and his mom. We hit it off from the start. Roland had been to the mainland, and had worked for Jim Nelson and Dode Martin (Dragmaster) and had them build him a dragster. At this point, he had Keith Black building him an engine for his car.

Roland was not meant to drive a Top Fuel car. When we all got back to the mainland, Roland tried to drive his new car at Long Beach. He promptly crashed. After we cleaned up the mess, Roland says, "Vipe (he called me Viper instead of Snake), what the hell happened?" I told him, "Shit. I don't know, you were smokin' down through the lights and you kept going."

The Snake thing came from a friend of mine named Joel Percell. He ran a car called the Mangler, with Danny Ongais driving. Joel started calling me the Snake because we won so many races by leaving the starting line before the other car.

After Roland crashed his car, I started driving for him, and Keith Black was doing the engines. We won the 1965 NHRA Winternationals. Roland and I continued as a team. We took the car on tour and I started making a living as a professional race driver. Things got faster, quicker, and more dangerous. Don Long built us a new chassis and we started to get name recognition. The Hawaiian and the Snake made good headlines in *Drag News*.

At the same time, the Snake and Mongoose thing began to build and we started match racing for big purses. Roland and I were doing very good as a team. Then, I think I started believing my own press clippings, and maybe my head got a little big for my helmet. I decided to go on my own, and Roland put Mike Snively in the car, and they went on to win a bunch of races.

When the Ford Motor Company offered several Top Fuel teams the new SOHC engine, Lou Baney got one of the early models. Working with engine builder Ed Pink and sports car great Carroll Shelby, Baney created the Super Snake, eventually driven by The Snake. *Bob Plummer*

Bob Spar, of B&M Automotive, asked if I would like to drive their Top Fuel car. It would be equipped with their latest innovation, called the Torkmaster automatic transmission. I would actually be in business for myself. B&M would provide the car and I would do the booking, driving, touring, tuning, and all the rest. So, with my wife, Lynn, at my side and our dog in the back seat, we hit the road. It was a real learning experience and I found out quickly how much better Lynn was at managing money than I was.

From B&M, I went to driving the Lou Baney and Ed Pink Top Fuel car, powered by the Ford overhead cam engine. They had fired McEwen, something that rubbed on McEwen for years after. Pink built unreal engines; they were perfect and had a ton of horsepower. Baney, as anyone would tell you, was the greatest, and more fun to be with than you can imagine. We started winning races. We got Carroll Shelby involved, along with Wynn Oil, and the car became the Shelby Super Snake.

Then Baney decided we should go on tour. Pink stayed home and sent us out on our own. Baney and I didn't do too good in the tuning department and soon we had Pink's fabulous engine in the toilet. Finally, as we were running down some road in the middle of nowhere, Baney says, "Snake, let's go home to California." I was ready, so we came home.

On the way home, Baney kept telling me the only way to make money in drag racing was to own your own stuff.

When we got home, I kicked around a little and

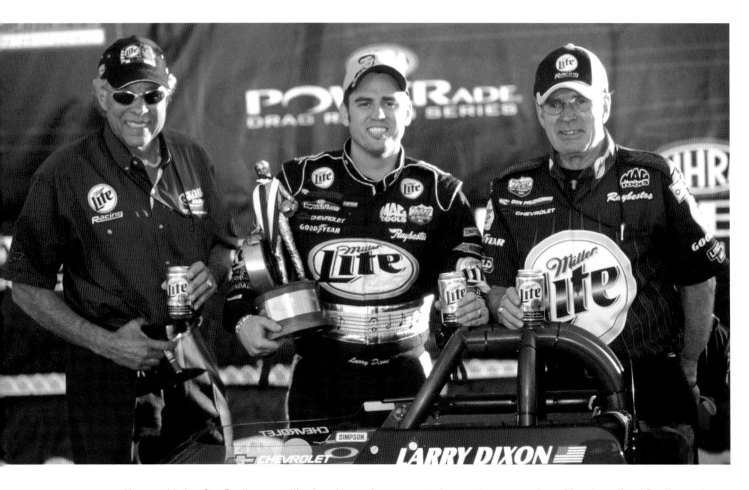

Above and below: Don Prudhomme still enjoys drag racing success today as a team owner. Larry Dixon has piloted Prudhomme's Miller Lite Top Fuel car since 1995. Together, they've won two national championships, in 2002 and 2003.

actually drove another Pink car, the Ansen Pink Top Fuel car. That was the same car Fuller, Zeuschel, and I had run a couple years earlier.

The idea of owning my own car came together around late 1967 or maybe early 68. I had seen Garlits running Wynn Oil as a sponsor, and Baney had some dealings with them on the Super Snake car, and they were based in Southern California, so I figured why not hit them up for sponsorship. At the very same time, I had bought a Don Long car from Roland Leong. Roland had decided to go Funny Car racing and give up the dragster.

Keith Black offered to help me by providing engines for the car if I could come up with a sponsorship deal. He would give me engines until I could pay him back,

I went to Carl Wynn and asked for ten grand. He said sorry. He did offer me seven grand. I jumped at the chance. So it went that Keith Black became responsible for financing me into my own business. The car was named the "Wynn's Winder" and, with Keith building the engines, I took the car on tour. We ran match races and appearance races—everywhere and anywhere. I started getting up to $1,200 per appearance and ended up paying Black back for his initial investment within a year.

I was so busy trying to make a living that I didn't see the storm clouds forming on my horizon. Running match races, appearance races, and trying to run NHRA National events began to wear on me. The pace of doing all the traveling and the labor connected with running a Top Fuel car took a big toll on my well-being.

We had a very bad scene at the Nationals in the late '60s. I had been running up to 50 dates on tour and I crashed the car really bad, sending me to the hospital. We took the car to the Ramchargers shop in Detroit to do the repairs. Then we went to the Nationals, which was the roughest race of the year

and required you to pay your own expenses.

I was underweight, beat up, and totally exhausted. Anyway, during a qualifying run against Jim Nicoll, he blows an engine, cuts the car in two pieces, and sends the cockpit, with him inside, over the guardrail. The front of the car flies right in front of me and I think that Nicoll is a goner. When I get out, the TV cameras caught me off guard and I said something about quitting. It was a bad deal, but I didn't give up or quit.

In 1969, McEwen came up with his idea for the Mattel Hot Wheels deal with the Snake and Mongoose characters. McEwen had kids and he knew about toys. I agreed, and we put together the program. It was the best thing that ever happened to either one of us.

By the 1970s, we had everything going on— Funny Cars, Top Fuel cars, rear-engine cars, and the Hot Wheels deal had gone crazy. I would never look back and things would never be the same. Corporate money had hit and drag racing was about to go big time.

Much of my career came after the time period contained in this book, and that's okay. The '60s were a great time in California but, today, I like where I am in my life. In the old days, when Lynn and I got married, her parents wondered about her marrying a drag racer. The '60s were fun, but the money was hard to come by and it was a tough life if you did it for a living. The only reason we made it was that I loved racing so much I couldn't quit, and Lynn supported me and loved me, so I overcame the obstacles.

Now I am very proud when I tell people I'm a drag racer. Drag racing is as big as Indy Car racing, and right up with NASCAR. It's fun to make up for the lean years, when we ate tube steaks (hot dogs) and towed over the interstate hoping for some appearance money.

CHAPTER THIRTEEN

RUN WHAT YOU BRUNG & BE SURE YOU BRUNG ENOUGH

The dreaded Ridge Route Terrors team of Warren, Coburn, and Miller were frequent visitors to Northern California and Fremont Drag Strip. The trio would go north and take home the money, then head south and do the same thing. *Steve Reyes*

Without reservation, there is agreement that not all Top Fuel milestones were the result of events consummated in California. Within the period of 1950 to 1970, Eastern racers evolved their own history. Names like Setto Postoian, Don Garlits, Chris Karamesines, Art Arfons, Pete Robinson, Connie Kalitta, Joe Schubeck, and the rest of a cast of thousands made their own special reputations as hard-running racers. It didn't take long for California to become diluted with invaders from east of Phoenix. The West Coast

were challenged and, in many cases, they received a butt whipping from their Eastern guests.

All of the arguments by the Eastern racers, that they had a world in Top Fuel separate from California and its claims, are valid and true. However, there is one undisputed challenge that justifies the legacy of California and its right to lay claim to Top Fuel leadership during our chosen period of time: if you want to prove you're a racer, then show up at the Smokers meet.

BAKERSFIELD AND THE PLAYERS

There is a bustling and fast-growing city located about 90 miles north of Los Angeles. It is known best for its agricultural heritage and rich petroleum production. Families are closely knit and pickup trucks are the vehicles of choice. Today, it can be reached by the interstate from Los Angeles in less than two hours. Most travelers consider the town a great place to stop for gas, have a good meal, or bed down for the night in a modern motel.

Above, left, and opposite page: In the old days, racers used to say, "You better run what you brung and be sure you brung enough." Well, back then dragsters came in all forms, including two engines side by side, two engines in tandem, and everything in between. *Don Brown*

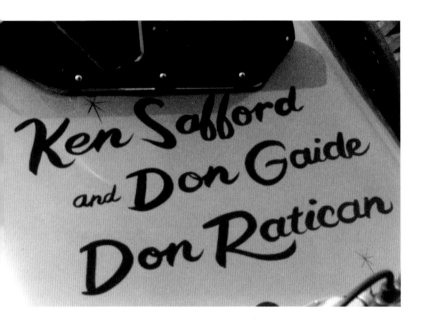

Above, right, and opposite page: Whether rebuilt, restored, or original survivor, a movement to preserve the famous dragsters of the 1950s and 1960s is under way and gaining momentum. At the 2006 Hot Rod Reunion, held at the original site of the U.S. Fuel & Gas Championships in Bakersfield, many of these legendary Top Fuel cars were in attendance. Seeing them again was a joy for all who loved the era. A random look included the Hemi-powered machine of the Frantic Four, Norm Weekly, Ron Rivero, Jim Fox, and Dennis Holding; the unreal, blown Oldsmobile fueler of Ken Safford, Don Gaide, and Don Ratican; the Dave West recreation of the Beebe and Mulligan "Fighting Irish" Top Fuel car; and views from inside and out of the "Chizler" car of Chris "The Greek" Karamesines. *Tom Madigan*

The city is Bakersfield, and the atmosphere it exudes is that of a high-energy, twenty-first-century urban community. However, the town's image belies the fact that it is home to one of the most historic events in the chronicles of drag racing. The event was called the U.S. Fuel & Gas Championships presented by the Smokers Car Club and it has always been considered the race for racers.

Try as you might, you will find no other place on the face of the earth that can lay claim to Top Fuel leadership during the decades within which our story is concentrated.

The whole history of the event began during World War II, a long time before there was a high-speed interstate highway linking Los Angeles and Bakersfield. Sometime during the latter stages of the war, the Defense Department constructed a large patch of asphalt to be used as a touch-and-go training site for B-24 bombers. It is unclear how

much the site was used and, at the conclusion of the war, it was abandoned.

In those early days, Bakersfield epitomized the California lifestyle. People were easygoing, there was no big hurry, and strict rules were something city people used to keep from running over each other. Racing was a big part of the central California landscape. Midget racers like Bill Vukovich, Johnnie Parsons, Sam Hanks, and Johnny Boyd traveled up and down the state, running seven nights a week at fairgrounds and bullrings and enjoying the postwar craze for action. Hot rodding, street racing, and running the dry lakes also played roles in the obsession.

As for its part, Bakersfield harbored a strong contingent of racers. In 1947, a group of enthusiasts formed a club called the Bakersfield Smokers Coupe and Roadster Club. Then in late 1949 or early 1950, the club officials, including Tom Croson, Jim Bowers, Bernie Mather, Jim Nugent, Jack Delaney, Hut Watkins, Harold Hann, and local speed shop owner Ernie Hashim, discovered a 200-acre plot of land, with a large portion covered in asphalt. It was the old touch-and-go training site.

The Land Company, the owners of the property, were willing to lease the asphalt portion to the club. The location was on the Maricopa Highway five miles west of Highway 99, a major north/south route from Los Angeles to Sacramento. At this time in history, there were no interstate highways, and U.S. 99 was a narrow, dangerous roadway overwrought with long-haul truckers. It traveled along a particularly treacherous piece of twisting roadway known as the Grape Vine, then climbed over a mountain range called the Ridge Route. At best, Highway 99 was challenging.

As for the acreage discovered by the Smokers, it offered nothing but open space, brutal summertime heat, harsh winds, biting cold winters, and little promise of improvement. Somehow, the Smokers prevailed and, in October of 1950, the very first Smokers drag race was held. According to John Bowser, present-day manager of the strip, the early days were given to locals and a few farm boys from Stockton and Fresno.

As the 1950s rolled on, drag racing began to grow and purpose-built drag strips started to appear. Meanwhile, the Maricopa track run by the Smokers stayed low key. At some point, and the exact date doesn't really matter, part of the original air strip was sold and converted to farm land. The Smokers moved their operation to another airstrip, located a short distance from Maricopa in the town of Famoso, and races continued on a local level.

California had always bragged about the advantages the state had over the rest of the country when it came to drag racing. Forty weekends each year, the weather was good enough to race. And, as we've already discussed, many, many speed parts manufacturers were located in California, making it easy for teams to get the latest innovations.

Racers around the country resented California and all its boosters, and one racer in particular decided to test the status quo. The racer in question was Don Garlits and he hailed from southern Florida with a reputation for hard running. Garlits claimed to have run some big numbers in top-speed readings at his local tracks. Of course, California racers shrugged off the readings as bogus. This war of words was about to change history and, as it did, it pushed a tiny local drag strip into the pinnacle of Top Fuel folklore.

The Smokers Car Club conceived a brilliant plan: why not pay the Florida vagabond, the racer others called the Swamp Rat, to come to California and prove himself? Come out and race the big boys!

Garlits, who to this day is unafraid of any challenge, agreed to come out and race. However, the Swamp Rat made his living racing his car and he wanted his appearance money to be secure before he would make the trip west. With the help of Ed Iskenderian, Don Garlits was ensured his paycheck. To promote the matching of East against West, the Smokers established the inaugural U.S. Fuel & Gas Championships. The year was 1959.

There was no way to anticipate what was about to happen.

The idea of East meets West, the gunfight at the OK Corral, High Noon, an outlaw in our town, all the classic clichés that come to mind produced an effect hard to understand, even these many years later. When talking to the old-timers, they say it was a scene equal to Woodstock. The barren land was covered with parked cars. The crowds were so intense, officials wondered if they would simply be overrun by spectators.

Local vendors brought lunch trucks loaded with food, only to be emptied in minutes. Portable restrooms were overflowing with uncontrolled volume. Money, from the $2 admission and $2 pit passes, was tossed into wooden fruit boxes and trash bags, then loaded into the trunks of track vehicles. There was only a steel cable and a few hay bales to act as a buffer between the spectators and the racing machines. And, there was the ever-present wind. Controlled chaos is the only way to explain the first Smokers Championships. To the delight of the California crowd, Garlits got beat and the now-leg-

THE KILLER CARS ARE COMING!!
WHO? EVERYONE!
SMOKERS, INC. MARCH 4, 5, 6 and 7
WATCH THE WORLD's FASTEST DRAGSTERS "RACE" SIDE BY SIDE!!!
ON SATURDAY MARCH 6
STARTING AT 10:AM
TO GAIN POSITION FOR THE
TOP FUEL ELIMINATOR RUNOFF
PLACE: BAKERSFIELD!

The race that all Top Fuel drivers wanted to win was the U.S. Fuel & Gas Championships at Bakersfield, presented by the Smokers Car Club. Started in 1959, the March meet was the Promised Land for Top Fuel racers and they all came ready to fight. *Steve Reyes*

endary Art Chrisman, driving the Hustler One fuel dragster, was crowned Top Eliminator.

Some called it the greatest drag race ever run. Maybe so, but one truth was evident: this would not be the last Smokers U.S. Fuel & Gas Championships.

With the 1960s came an explosion in the world of Top Fuel, and the Smokers Meet became a lightning rod for those who burned nitro.

It is very difficult to explain why the Smokers Meet became such a happening, but every year when the month of March rolled onto the calendar, every California Top Fuel car and every touring Top Fuel team from around the country rolled into Bakersfield. The undisputed challenge mentioned at the beginning of this chapter is what drove all those teams to show up for the March Meet.

The city of Bakersfield greeted the racers with open arms, although there were times when the police didn't find too much humor in the herd of wild-eyed racers running their streets. Motel owners

bit the bullet and allowed racers to rent rooms. They looked the other way when they found guests rebuilding a Hemi on the dresser or dumping 20-50 racing oil in the toilet. Firing up a Top Fuel engine at 2:00 a.m. was another trademark of the racers that innkeepers understood as a necessary inconvenience.

Overall, the racers stayed within the bounds of reason, with fighting and drunkenness held to a minimum.

Bakersfield offered the participants everything a Top Fuel shootout should have. No matter what any Top Fuel driver tells you about great races in other locations, the truth is that if you ran Top Fuel in the 1960s, Bakersfield was the place you had to go in order to prove your mettle, to show your soul, and to check the circumference of the bravery sacks between your legs.

Anywhere else didn't count. Bakersfield became the racers' race, the cradle of the Top Fuel racing universe. It provided competitors with every aspect of the sport: speed, courage, loss, victory, hardship, pain, suffering, joy, and disappointment. Most who raced there thought of themselves as too quick to die. Sometimes they were proven wrong.

To overcome the challenge of Bakersfield meant you were the bravest of the brave, the quickest of the quick, and you carried the gods of speed on your shoulders. There were no favorites and no pity. You came to the starting line and agreed never to blink and never to lift.

As if to justify the title Fuel & Gas Championships, in 1961, Lefty Mudersbach, driving the unblown, twin-Chevy-engine Chet Herbert Top Gas dragster, beat Jack Ewell and his Top Fuel Hemi in the final.

In 1962, a star was born when the Viper, a.k.a. the Snake, neé Don Prudhomme, driving a Ken Fuller chassis and a Dave Zeuschel Hemi, blew off the field, proving he would be a driver to be reckoned with in the future.

If historians see the first U.S. Fuel & Gas Championships as a happening with unheard of dimensions, then they definitely should take a look at the 1966 and 1967 races, too.

In 1966, well over 100 Top Fuel cars attempted to qualify for a 64 car field. For those who wonder, 1966 was a pinnacle for Top Fuel racing. Cars and teams that ran only once a year came to Bakersfield. Teams with no budget borrowed money to come, teams with no chance of winning showed up, and the racers from

Bakersfield and the U.S. Fuel & Gas Championships was always the place for a Top Fuel driver to prove how brave he could be. Sometimes the track won. Don Bowman surveys the damage to his car after a crash at the 1967 March Meet. *Steve Reyes*

The late Mike Snively, dressed in an early version of the aluminized firesuit, packs his drag chute, as young Bill Simpson checks things out. Simpson, a pioneer in creating safety equipment for race drivers, was also a top-flight driver in his own right. Simpson raced fuel dragsters and then moved on to race in the Indy 500. *Roland Leong Collection/Petersen Publishing*

back East came with blood in their eyes.

Bakersfield was the badge everyone wanted. The crowds, the harsh conditions, the crashes, the blower liftoffs, the fist fights, and spending your last dollar; none of that mattered. What counted was rolling to the starting line with a load of nitro and the magneto on kill, then dropping the hammer, blazing the tires, and becoming the meanest bear in the woods. If you won Bakersfield, you were a racer.

The late Mike Sorokin, driving the Surfers Top

Fuel car, won both the Saturday race and the Sunday race in 1966. Of the 64 cars that qualified, 53 were from California and 11 from someplace else. The field had 58 Chrysler Hemi engines, two Ford OHC Cammers, and there were four Chevy engines.

Don Garlits, who had won in 1965, went out in round two, losing to Jack Ewell.

The 1967 Bakersfield event was more of the same, with a huge field and two days of competition. Interesting points of the event included the

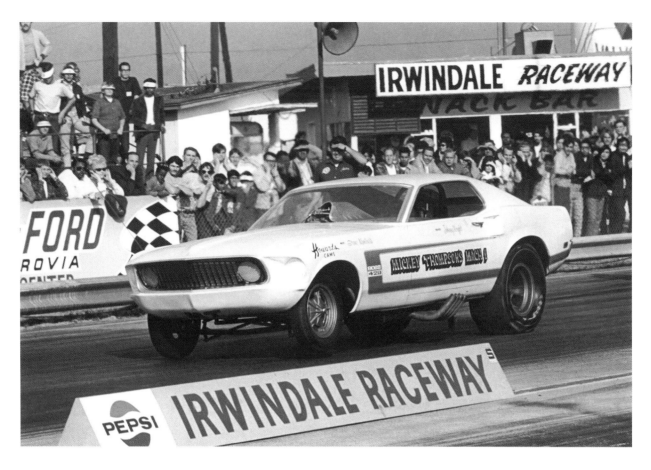

Once the Funny Car got a foothold, the days of the big Top Fuel shows were numbered. Many popular Top Fuel teams went Funny Car racing, including Mickey Thompson (shading his eyes just behind the car). Shown here is driver Johnny Wright making a pass in Mickey's Ford Mach I Mustang Funny Car. *Ed Justice Jr.*

fact that California cars still outnumbered the outsiders. There were a bunch of new names, like Jerry Ruth, Pete Robinson, Leroy Goldstein, Kenny Safford, Gary Gabelich, John Mulligan, Steve Carbone, and Wild Bill Alexander making headlines in Top Fuel.

Don Prudhomme had switched from a Chrysler Hemi to the Lou Baney-owned Brand Motors OHC Ford, replacing Tom McEwen in the driver's seat. The Hawaiian, Roland Leong, entered two cars—one driven by Mike Snively and the other handled by Mike Sorokin. Floyd Lippencotte, Jr., gave up his ride in the Freight Train to drive the Top Fuel car of Don "The Beachcomber" Johnson. Absent from the final 32 cars in 1967 were Tommy Ivo, Don Garlits, and The Greek, Chris Karamesines.

The late Mike Snively in the Hawaiian Number One car took the title, but there was an underlying bit of foreshadowing in the 1967 Smokers meet. The Funny Cars had a huge impact at the event. Did it mean the demise of Top Fuel as the number one attraction? Time would tell.

The Smokers kept the U.S. Fuel & Gas Championships in the spotlight for many years, and throughout the 1970s it remained one of the premier events in the country. Although Funny Cars began to take away from the Top Fuel glory, it was still the race to win.

DIGGER RALPH

When it comes to Top Fuel racing and Bakersfield, few in the sport equal Ralph Guldahl, Jr., otherwise known as Digger. I have known Ralph for more years than I can remember. Ralph has been addicted to Top Fuel since the 1950s. Although he could have followed in the footsteps of his father Ralph Senior by becoming a World Champion Golfer, he chose the magazine business and his love of nitro.

For more than forty years, Ralph labored as a magazine editor, covering major drag racing events all over the country. At present, he works for the Edelbrock Corporation, tending to the company's archives. But it was during the 1960s when Ralph enjoyed his finest hours, covering the Smokers Meet

Not all big names in Funny Car racing came from the ranks of Top Fuel teams. The late "Big John" Mazmanian came from the Supercharged Gas Class. *Ed Justice Jr.*

Tony Waters of Bakersfield began running fuel cars in the 1950s and stayed true to the calling for many years. He once ran his modified roadster against the best dragsters at the first U.S. Fuel & Gas Championships in 1959, finishing runner up to Art Chrisman. Don Edmonds is shown here, driving Tony's 1967 Top Fuel car. *Steve Reyes*

at Bakersfield. It seemed only fitting that Digger offer up a story or two about the March meets.

RALPH GULDAHL, JR.

It would take ledgers thicker than the encyclopedia to record every story and every player who raced Top Fuel at Bakersfield.

In the '60s, those who came to the Smokers Meet were a living, breathing culture living in their own world. Nitro makes you operate in a different level of consciousness. The world of the '60s offered up rock & roll, LSD, hippies, love, psychedelic images, and a culture counter to the normal. Top Fuel drivers had Bakersfield and 98 percent nitro.

Of all the stories, there are several that stick in my memory. First, in the early days, it was the original Smokers Car Club that made the race a success. They would do everything, from putting up the grandstands to technical inspections, selling tickets and pit passes to preparing the track and selling food. The second big story was the fact that the racers from around the country came to California. Racers came from the Midwest, East Coast, the South, Texas, and Florida. They all knew that the biggest gunfight of the year was in Bakersfield in March.

At one point, Bakersfield was an outlaw track running fuel when it was banned at other tracks. To accentuate its image, the Smokers had one of the great announcers of all time. His name was Bernie Mather and he was as hip as you could be. He talked BeBop and Hep Cat. He called the guys cats and the girls chicks and he dug jazz and hot girls in the pits. He liked using nicknames for the drivers and stirred the crowd with his wild ranting.

There was a narrowing of the track after the shut-off area where drivers would stop and load up their drag chutes and check the engine over. The problem was that, if a car came through the lights and lost brakes or chute, it would come screaming into the narrow area, called the finger, at high speed and crash into the sitting cars. Bernie would always caution drivers, "Don't linger in the finger."

Another moment that sticks out in my mind was 1963. Chris Karamesines was racing with a very heavy heart. His long-time friend and partner, Don Maynard, had been killed in a highway accident and Chris was in a mourning period as he ran the Smokers event.

As if crying out that Top Fuel drivers care for their own, Chris set low ET of the meet at 7.99 and dedicated the accomplishment to the memory of his friend. It brought chills to the spine.

THE RIDGE ROUTE TERRORS

As our tale is more about human endeavor than mechanical genius, the story of Bakersfield, the Smokers, and the U.S. Fuel & Gas Championships would not be whole without talking about those local folk who made Bakersfield their home.

From the aforementioned original club officers to their crew of Jack Hatchman, Bob Trubey, Bud Vichi, and Don Swan, from Ernie Hashim and his speed shop with its connection to the manufacturers of M&H drag slicks to local racers Tony Waters and Bill Crossley, all the locals played a role in the early days. Then there was the late Jack Williams, one-time track manager and Top Fuel driver. Williams passed the torch to the new crew of John and Blake Bowser and Bill McNatt, who run the track today. Certainly the locals made the Smokers Meet a piece of history, but there is one trio of names that took the town of Bakersfield one step further.

The three were Roger Coburn, Marvin Miller, and James Warren, and they represented a Top Fuel dragster team known as The Ridge Route Terrors. If ever a team expounded the true spirit of the sport, an absolute sense of purity for the idea of drag racing, it would be these three.

They got their name from the fact that they would tow into Southern California over the highway known as the Ridge Route. Once in Southern California, they raided local drag strips, took the prize money away from the locals, and returned north. The driver, James Warren, is a tall, lanky man. Now in his late 60s, he is one of the most unpretentious human beings on the planet. During his career, James was always ready to help a fellow racer. He was never one to take advantage of a situation. James wanted to win on his talent, not on the other driver's bad luck.

At the 2006 Auto Club NHRA Hot Rod Reunion, James Warren offered a few well-chosen remarks about his old team. It was a very rare opportunity, because James is not a talking-head sort of person.

JAMES WARREN

We actually started running circle track cars in the early days. There was no money in drag racing, and running the dirt tracks you could pick up a few bucks here and there. When we finally went drag racing, we started with a Chevy. At the time, the tires were just right for a Chevy and not good enough for a Chrysler Hemi. So, when we raced the Chrysler cars, I could get off the starting line quick while the Hemi cars would smoke the tires all the way down the strip. By the time they got hooked up, we were gone. It was great fun to sneak down to Southern California and beat the Chryslers, grab the money, and run.

Once the tires got better, we went to a Chrysler.

Back in the 1960s there wasn't any sponsor money, so you had to have a team where each member kicked in something to make it work. We had a perfect combination. Roger is my brother-in-law and Marvin was my boss. He was manager of Rain for Rent, a company that provided portable irrigation systems for farmers. I was picked as the driver because Marvin and Roger didn't want to drive.

We loved racing the guys from back East because they were tough and always wanted to prove they could beat the California guys. We also enjoyed heading south and running Southern California. That's how we got the title. Some magazine writer said we came down and terrorized the Southern California racers, so they called us the Ridge Route Terrors. In reality, although we based out of Bakersfield, I always thought of Long Beach as the toughest track to run. You had to be on your game every time or you would go home early.

Being based in Bakersfield, the Smokers Meet was the biggest event of the year. We won the Sunday portion of the meet in 1966. We won overall Top Fuel title in 1975, '76, and '77, but that was with a rear-engine car.

We toured some, and went to the NHRA Nationals a few times, finishing runner-up to Don Garlits one year.

In the '60s, racing Top Fuel was for pride and fun. The money wasn't much, although you could keep a car going and pay expenses. Later, when the big sponsors came in, things changed. We had a great time and that's what is important in my book.

CHAPTER FOURTEEN

OH NO, HERE COMES GARLITS

The story of California Top Fuel between 1950 and 1970 could not be complete without Don Garlits. Garlits came to California to prove himself. And he did, over and over, beating the best in the west. *Don Brown*

From midway through the 1950s, into the 1970s, and beyond, California Top Fuel racers confronted the ever-present dread of facing off against a fearsome renegade from the swamps of Florida—Don Garlits. Whenever a major Top Fuel drag race played out on California soil, Garlits was there, hunting, stalking his prey, ready to make a clean kill.

There was no doubt that Garlits, who the fans called the Swamp Rat, was feared, hated, and admired, all at once. He was the nemesis of those wanting to claim supremacy in the ranks of Top Fuel competitors. California racing fans denounced him as an outsider. He didn't even have chrome on his race cars. For a racer, if you had to face him, the challenge was demanding. He was a tough, mean, hard driver and he would never give an inch.

There were plenty of others who came to California from back East: Karamesines, Robinson, Schubeck, Postoian, Kalitta, Arfons, and Collett. They were tolerated. Garlits was shunned. When tales of the Swamp Rat first filtered across the California border, word was that he raced at strips with phony clocks, that he somehow cheated his rivals.

Finally he came to California, and the locals beat him at Bakersfield, scoffing and mocking his attempt at challenging the West Coast. But he never quit, and he learned his lesson well—within a week of Bakersfield he had won his first California Top Fuel race. Then he came back, again and again, beating the best, setting records, and winning championships. Don Garlits won respect from the California racers and went on to become one of the greatest Top Fuel drivers of all time.

Garlits won that respect by his sheer determination. He was a real racer, and no one could deny that fact because he did everything—building engines and chassis, driving the car, towing the car, and paying the bills. Garlits never asked for any special treatment, nor did he ever give any. Unlike the California racers, Garlits did not have the latest technology within his easy reach. He was not surrounded by legends of fellow racers working to build a better machine. He didn't compare notes with others. He was isolated.

Of course, Don Garlits is not a superhuman entity. He had a small group of loyal supporters. Strongest of those who believed in his abilities was his lovely wife, Pat, who traveled with him and took on the job of mother, teammate, soul mate, and fearless defender. There were also his brother Ed, his longtime crew chief Tommy "T. C." Lemons, bad boy Connie Swingle, his some-time touring partner

Marvin Schwartz, Art Malone, Dick Maxwell of Chrysler, and California patron Ed Iskenderian, who all aided Don in one way or another. But the truth of the matter remains that he made the decisions, and he put his skin on the line.

His success depended on his abilities to create new innovations, to prepare the car for battle, and to call up the skill to drive better than the competition. The late Tony "The Loner" Nancy once said, "When the old man rolls up to the starting line, you know he has been in that chair so many times that nothing is going to rattle him. You have to beat him by being better."

My introduction to Don Garlits came in 1961. I was sitting in a coffee shop in Bakersfield eating pancakes before heading to my first U.S. Fuel & Gas Championships. As I got ready to leave, I saw a black and white 1961 Chevy Suburban parked at the curb with "Don Garlits Garage/Tampa Florida" lettered on the side. Going out the door, I offered a greeting to Garlits and he nodded in response. We both left and headed for the strip.

Garlits named and numbered each of his Top Fuel cars. By the time he got to Swamp Rat V, he had become one of the most feared racers in America. Every California Top Fuel racer had the same opinion of Garlits—Big Daddy was tough to beat every time you raced him. *Don Brown*

Proving that he is human after all, Big Daddy gets a holeshot laid on him, something that could be considered a rare occurrence. Garlits never complained about getting beat. He just got even the next time around. *Don Brown*

Years later, I interviewed Garlits at his museum in Ocala, Florida, as a sidebar story to a magazine article on the NHRA Gatornationals. In 2005, I attempted to conduct another interview in California, but circumstances prevented us from meeting face to face and I was forced to find an alternative method. The solution was to send a tape recording with a list of questions to my good friend Steve Reyes, who lives within a few miles of the Garlits Museum. Reyes is one of the greatest drag racing action photographers of all time, and many of his masterpiece shots can be found in this book. Steve agreed to conduct the interview with Garlits.

However, despite the wealth of information contained in the resulting tape, I felt something was missing. During our first meeting in Ocala, Garlits had told me a story concerning the accident at Long Beach when he lost part of his foot. The story struck me with such emotion that I felt compelled to include it in this book. But, I didn't want to relay the story without first confirming with Garlits that he wanted to share his experience with the world.

In October, 2006, while attending the NHRA California Hot Rod Reunion, my wish was granted. Don Garlits and I sat in a restored version of his 1961 Suburban and he recounted the story, once again, of how he overcame that terrible accident with help from his faith in God.

On March 8, 1970, at Long Beach Lions drag strip, Don Garlits raced Richard Tharp in a Top Fuel elimination race.

What's wrong with this photo? Nothing, except a rare change of color for Don Garlits as he runs the 1967 NHRA Winternationals in red instead of his traditional black. *Don Brown*

As the two cars left the starting line, a two-speed transmission Garlits had recently designed exploded, blowing his Wynn's Charger car in two and severing Don's foot just about in half. He was rushed to a local hospital and remained there for six weeks. Doctors closed the damaged portion of his foot with seventeen steel staples and wire clamps, creating pain cycles of incredible magnitude. Don told me that his pain nearly drove him to the point of hysteria.

The doctors and nurses wanted to fill him with painkillers. A few years earlier, he had experienced a very bad reaction to painkillers while combating terrible burns suffered in a blower explosion at Chester, Pennsylvania. He didn't want a reoccurrence, so he declined the pills. The doctors and nurses warned him that he was making a big mistake. The result of not taking the painkillers caused Garlits to shiver with chills and, at the same time, soak his bed with sweat. His condition required a bed change two or three times a night.

Finally, a nurse offered Don one more chance to take the medicine. When he declined, she told him, "goodnight, Mr. Garlits," walked out without changing the bed, and left him to his misery. Later that night, Don told me that he cried out to God for help, in the same manner a child might cry out to a parent. Suddenly, he said, a warm feeling came over

him. He felt at peace and could sleep the rest of the night without pain. The doctors were skeptical, but they didn't laugh out loud. They were, however, convinced that something was going on. Don said they finally stopped doubting him when he felt little pain as they used wire cutters to remove the clamps and staples from his foot.

Don Garlits is unabashed about his faith in God, and hearing about that time in the hospital brings home the fact that he is a man with more to his life than drag racing.

Then he started the Don Garlits-against-California portion of our story, and his mood became considerably lighter. Keeping his remarks within the context of the 1950s to the early 1970s, "Swamp Rat" Don shared some of his favorite stories about racing the California Top Fuel hotshoes.

DON GARLITS

This whole thing about California started way back in 1955, when the NHRA Drag Safari came south to put on a drag race. I was in a car club called the Strokers at the time and I won Top Eliminator at the event. When the race was over, the club president presented Pat and me with a tea set as a gift for our wedding anniversary.

As I accepted the gift, the president remarked that I should retire because I would never be able to

In the early days, Wally Parks and the NHRA would send out teams they called the "Safety Safari" to set up events at local tracks in places where the locals had no equipment. Later, the NHRA formed permanent divisions around the country to do basically the same job. The theme was always "Safety First." *Don Brown*

beat the California racers. I was furious and thought, *What does this guy see when he looks at me?* It fired me up and, less than two years later, I beat Cook & Bedwell in a match race. They were the best California had to offer at the time.

In 1958, I tried to put together a tour of several strips, but the promoters were reluctant to send money to me before we came out, so we didn't put

things together until 1959. My friend Ed Iskenderian stepped in and he held the money for me to pick up when I got to California. Ed allowed us to use his shop as a base. We ran the U.S. Fuel & Gas Championships at Bakersfield. It was a disaster— we blew a rod in eliminations and got beat. The crowd loved it! We ran an unblown engine, but in order to get the top speeds everyone was running,

Above and below: California beckoned racers from other parts of the country to come and mount challenges. One of the most competitive of the 1960s was Bobby Langley, a record-holding driver from Texas. Langley was also noted for his Scorpion dragsters, which featured outlandish body styles and wild paint schemes. *Don Brown*

I knew we needed a blower. So, with Isky's help, we put on a blower for the race at Kingdon. I ran over 180 miles per hour and beat Tony Waters and his blown DeSoto.

Everyone thinks I was the first one from the East to race California. Not true. Bobby Langley and Setto Postoian came out before me. We came back in December of 1959, but I was recovering from burns,

so Art Malone was driving and we beat Chrisman and the Hustler One at Riverside.

The funniest thing about Riverside was that Ed Iskenderian had his CPA working the gate receipts at the track. The track didn't want to pay us an appearance fee, so we settled for 10 percent of the gate. Usually the promoters were bad about gate percentage, but Isky's guy kept them honest and we got about $7,800. We had asked for $4,500 to begin with.

There are serious misconceptions about me and my relationship with the California Top Fuel racers. Actually, we looked forward to coming to California. Everyone from the East and South came out in the winter to get what we called the California Tune Up. You could load up on equipment, new chassis designs, talk to manufacturers, and race a bunch of tracks and get appearance money. The fans are the ones who liked to hate me. But hey, they paid their money and, if they wanted to get excited and yell, it was fine by me.

In 1963, I brought out a very lightweight car called Swamp Rat V. It was so light that it would spin the tires the length of the strip. Bruce Crower suggested a wing to produce down force. He had a

In order to gain a traction advantage on the rear wheels Tony Nancy ran a rear-mounted wing on his front-engine Top Fuel car, something very unusual for the time. After several runs he gave up on the wing and returned to a conventional setup. *Steve Reyes*

friend build me a wing. We showed up at Long Beach and when we pushed down to fire up, someone in the crowd yelled, "Hey you f**kin' fink, why don't you take that Piper Cub back to Florida?"

The fans in California were very loyal back then. They loved their guys to win and they took it out on me. One time at Bakersfield, the crowd tossed beer cans at us and called me Garbage Don and Swamp Rat and, when I would get beat, they went nuts. It was tough at first, but in the end they became fans.

In 1965, we came to Bakersfield with three cars: Marvin in one, Connie Swingle in another, and me in a third. I ended up winning, and won again in 1971.

California was good for those of us who made a living in Top Fuel. A group of us—Kalitta, The Greek, Bob Sullivan, Joe Schubeck, Vance Hunt, and a few others—could run all the big strips like Long Beach, San Gabriel, Pomona, Half Moon Bay, Fremont, plus a bunch of smaller strips, and make enough money to make a full season profitable. Overall, the California racers treated me really good. When I had my accident at Long Beach, Mickey Thompson jumped in to help me and Tom McEwen came to the hospital every chance he got. I couldn't believe the support California racers gave me.

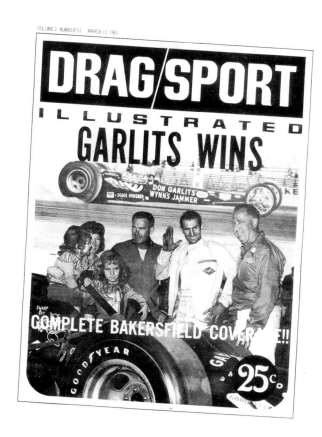

During the 1960s and 1970s, Northern California drag strips like Fremont, Half Moon Bay, Sacramento, and San Jose were home to many local racers. These racers supported the tracks on a weekly basis, competing in cars like this very neat blown Oldsmobile Top Fuel dragster. *Steve Reyes*

From the beginning, one of the rewards of going fast was the big trophy and the trophy girl who presented the giant, gold trinket. Most drivers would kiss the girl, then try and sell the trophy back to the promoter for cash or a case of racing oil. *Don Brown*

When the subject turns to good guys in drag racing, the late Jim Davis of Northern California is near the top of the list. Little known outside of California, Jim Davis was a chassis builder, Top Fuel racer, and all-around credit to the sport. He and his wife were killed in a motorcycle accident a few years back. *Steve Reyes*

Of all the California Top Fuel racers, the one I loved to beat was Prudhomme. He was the young gun, and over the years he developed a great reputation. He was a tough, hard racer. We both knew that, when we raced, it meant something special to the winner.

The best story about our rivalry happened at Half Moon Bay, running the Drag Racer Magazine Challenge. Prudhomme had been running so strong with his Torkmaster car that the promoters were sure he would win, and they pre-engraved the winner's trophy with his name. I won and they had to swap the name tags, only the tags didn't work, and it was easy to tell something was wrong. That is my favorite trophy.

I don't mean to say that everything about California was perfect. Wally Parks and I didn't always agree on things, and I had a few altercations with racers who didn't like getting beat. Every Top Fuel racer in California wanted a piece of me. They thought putting Big Daddy on the trailer was a proud day.

Although he broke top speed and low ET records everywhere he ran, Garlits had a tough time at the NHRA Winternationals during the 1960s, winning only once, in 1963. He picked up the pace in the 70s, winning the event three times. *Don Brown*

There were always theories on how to make cars go faster. One theory suggested that Zoom headers created downforce. One thing was for sure: Zoom headers cleaned the tires. Frank Martinez, in the Northern California Top Fuel car "The Wailer" at Fremont, offers a demonstration in 1966. *Steve Reyes*

It wasn't just me. Kalitta and Roland Leong had their moments, and Connie Swingle had his share of altercations with the California stars.

Funny, the only case of sabotage on my car didn't involve California racers. One time, we had our car in a stall at Keith Black's shop. We took the car to Irwindale and, on the first pass, the engine laid down and I jumped off the throttle before it blew. When we checked the fuel line, we found a newspaper rolled up inside the line. It was a Dallas paper.

Thinking back, the '60s, and even the late 1950s, California was always good to me. I loved running the northern strips like Fremont and the racers were very hard runners. Ted Gotelli, Sammy Hale, Bob Haines, Jim Davis, and the crew from Vic Hubbard's were all hard racers. However, Bakersfield was the one race everyone from outside of California wanted to run. It was the place to come if you ran Top Fuel.

I'll tell you one thing—if I didn't have good memories of California, I wouldn't be here at Bakersfield in 2006 talking to all the old guys. Like it or not, during the '60s, California was the place for Top Fuel racers to test their mettle. And that's a fact.

CHAPTER FIFTEEN

WHAT'S UP, BRO?

There were several versions of the Hawaiian Top Fuel dragster. This 1965 model features a Ken Fuller chassis and Keith Black Hemi engine, and was driven by Don Prudhomme at the NHRA Winternationals. *Roland Leong Collection*

Racing fans call him the Hawaiian, but racers know him as just Roland. Roland Leong played an enormous role in the amplification of the California image in Top Fuel racing around the country throughout the 1960s and into the 1970s. His climb from green kid to championship-winning car owner and crew chief was completed in spectacular fashion. Yet, despite his accomplishments, Roland Leong remained shy about his dedication to his chosen profession.

The truth is, understanding just how much influence Roland had on the world of drag racing is very difficult. In traditional Hawaiian mystique, he resides within his own persona, opening his feelings only to those closest to him. And, on occasion, to fellow racers.

Roland and I became friends in the early 1970s, when I was an editor at *Popular Hot Rodding* magazine. Since that time, we get together every decade or so, catching up on the years that have passed.

What always amazes me is how Roland can pick up a conversation right where it left off, no matter how long ago that was.

Roland never rose to the top as a driver; stories of his exploits as a Top Fuel driver are good for few bench-racing tales. He did, however, make a tremendous contribution as a car owner, crew chief, and businessman. In the mid-1960s, Top Fuel cars carrying the logo of the Hawaiian were some of the best to ever represent the glory days of California drag racing and, in the seats of those cars, two of the best drivers in the sport.

Roland talked about the rise and fall of California Top Fuel racing during a conversation at his home in Los Angeles during the spring of 2006.

ROLAND LEONG

Growing up in Hawaii, we only had one drag strip and it was only open once a month, so street racing was a big deal. We all read *Hot Rod* magazine and wished we could go to California and race with the heroes shown on its pages.

I guess I was kind of a wild kid and my mom wanted to keep me out of trouble, so my parents invested in a local speed shop and put me to work.

Keeping the rear tires of a Top Fuel dragster in the tracks made by a burnout is the only way to get maximum traction. Top Fuel owner Roland Leong concentrates on bringing his driver into the perfect starting position. *Steve Reyes*

The shop manager was a racer and it didn't take long to start learning the score. As the business got better, I decided to build a gas dragster. So, my mom and I contacted Jim Nelson of the Dragmaster Company in Carlsbad, California. Jim and his partner Dode Martin built us a complete, blown small-block Chevy dragster and shipped the car to Hawaii. Then Jim came over and helped me learn how to drive the car and took us racing until we got the hang of things.

Soon, I got the urge and wanted to go to California where all the action was happening. Nelson became part of the plan. I ended up working at the Dragmaster shop and living at Jim Nelson's home. I started at the very bottom—sweeping floors, washing parts, and painting chassis. But, my hard work paid off. Jim and Dode began teaching me engine building, chassis set-up, and I started going to the races to learn the trade. I was hooked from the start and quickly started racing my own car, having it shipped to California from Hawaii.

Next, I started running engines from the shop. At the time, Dragmaster had a deal with Dodge to run the Dart engine, so we put one in my chassis.

I was still a kid, and I would get homesick about every six months and fly back to Hawaii, stay for a few weeks and then miss racing and return to California. Finally, Nelson had enough and told me to make up my mind or find a new job. I started staying in California for longer periods. When the Dragmaster team started building cars for Mickey Thompson, he came to me and offered to put a Ford engine in my car if I would run the NHRA Nationals back East.

I told my mom I was going to Indianapolis for the Nationals. She asked who I was going with and who was going to drive the car. I had no idea, so she flew Danny Ongais over to the mainland and he went with me and started driving.

After Indianapolis, Jim Nelson wanted to quit driving so Danny took over driving the Dragmaster Dart car for Nelson and Martin. When they gave up racing, Danny and I put together a Chevy-powered Top Gas dragster and ended up winning the NHRA Winternationals at Pomona in 1964. We also won the *Hot Rod* magazine meet at Riverside Raceway. Everyone remembers the famous photo of Danny pushing the car the length of the strip for a win, after it broke leaving the starting line.

At the same time I was running with Danny, I built a Dodge-powered gas dragster and took it back to Hawaii. I won a couple of races and was lucky enough to meet Don Prudhomme and Keith Black when they brought their Top Fuel car over for an exhibition race. All this convinced me that I would become a Top Fuel dragster driver.

Back on the mainland, I contacted Ken Fuller and had him build a Top Fuel chassis. I then asked Keith Black to build a Chrysler Hemi. Next, I asked Wayne Ewing to fabricate a body and put together the first Hawaiian Top Fuel car. I wanted the car to look like the Greer, Black, and Prudhomme car, only longer. When completed, we took the car to Long Beach for initial testing with me as the driver.

Keith Black had made it a habit of always warming his engines on straight alcohol. With my car, he

decided to go with a low percentage of nitro. He told me to mix a 20 percent blend for the test. I didn't have a clue and, instead of 20 percent, I came up with about 50 to 60 percent.

When I made my first run, the car had so much power I quickly surpassed my experience for driving and big problems were coming fast. My run was over 180 miles per hour, but I couldn't find the chute release and the car ran off the end of the strip, clipping a sign post and sending the marker stating "end" flying into the push truck of Gary Cagle, who had parked at the end of the strip after making a run a

Posing with his parents, a young Roland Leong shows off his Dragmaster dragster, built by Dode Martin and Jim Nelson, then flown to the Islands and raced in the Top Gas class. When Roland came to the mainland, he lived with and worked for Jim Nelson at the Dragmaster shop. *Roland Leong Collection*

Before Roland Leong came to the Mainland and made his name as The Hawaiian, he created a stir on the islands. In 1963, Roland set the top speed record in Hawaii with a blast of 180 mph. Here he is with his parents and the dragster that did it. *Roland Leong Collection*

By 1991, Roland Leong had left Top Fuel and gone Funny Car racing. Here he shows his mom, Teddy (left), and his sister, Marilynn (right), how to mix up the right percentage of Nitro using a handheld hydrometer. *Roland Leong Collection*

few minutes before mine. I ended up on the railroad tracks about a quarter mile from the end of the strip. The car was bent up and I was shaken up.

Back in Black's engine shop, he told me he couldn't go to the races with me anymore. I asked, "Why not?" He answered, "You scare the shit out of me. Besides, what would I tell your mom if you get killed?" Keith had given up running the GBP car and he suggested that I get out of the driver's seat and put Don Prudhomme in, because he was looking for a ride and he was a better driver than I was.

We made a great team and started by winning the NHRA Winternationals. In fact, the car ran so good that we decided to go on tour. Prudhomme had been out on tour with Tommy Ivo, so I had him do all of the bookings. The big prize for us winning the 1965 Winternationals was a new Ford pickup truck equipped with a camper. When we decided to go on tour, we had our tow vehicle. I asked Rod Pepmuller to build a trailer, and away we went.

I was so naïve and had never really experienced much. It was the first time I really was on my own.

An example: our first match race was in Rockford, Illinois, against a jet car. I had never even seen a jet car, let alone raced one. When we got to the starting line, that thing scared me to death so I stayed inside the push truck and just waved Prudhomme on up to the starting line. He was staring at me, wondering what the hell I was doing.

Prudhomme was awesome as a driver, and we won about 90 percent of our match races. We started to get a big reputation and everybody wanted to beat the Hawaiian from California. When it came time for the Nationals in 1965, I flew Keith Black to Indy to do the tuning on the car. We won Top Fuel. It was the first time a Top Fuel car won both the Winternationals and the Nationals in the same year.

Unfortunately, on the way back to California we crashed the push truck and trailer and ended up getting home with a battered race car. Paying for the damage took a lot of our winnings.

At the end of the season, Prudhomme came to me and said he had a deal with B&M to run the Torkmaster car on his own. It was a good deal for him, at least he thought so, and I wished him luck and went looking for a new driver. I had known Mike Snively since my days at Dragmaster, so I called him and he jumped at the chance to drive a Top Fuel car.

When it came time to go on tour, I discovered that I needed to wise up. I would call a track promoter and try to book the car, and I would be told that the track already had Don Prudhomme booked in. I forgot that he had always booked the Hawaiian car, and track owners automatically figured if he called it must be my car. There was some confusion, but after we won the Winternationals in 1966, track owners knew the difference between Prudhomme and Snively. It was also the first time a Top Fuel car won the Winternationals back to back (1965-1966).

For the second straight time, on our return trip to California we crashed the tow rig. It was at night and I was sleeping in the back seat of our station wagon. When I woke up, we were upside down in the middle of the desert. The trailer had broken off and we couldn't find it. We didn't find the trailer until morning, on its side about a hundred yards from the tow rig. It was one more costly mistake that dipped into the budget.

Back in California, Keith Black offered us a new deal. Because of his ties to Chrysler Corporation, the company offered Keith a new 426-cubic-inch Hemi to begin running in a Top Fuel car. Garlits had one, the Ramchargers had one, but nobody on the West Coast had one. Chrysler agreed to pay all the expenses incurred in running and testing the new engine. Black

A youthful looking Roland Leong works on the 1965 version of the Hawaiian Top Fuel dragster. Don Prudhomme drove this car for Roland, then left to pursue his own effort and was replaced by Mike Snively. Between the two drivers, Snively had the most success with the Hawaiian.

asked me to build another car. So, I put together two cars, Hawaiian I and II, with Snively taking the 392-cubic-inch engine and car on tour and the 426 staying in California with Mike Sorokin driving.

We ran Bakersfield with two cars in 1967. Sorokin got beat by Dave Beebe in the fourth round, but Snively got Beebe in the final. Later, I decided to go back to running only a single-car program and put Snively in the 426 car, and Sorokin went to another team. Sometimes I think I should have kept both cars running because of what happened to Sorokin.

One night, at OCIR, I had Snively in my car and Sorokin was in a competitor's car. It turned out to be *continued on page 184*

continued on page 184

DEATH OF THE ZOOKEEPER

Imagine being strapped into a machine traveling 200 miles per hour with a hurricane of fire blowing directly into your face, cooking your body as you are unable to defend against the inferno with your outstretched arms. That is exactly what happened to John Mulligan, when an exploding clutch created a fire so intense that it forever changed the face of drag racing. John Mulligan's death impacted the sport of Top Fuel drag racing so violently that it would never be the same.

The Beebe Brothers, Dave and Tim, have a long and colorful history in the world of drag racing, as did John Mulligan. But it was when they joined forces that history was made. At one point in drag racing history, John "The Zookeeper" Mulligan and Tim Beebe had the most feared Top Fuel car in the nation. They were the world's fastest Top Fuel car. Then in the blink of an eye it was over.

By all accounts, substantiated by drivers like Tommy Ivo, Tom McEwen, Ken Safford, and Don Prudhomme, John Mulligan was one of the most liked and most respected drivers in the history of California Top Fuel racing. His death was a tremendous shock to all who knew him, and the loss is still felt today. Close friends like journalists Don Prieto, Jim McFarland, and photographers Jere Alhadeff and Steve Reyes still choke up when remembering Mulligan. Tim Beebe, partner and crew chief of the original car and a witness to the event, offered his view of that day in 1969.

TIM BEEBE

We had switched from a 392 Chrysler Hemi to the 426 model in order to keep up with the other top runners. We had worked with the Ramchargers, who had been working on the engine since 1965. So, we installed a 426 that had been purchased by Marv Ritchin of M&H tires. We ran at OCIR, then headed back East. In September, we showed up at the NHRA Nationals.

John and I had gotten back together after both of us had gone in different directions. At one time he drove my car then left for a different deal, and my brother Dave took over driving. Later, John and I decided to build a new car to take on tour. It was that tour that ended at Indy. The new car was a Woody Gilmore, and it ran really stout, handled great, and we knew that it would run some big numbers. Our secret was in the tune-up. Nobody, not to this day, knew what I was doing with the fuel system and the clutch set up. We did a lot of work with M&H, so a combination of good tires, my tune up, and John's driving and we were setting records everywhere we ran.

At Indy, right out of the box, we set an NHRA qualifying record with a 6.43 ET. I knew there was more, but I wanted to wait for eliminations.

We got Tommy Ivo in the first round. John had been experiencing some tire shake, but we really didn't know what that was or how it affected the car. John figured he could run a .30 something against Ivo.

On the run, John got out on Tommy and it looked like a "you lose pal" run. About halfway down the tires got a bite on the track and started shaking. The shake broke the driveline coupler and pulled the main shaft out of the clutch. The clutch came apart and one of the studs cut a hole in the aluminum pan. The problem was, when we went from the 392 Hemi to the late-model 426 Hemi we had to use the 392 flywheel, so we had to cut the motor plate out. So, when the clutch came unhinged it exposed the studs, and one cut the pan.

It was one of the worst fires ever seen. The clutch can and the bell housing got distorted and hung the throttle WFO and pumped more oil on the fire. John couldn't see and the car hit the guard railing and came apart. The fire had burned though John's belts and, when the car hit, the force ejected him onto the track. Ivo once said, "John looked like a bird that got hit by a car. He just lay quietly, not moving."

John was burned badly, but there seemed to be some hope at first.

At the hospital they tried, but they were not ready for such terrible burns. Don Prudhomme stayed with me and so did Tom McEwen. They were so worried and wanted to help but there was nothing to do but wait. John actually started to show improvement and the hospital let him have visitors. You know how much he loved Pepsi, he started asking for me to bring him a Pepsi.

The problem was that everyone started coming in without a hospital gown or mask and somehow John got an infection. A.J. Foyt called and told me to get him to Houston to a burn center. John's dad wanted him to stay. In hindsight, it would have been too late. John lived 13 days and died of complications from the burns. In today's world of medicine, John may have survived.

There were all kinds of stories about what happened that came around after the fact. Some said the engine blew. Not true; the engine ran two weeks later in Tom McEwen's Funny Car. Other stories had us running Hydrazine. That's bullshit, we ran 85 percent Nitro. Still others said John died at the track. Wrong again! It was an accident, nobody's fault, it just happened. Tire shake broke the coupler and the clutch came apart, and that started the fire.

John was a great guy, everybody's friend. He loved racing a Top Fuel car, and I loved watching him. He did not die in vain. Because of John, Top Fuel drag racing made a lot of changes in safety regulations, so what happened to him wouldn't happen again.

Everyone who ever met John liked him instantly and had to take a deep breath when told of his passing. With all of the animals around Top Fuel racing, like the Snake and the Mongoose, there had to be a Zookeeper, and John Mulligan obliged.

Jet vs. Top Fuel dragster. The Waters & Edmunds fueler blasts off against the "California Kid" jet car at Fremont Drag Strip in 1966. About racing jets with a Top Fuel car: Don Prudhomme once remarked, "Don't let a jet get in front or they will burn you down."
Steve Reyes

continued from page 181
a bad night. First, Snively blew a clutch and almost cut the car in two. In fact, part of the floater plate ended up in the cockpit with Snively. A while later, I was in the staging area talking to Sorokin as he prepared to make a run. He took off and the clutch exploded and cut the car in two. Mike was killed. I was devastated. We had just finished a conversation and, a few minutes later, he was gone.

Suddenly Top Fuel racing had a real problem. We had to find a solution to the exploding-clutch conundrum. There were no computers with data acquisition equipment, no space-age metals, or staffs of engineers to solve problems, only racers with homegrown knowledge. For us, Keith Black

and Paul Schiefer came up with a three-disc slider that would help prevent explosions. Keith called me and told me he had the answer. As I mentioned, we were the only team running the new 426 Hemi on the West Coast. There was a 5/8-inch difference between the crankshaft flange on the 426 and the 392, so we could run a three-disc setup without any modifications and without being detected. It cured our problem of clutch disintegration, reduced tire spin, and produced better times, too.

We kept the clutch thing a secret for a time but, for the sake of the sport, Schiefer came out with a three-disc clutch with adjustable pressure
continued on page 188

After Don Prudhomme decided to go it alone, Roland Leong asked his old friend, Mike Snively, to jump into the driver's seat. The team of Leong and Snively clicked and they won many National events, including the 1966 NHRA Winternationals. For reasons unknown, Mike Snively took his own life, and a true champion was lost. *Roland Leong Collection*

LIVING WITH THE BOMB—
Some Thoughts on Top Fuel Clutch Evolution from the Mid-'60s to Mid-'70s

There is no doubt in anyone's mind that Top Fuel cars experienced a very steep—and deadly—learning curve when it came to clutch development during the decade of the 1960s. It is imperative that those reading this story understand the full impact of the problem. To get an accurate perspective, I called on the services of Jim McFarland, Hall of Fame journalist, automotive engineer and a firsthand participant in the evolution of clutch design during the problem years. Jim guided the direction of the following sidebar to our story, and provided much of the technical information.

By the mid-1960s, Top Fuel clutch development had reached a point where multiple discs and high degrees of centrifugal, lever-assisted clamping forces were the standard package. The use of two- and three-disc systems provided significant improvement in the ability of such clutches to hold and transfer power levels in the 2000-horsepower range, considered high for this period in Top Fuel car evolution. Composite disc lining had long since been replaced by sintered-iron facings, and intermediate plates (called floaters) were used to increase torque-holding surface areas and to separate the discs. The resulting package was comprised of discs and floaters all held together by pressure plate springs and the dynamics of centrifugal release levers.

Then, some time in the mid-'60s a "mistake," made by a well-known racer during reassembly of his car for a weekend race, dramatically and forever changed Top Fuel clutch packages. By incorrectly installing the three discs in his clutch system (actually backward), the resulting interference among the disc hubs prevented a total engagement of the system. The result was a virtually smoke-free (no tire spin) run down the drag strip that trimmed the car's elapsed time and immediately opened an opportunity for unbridled experimentation by racers—who subsequently created a ticking bomb that was capable of tremendous damage. It was not until after a series of clutch failures that the secret of how the "smokeless" run actually occurred became known.

Although the clutch assemblies were contained within bell-housing covers (or clutch cans; some made of steel while others were aluminum with a steel lining), these covers were nowhere near capable of controlling the forces of an explosion when a clutch assembly disintegrated at high rpm. Cars were cut in half, white-hot discs and floaters were sent into the air, and drivers were maimed or killed.

Racing clutch manufacturers were sent into quick action upgrading and redesigning critical components. In retrospect, the latter 1960s were a period of transition for the very way high performance and racing parts were designed and built. Until this point in the evolution of drag racing, parts iterated pretty much by a process of "cut and try," as opposed to fundamental engineering or scientific processes.

When the "slider clutch" concept first emerged in this period, it was, as previously stated, due to an incorrect and accidental assembly of a Top Fuel clutch. The ensuing period of racer experimentation proved to be costly, and not very accurate.

However, the situation was quickly addressed by two of the then-leading manufacturers of Top Fuel clutch packages: Schiefer Manufacturing Company and Crower Manufacturing. Paul Schiefer, a pioneer and innovator in high performance and racing clutches and flywheels, quickly engaged outside engineering and testing lab services to evaluate and help

correct the problem. Concurrently, the creative Bruce Crower was personally engaged in completing the development of his multiple-disc "Crowerglide" clutch system. In both designs, additional clutch discs and floater plates were added to increase frictional surface area and to aid in heat dissipation, high temperatures being a potentially damaging component of such clutch packages. Aerospace materials were incorporated into clutch disc facings and in pressure and floater plates, adding to the safety factor of the new generation of slider clutches.

While the Schiefer-designed pressure plate employed adjustable, counterweighted centrifugal levers to provide high-rpm clamping forces, the Crowerglide incorporated a system of levers of a different style that accomplished a similar purpose.

The tremendous efforts of Schiefer and Crower found solutions to the problem of clutch failure and the dangers to drivers. But more importantly, these efforts ushered a new level of product research and development into the maturing drag racing parts-producing community. Thankfully, innovators like Bruce Crower and Paul Schiefer, together with safety equipment pioneers Jim Deist and Bill Simpson, made Top Fuel racing a safer sport. The NHRA also played a pivotal role by requiring the use of ballistic blankets for clutches and superchargers to prevent debris from flying everywhere after explosions.

A smiling Roland Leong, his mom, and crew celebrate after winning the Top Fuel title at the 1966 NHRA Nationals in Indianapolis. From left to right: Danny Broussard, driver Mike Snively, engine builder Keith Black (front with sun glasses and turned head), Roland, chassis builder Ken Fuller (with his head turned), and Roland's mom, Teddy. *Roland Leong Collection/Petersen Publishing*

continued from page 184

springs, longer stands, and extended studs for the flywheel. Other clutch manufacturers followed in curing the problem.

We continued racing and upgrading our equipment. Ken Fuller had built my chassis for a number of years but, in 1967, I moved to a Don Long chassis. Fuller was not very happy.

We took the new car, sans full body, chrome, paint, and lettering, to the *Hot Rod* magazine race at Riverside. After the second round, Keith Black comes up and says I should cut the uprights out of the front portion of the chassis for more flex. So, I cut them out and the car goes quicker, and we win the event. *Hot Rod* wants the car, complete, for a cover shot.

So, we take the car back to the shop to build the body, paint, and chrome. Don Long sees what we did and he tells us to weld the uprights back in place or get the car out of his shop. After the cover photo, we go to a race in Carlsbad and I cut

Keith Jackson of ABC's Wide World of Sports interviews driver Mike Snively—as owner Roland Leong looks on—after the Hawaiian team's 1966 NHRA Nationals victory. *Roland Leong Collection/Petersen Publishing*

One of the hardest-running Top Fuel cars to come out of California during the rocking '60s and early '70s was that of Dennis Baca. Just check out the injector butterfly and you will see that it is WFO as Dennis unloads the clutch on a run at Ontario Motor Speedway. *Tom Madigan*

the uprights back out of the chassis. Long shows up at the race and gets pissed. Now I have both Fuller and Long mad at me. It took a while to get back in their good graces.

After Snively won Bakersfield in 1967, I decided to make racing a business. There were no big sponsors back then, so the only way to make a living was appearance money and match racing back east. We did have one great source of income when we got onto a tire testing program. Once we got a name, free parts and small sponsorship deals helped, but tire testing really paid good. You would get paid per run, plus payment for all of the parts you used during the tests.

We tested for both Goodyear and M&H. However, on one occasion, things got kind of ugly. We were running the NHRA Springnationals with M&H tires. After we made our way through eliminations, Goodyear offered us their newest compound and we switched tires. Marvin Rifchin of M&H had his technical guy check tires between rounds and, when he saw the Goodyear tires, he told us we would never run M&H again.

Marvin and I still laugh about that. By the end of the year, I was back on M&H.

By 1969, I saw the writing on the wall and built my first Funny Car. More and more teams were going the Funny Car route, including McEwen and Prudhomme. Top Fuel started losing its grip on fan loyalty. Funny Cars were getting all of the ink, and fans loved the burn-outs. For California teams, Funny Cars were the answer—you could get more bookings, run more match races, and earn more money. Sponsors loved the Funny Cars because there was room for big logos on the side. Fans identified with the cars; Dodge, Ford, and Chevy, you couldn't do that with a Top Fuel car.

For me, the 1970s meant Funny Car racing. I never went back to Top Fuel. I carried the Hawaiian Punch logo on Funny Cars for nine years.

As for Top Fuel, the '60s was the wildest time for running a dragster in California. By the late '70s, rear-engine cars, smaller fields, and a huge increase in costs forced many of the small teams out of the picture. Funny Cars went big and Top Fuel went expensive. But, I'm glad I had a turn at those glory days. Time moves on.

CHAPTER SIXTEEN

BIG MONEY IS COMING

Top Fuel racing became a fierce rivalry between two distinct cultures—East versus West, Right Coast versus Left Coast, California versus the rest of the country. Here, the East's Art Malone puts a holeshot on the West's Tommy Ivo at the 1965 NHRA Winternationals. *Don Brown*

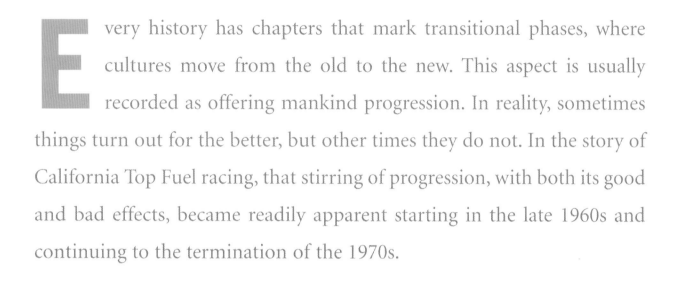

Every history has chapters that mark transitional phases, where cultures move from the old to the new. This aspect is usually recorded as offering mankind progression. In reality, sometimes things turn out for the better, but other times they do not. In the story of California Top Fuel racing, that stirring of progression, with both its good and bad effects, became readily apparent starting in the late 1960s and continuing to the termination of the 1970s.

There were many contributing factors to the meta-morphosis of Top Fuel. Most noticeable was the introduction of the fuel-burning Funny Car. As speeds climbed well over 250 miles per hour in the late 1960s, the hideous nature of the front-engine, fuel-burning dragster rose to a point where every race produced incidents of catastrophic brutality. The solution would be rear-engine cars with cookie-cutter personalities.

Then came the costs involved with going fast. As speeds increased, the price of winning went through the roof. Manufacturers of specialty parts realized that they were no longer in business to break even, but needed to make profits. For the racer, everything from tires to engine parts to fuel and travel began to climb. Many of the local teams, made up of groups of friends using their own money to run, found out they could no longer afford the price of racing.

Lurking in the shadows was a monster that finally rose up and seduced many of those crying for help. Large corporations realized that drag rac-

One of the Top Fuel drivers who transcended the evolution from front-engine to rear-engine cars is 1979 World Champion Kelly Brown. Brown (center with Top Gas Champion Jack Jones right) started out in the 1960s driving an unblown Junior Fuel dragster. He moved up to Top Fuel and won four National events in 1978, driving for Leland Kolb. *Kelly Brown Collection*

ing appealed to the youth market, so they voraciously diverted dollars from other forms of racing into drag racing. Both the NHRA and AHRA secured television contracts and, suddenly, millions were exposed to drag racing. The syndrome of money-equals-fast had begun. Drag racing would never be the same. As for the competitors, some would linger and others would fade into obscurity.

One Top Fuel driver lived both the old school and new generation of racing. He ran, and beat, the best. He became World Champion in Top Fuel as part of an independent team defying corporate dollars. He lived the transition of Top Fuel in California.

The Unsinkable Kelly Brown accomplished much during his career: Top Fuel Champion, winner of the NHRA Nationals, driver of front- and rear-engine fuel dragsters, Funny Car driver, open-wheel road racer, movie actor, stuntman, and one of the most popular drivers in the business of automotive TV commercials.

I met Kelly Brown, KB to his friends, during my brief stint in open-wheel racing. Both of us were well acquainted with Top Fuel racing and we both knew most of the same people. Drag racers were not very popular on the road-racing circuit, so we had much in common.

Many years later, through some quirk of fate, we both ended up living the rural life in Northern California. Kelly was eager to offer his memories on Top Fuel, from the front-engine experience through the rear-engine revolution to the Funny Car invasion and winning a World Championship after coming back from retirement.

KELLY BROWN

My introduction into drag racing came, like many California racers, with a trip over the Ridge Route to Bakersfield in 1959 for the first Smokers U.S. Fuel & Gas Championships. We camped out and spent the weekend watching the fuel-burning machines do their thing. I was hooked from my first whiff of nitro.

I became close friends with Manette Prudhomme, the late brother of Don. We would go to San Fernando nearly every weekend to watch Don drive. When Don began driving the Fuller/Zeuschel/Prudhomme car, I went along as a crew member and, in 1962, was a witness to Prudhomme winning Bakersfield.

By 1964, I started driving. First in a blown gas Chevy dragster, then an unblown fuel car, and as my experience grew I was offered a ride in a blown fuel digger called The Outcast. My first Top Fuel race was against Art Malone. Of course, he blew my dress up. By 1966, I had progressed to a Chrysler Hemi and finally won my first Top Eliminator at Long Beach.

Driving a Top Fuel car in the mid-1960s was an experience very difficult to communicate to the real world. No one, other than a driver, could come close to getting the picture. It was a matter of putting the hammer down and boiling the tires for the full quarter mile. Sometimes you could backpedal the throttle enough to get a grip, but most of the time it was balls out. Every run, you got oiled down. Sometimes a blower would lift off in your face and scare the shit out of you. Fires were common, and clutches became the drag race version of a hand grenade.

The rear-engine Top Fuel dragster changed everything. The driver was safer, the cars were more stable, and speeds went higher, and ETs went lower because of better traction. Carl Olson, in the Kuhle and Olson car at Ontario 1971, offers an example of the new breed of car. *Don Brown*

It was so easy to get caught up in the California image. California Top Fuel drivers had access to the latest parts, great engine builders, and a long list of drag strips to race. On any given Saturday night you could have a 32-car show, and that happened only in California.

Something that has been forgotten about the '60s in California was the fact that everybody had a different combination. Today, you buy a chassis, buy the same engine as everyone else, and depend on computers to call the setup. In the heyday of Top Fuel, each team ran their own deal—blowers, injectors, header design, clutch package, and camshaft. Engines included Oldsmobile, Chrysler, Ford, Chevy, De Soto, two in tandems or two side by side; you had to build your own package. Once cars started running over 200 miles per hour, then we all figured the sky was the limit. The sky was the limit—230, 240, and 250 miles per hour all came within a five-year period.

Known best for his abilities as a World Champion Top Fuel driver, Kelly Brown also made a name as an open-wheel racer and as a stunt driver in movies and TV commercials. *Kelly Brown Collection*

Two years with Brissette and Yeats provided 10 years of experience. Those two guys raced hard and knew how to set a car up to win.

Next, I took a ride in a super lightweight Frank Huszar-chassis car tuned by a fellow named Dave MacKenzie. On our first outing, we finished runner-up at the *Hot Rod* magazine meet at Riverside. I started winning on a regular basis and, like many of the California racers, decided to hit the road. For a California racer, match racing and touring back east was the only way to make a real living out of racing. I had one thing going for me that other racers didn't—being in the movie business allowed for time off. I worked a gig and then would be off for a month or two, so I raced the major events and then slipped back to California and did my thing.

In the late 1960s, Don Prudhomme decided to go out on his own and left the Lou Baney/Folger Ford Top Fuel car looking for a driver. I called Lou and asked if I could be considered. He had a list as long as his arm of guys who wanted to drive that car. At the time, I didn't know Lou that well, but he gave me the ride and I have to say that he was one of the greatest men I have ever known. His sense of humor was a perfect offset to the rigors of racing and his wife, Millie, and family were just as great. Lou was a racer down to his soul. He went back to the dry lakes and the earliest days of drag racing. He was a pioneer. I don't think Lou Baney had an enemy in the world.

Ford Motor Company had put out a few Cammer engines as part of their overall racing program. The one Baney ran in his car was the result of his relationship with Chuck Folger. Chuck owned a dealership in Monrovia, California. However, his connections to Ford went far deeper. Chuck was one of the chief engineers on the Ford GT-40 LeMans project and, therefore, had an inside track to the Cammer engine. The car was a combination of a Don Long chassis with Ed Pink building the engines. Lou did the tuning at the track.

Although I stayed in California, I started getting better rides. And, when I climbed into a Woody Gilmore-built car owned by Jim Brissette and John Yeats, I became accepted as a real Top Fuel driver. It was amazing. You had to earn your respect from the other drivers by beating them and proving you would never lift the throttle just because of a few parts flying, a little oil covering your goggles, or a fire blowing in your face.

With Ed Pink doing the engines, we had no worries about horsepower, but the Cammer had several built-in issues. With all of the gear drives on the front of the engine, if you burned a piston it was impossible to tear the engine down and get it back together between rounds at the track. So, you had to bring a spare engine or hope nothing broke.

The advantage of the SOHC engine was its ability to turn high rpm. It would run 10,000 rpm on a regular basis. So, if I stayed even with a Chrysler Hemi at half track and didn't burn a piston we would win. We were runner-up at the NHRA Springnationals in 1969. Ford Racing then requested that Baney switch from the Cammer engine to the new 429-cubic-inch Shot Gun

Fire put the fear of God in every Top Fuel driver who ever sat behind a blown Hemi engine. Here Bob Noice in the Jim Brissette Top Fuel car unloads a motor at OCIR in 1969. *Steve Reyes*

When Top Fuel cars broke the 200 mph barrier, rumors had the secret being chassis design, tire compound, and clutch improvements, along with exotic fuels. But another reason, touted by some, was the down force produced by "zoom" headers when the engine was at high rpm. Not only did the headers exert downforce, but they cleaned the tires of debris as the car accelerated down the track. *Don Brown*

In the mid-1960s, Lou Baney and the Ford Motor Company joined with Brand Ford, a local dealership, to run the SOHC SONIC Ford engine in a Top Fuel dragster. McEwen started as the driver, but Baney and engine builder Ed Pink decided they wanted Prudhomme to take over. It didn't set well with the Mongoose. *Jim White; Tom McEwen collection*

When car owner Lou Baney was badly burned in 1969, he parked his SOHC Ford powered Top Fuel car and put his driver, Kelly Brown, out of work. Kelly was then hired by Leland Kolb, and the pair won 9 out of 11 races. Using a Keith Black "de-stroked" Hemi, the team of Kolb and Brown was runner-up at the 1969 NHRA U.S. Nationals. *Kelly Brown Collection*

push rod engine. Baney declined and went to a Chrysler Hemi. It was all immaterial because Ford pulled out of racing at the end of 1969.

Shortly after the Ford story, Baney was seriously burned at the races and had to take some time off, so I had to move on. I was contacted by Leland Kolb, who ran out of the Keith Black engine shop. Black had just completed building a destroked (396-cubic-inch) late-model 426 Hemi for Kolb and the engine was installed in a Woody Gilmore chassis. Leland wanted me to do the driving. It was an awesome combination. We won nine out of our first eleven races and, in 1969, were again runner-up at the NHRA Nationals, this time to Don Prudhomme. That was a real trip—two California racers from Van Nuys racing at the Nationals. I thought, "Man, if the crowd at Bob's Big Boy could see us now."

It was obvious to me that Top Fuel racing was changing its image. When Detroit manufacturers like Ford and Chrysler got involved, more and more equipment makers wanted to climb on board. The TV coverage appeared and sponsorship really took hold. Name placement became a big deal. Sponsors dumped in money and in return they wanted their name on TV or in magazines. Marketing people, who knew nothing about racing, started calling on Monday morning asking the racers why they didn't win.

By the end of 1970, Leland had slowed down and I had started racing SCCA open-wheel Formula cars and had all but given up Top Fuel racing as a career. Then Ed Pink called telling me he had a customer out of North Carolina named Barry Setzer who wanted to build a Funny Car. Ed hired me to put the team together and to drive the car.

I could see that Funny Cars were the wave of the future; Prudhomme, McEwen, and many other Top Fuel drivers made the switch. The first time we tested the car at OCIR I about freaked out. When the

It's not hard to understand why the Funny Cars became popular. Fans could identify with the manufacturers (Ford vs. Dodge vs. Chevy) and sponsors had plenty of room for logos, as demonstrated by Mark Higginbotham and his Vega. *Ed Justice Jr.*

The idea of rear-engine Top Fuel dragsters goes back to the 1950s. This short-wheelbase digger, carrying a blown Chrysler Hemi, proved to be a handful for the driver, but it was still a good idea. The rear-engine fuel dragster finally became established in 1970, when Don Garlits created his first version. Everyone else got the message. *Steve Reyes*

Kelly Brown, known simply as "K.B." by his friends, became the NHRA Winston World Champion in Top Fuel in 1978, driving the Brissette and Drake car. Then in 1979, driving the "Over the Hill Gang" rear-engine Top Fuel car, K.B. won the U.S. Nationals at Indy. *Kelly Brown Collection*

crew set the body down, I was enclosed in a box and figured that I would not be able to keep the car in one lane. The car seemed so much wider than a Top Fueler that it took some getting used to.

As drag racing moved into the '70s, the sport as I had known it changed right before my eyes. Top Fuel was going rear engine, Funny Cars were capturing the fans' attention. The cost of racing was escalating as fast as the speeds being recorded. And, California was losing its image to other parts of the country.

I continued to drive for Barry throughout the '71 and '72 seasons, then moved on to a project with Don Rackemann where he built a pair of Funny Cars resembling an old-fashioned bread truck. The cars were called the Wonder Bread "Wonder Wagons." The boxy shape of the body presented issues with aero-push and were later replaced with Chevy Vega bodies.

I retired after the 1974 season and went back to the movie business full time. At this point I was married, had children, and didn't see Top Fuel racing as a way to make a living.

In 1977, I went to a roller skating party held to celebrate Larry Bowers' birthday. It was very reminiscent of the days at the Rainbow Roller Rink in Van Nuys when a bunch of us wild kids hung out together. During the evening, Jim Brissette mentioned that he had built a rear-engine Top Fuel car with a Don Tuttle chassis. He said there was no budget and racing

The driver California Top Fuel racers hated dealing with because he was so tough to beat. Don Garlits came to California many times and defeated the best in the west. Whether despite or because of his tenacious nature, California racers respected Garlits and they all knew he was something special. *Tom Madigan*

would be limited to the West Coast, but would I like to drive the car. I jumped at the chance. It was a whole new experience. The car ran an Ed Donovan aluminum-block Hemi and I loved the engine in the rear—no oil downs, fires, or blower parts hitting you in the head.

At the 1978 NHRA Winternationals, we set low ET and won the race. We changed our plans about traveling and went to the Gatornationals and were runners-up to Don Garlits. We then won the Cajun Nationals, and the Molson Grand National event in Canada. I had to race Shirley Muldowney in a TV show called "Battle of the Sexes." She was a great sport and, although I won, we had a lot of fun. At the end of 1978, I won the World Championship in Top Fuel.

In 1979, I again switched teams to a group of old friends—The Over the Hill Gang (Sonny Dias, Bill Schulz, Gary Reed, and Jim Thomas)—to run one season. We won the NHRA Mile High Nationals, Springnationals, repeated at the Cajun Nationals, and then the 25th Nationals at Indy. Couldn't get any better.

After '79, Top Fuel became a business and teams like the Over the Hill Gang couldn't afford to compete. I never ran Top Fuel as a professional driver after that. Top Fuel would never be the same.

The one feeling that I kept from my experiences was the thrill and unreal level of excitement that came with running a Top Fuel dragster at the U.S. Fuel & Gas Championship in Bakersfield. At that point in time, California was the center of the universe for Top Fuel.

CHAPTER SEVENTEEN

WORKING CLASS RACERS

One reason the front-engine Top Fuel dragster became so popular with fans was its sheer animal attraction of pure power and its attack on the senses. *Don Brown*

How the hell do you cram 20 years of California Top Fuel drag racing history into a reasonable amount of space? You don't! From the start, there was no way to include the totality of the story to be told. So, the real issue became what stayed in and what landed on the cutting room floor. In the 20 years this story spans, thousands of Top Fuel cars ran in California. Well, maybe hundreds. The Law of the Jungle sorted the strong from the weak. If you built a reputation, the word got out; if not, you raced without notice.

During the course of this project, I interviewed close to 50 individuals, some on tape and others just bench racing. Not everyone made the cut, but the prospect of leaving out any story worth telling had this author twisting in the wind. So many stories, yet so little space, became an issue. The marketing people wanted superstars and the average reader may not care about the no-names. What to do?

Many of those who, in the end, were not featured are friends or old competitors. Some are no longer with us. Names raced through my mind faster than a Final Round blast down the strip. I saw faces and heard voices: Dirty Eddie Potter, Bill Colburn, Jeep and Ronnie Hampshire, Larry Dixon, Sr., Jocko, Butch Maas, Steve Carbone, Bruce Woodcock, Gary Gabelich, Leroy Goldstein, Jack Ewell, Nick Marshall, Gerry Glen, Jerry Bivens, Chuck Griffith, Swinging Sammy Hale, Dusty Rhodes, Paul Sutherland, Bobby Tapia, Jim Dunn, Rick Stewart, Wild Bill Alexander, Jim Williams,

Bob Haines, Zane Shubert, and the list goes on. Everyone just mentioned gave racing their all. They were all brave, tough, and could run with the best. Every name deserves to have his story told.

The answer was to devote a single chapter to the competitors who didn't get all the glory. A segment dedicated to those working-class racers who ran for the pure satisfaction of the act and not for the glory. The following is a compilation of California Top Fuel from those who played a part, but remained in the shadows. Consider this chapter to be, as it was described by Roger Wolford, "An exercise in democracy."

FISTFIGHTS AT THE GREEN ROOM

There was an appreciable development in Top Fuel racing between the end of the 1950s and the mid-1960s with respect to engine technology. In the early days, racers built their own stuff. They did everything themselves. However, that trend became interrupted as higher speeds and lower ETs demanded more power. It became vogue to have an engine built by a professional.

There were many who tried to build engines, but only a few who gained reputations as winners. I was fortunate to have met five of these builders, all

One of the all-time best Top Fuel drivers during the 60s and 70s to call California home was the late Steve Carbone (far lane). Steve was a fearless competitor, and would never give an inch. At the 1971 NHRA Nationals, Carbone had the balls to outlast Don Garlits in a burn-down duel (a battle of wills to see who would stage his car first at the starting line) during the final race. Carbone took the title, winning both the duel and the race. *Ed Justice Jr.*

Above: One of the truly great drivers and all-around good guys to come out of the California Top Fuel ranks during the 1960s was "Wild" Bill Alexander, shown here in the "Cheetah" Top Fuel car. Alexander also ran "The Shudder Bug" and the "Freight Train" fuelers. *Steve Reyes*

Right: "Half the fun of being Publisher of *Hot Rod* magazine is hanging out with the legends of the sport like engine builder Keith Black," said Hibler. Harry and Keith became close friends, and remained so until Black's passing in the early 1990s. *Harry Hibler Collection*

The essence of Top Fuel racing in the 1960s. Here, the late Gary Ormsby (near camera) boils the hides and sends header flames into the night as he takes on Rick Zoucha at Fremont (1967). *Steve Reyes*

based in Southern California: Keith Black, Dave Zeuschel, Ed Pink, Sid Waterman, and Paul Pfaff. Keith and Dave are gone, but the remaining three offered up a few remarks about the Top Fuel wars and the way they came into the spotlight. Pink and Waterman, for the record, chose the Chrysler Hemi as their weapons; Pfaff picked the Chevy small block.

Sid Waterman represents the wild and wooly racers from Northern California. Although much of our story has been centered in Southern California, the north produced plenty of action too. Today, Waterman is noted for his fuel pumps. Waterman fuel pumps are used in every major market of racing, including Indy, Top Fuel, Funny Car, Champ Car, World of Outlaws, and NASCAR. You can't win without a Waterman pump.

Waterman began his drag racing voyage at Fremont Drag Strip as an announcer. It didn't take long to move from the microphone to the cockpit. Sid offers a few comments about his career.

SID WATERMAN

Northern California had its share of hard-running cars in the early years: Cash Auto, Ted Gotelli, Vic Hubbard, Champion Speed Shop, Ed Cortopassi and his Glass Slipper, and Masters and Richter.

In the battle of Northern California vs Southern California, Ted Gotelli's team was one most feared by the boys down south. Gotelli ran Ken Fuller chassis and big loads of Nitro in his engines. "Terrible Tempered" Ted employed top drivers like the late Denny Milani, Ron Hampshire, Ken Safford, Jesse Schrank, Bud Barnett, Jim McLennan, Pete Ogdon and Glen Leasher. *Steve Reyes*

I started up with Sid Masters and Rick Richter as a helper and tire wiper. But I knew that I had to have my own Top Fuel car. As it happened, Sid and Rick were great guys and I learned a lot from them. I wanted to move fast, so I contacted a chassis builder named Ken Fuller and told him I wanted to buy a front axle assembly for a Top Fuel car. He agreed, and when I picked up the front end and loaded it into my station wagon, Fuller asked me what I was going to do with the piece. I told him that a friend at a muffler shop was going to weld up a chassis, and Fuller blew it.

He yanked the front end out of my wagon and told me that he would never let one of his front-end units get put on a muffler-tube, piece-of-shit chassis. He agreed that if I bought enough chrome-moly tubing for two chassis, he would build one for me and one for him, and would then attach my front end. I suddenly had a Ken Fuller car. Bob Haines crashed the Masters and Richter car at Half Moon Bay trying to run 190 miles per hour. So, M&R put their Hemi in my brand-new Fuller chassis and we went racing.

After M&R, I teamed up with a car club called the Visalia Strippers and installed their blown Chevy small block, with Jet Car Bob Smith driving.

By this time, I was building my own engines. The learning curve was steep, but I didn't do it alone. I will always be grateful to Don Alderson of Milodon Engineering, and Ed Donovan, who helped me constantly to become better. I switched from Chevy to Chrysler, keeping the engine as stock as possible but using parts like Don's boxed rods, a C&T crankshaft, a camshaft from anyone who would help, and kept the nitro down to 60 percent. I would take the car to the track and rent a driver for the night. Lefty Mudersbach drove for me as well as Don "Cement Head" Yates. Every week a different driver, but I was learning.

I left Northern California and headed south. I got a job at C&T Automotive, then Schiefer Clutches, and finally Mickey Thompson. Mickey hired me after Ron Goodsell, driving my Top Fuel car, beat Mickey two straight *Drag News* Mr. Eliminator competitions.

Mickey said, "Anyone who can beat me two straight needs to be working for me."

He even bought out my sponsor's company (Clear Spark Distributor Company).

I continued in a rut of working full time, building engines on the side, and racing my car.

Then one year at the March Meet at Bakersfield, my life took a turn. Our car, The Outcast with Ronnie Hampshire driving, was stuck in the back of a 90-car

Northern California produced several outstanding Top Fuel teams in the late 1960s and one of the very best was that of Masters & Ricther. Chassis builder Ken Fuller put together this Masters & Richter Special, shown with Denny Milani driving. After Milani was killed in a Top Fuel crash, the team hired Bob Haines as their driver. *Steve Reyes*

field. It couldn't get a bite because we were running old tires. It was a sad state of affairs, because we were National top speed record holders at the time.

Anyway, this guy named Herb Robinson showed up and asked what the problem was. Herb was a rich guy who loved drag racing. I tell him the problem is tires. Herb says, "Go over to the Goodyear truck, get a new set, and charge them to my account."

We qualified third or fourth, but got beat. After the race, I go over to Herb and pay him back out of our round money. He says, "You know, I bought ten sets of tires for different teams and you're the only son-of-a-bitch to pay me back."

A short time later, old Herb called me and told me he had a brand-new engine-building shop, compete with all the equipment, ready to go. He and his partner had a falling out and no one was using the place. He asked me if I wanted to take over. I jumped, and became a professional engine builder.

The shop was located in Redondo Beach behind a topless bar, making my shop an instant hit with

racers. One of my first customers was Mickey Thompson, next the Atlas Tool car, Beebe Brothers, and a cast of many. In 1967, I sold my Top Fuel car and went full-time engine building. I tried to pattern my work after Ed Pink and Keith Black. Black was very good with setup and fuel systems, but I favored Ed Pink and the way he paid attention to detail.

By the late '60s, I moved to a larger shop in Gardena. I was part of the California Top Fuel phenomenon and we were building a lot of fuel motors. But there was more to it than just building engines—we all had fun racing, and every week something new would be discovered.

I did have one weakness: I was a soft touch and couldn't say no when someone was in trouble. Some of the racers would get run off by Black or Pink for not paying up, and they would come to old Sid for help. I would have made more money if I would have learned to be tough.

I established a reputation for building big-horse-power engines and some of the racers liked that my engines ran hard. I was the first to run nitrous and nitro together. I was a racer first, and an engine builder second. I wanted to win.

In 1979, I sold my engine-building equipment and bought Mickey Thompson's aluminum rod business. The Top Fuel teams started building their own engines and the profit margin was gone. I moved to Northern California and built my first fuel pump system. I gave up drag racing to concentrate on my business.

But, the old days in the '60s were the most fun. I liked the fact that you had to figure everything out on your own. There were no computers, engineers, or big-money sponsors.

Hell, in the old days at San Gabriel, you would win a couple hundred bucks and go across the street to the Green Room bar and drink beer and watch the fights. It was a great time.

THE OLD MASTER

In the race car business, he is known as The Old Master. Ed Pink is old school, with roots at the Dry Lakes of the Mojave Desert. He raced a flathead Ford in the 1940s and, from the late 1950s to the 1970s, he was one of a handful of Top Fuel engine builders you

went to if you wanted to win. Pink moved from drag racing to the Indy 500, then created his own engines for midgets, and is now involved in working with automobile manufacturers on racing projects.

But, back in the days when Top Fuel reigned, Ed Pink was a player. He offered a few stories about those days.

ED PINK

I'm a product of postwar dry lakes racing. I went to El Mirage in the late 1940s after Muroc was taken over by the military. I started by learning the hard way with a Model T four banger, then a Model A four banger, a '37 Ford coupe powered by the little V8-60, and finally a '36 Ford with a large flathead V-8. I met up with Chet Herbert, who had a six-cylinder GMC on fuel. I began learning about using nitro and how to set up a supercharger. But, the major development at that time was when I became friends with Bobby Meeks, Don Towle, and Fran Hernandez, the gang from Edelbrock.

In turn, the guys introduced me to Vic Edelbrock, Sr., and from that point forward, my education began in earnest. Vic Senior was one of the smartest engine builders I ever met, and he taught

The "Old Master," Ed Pink, didn't start out as an old anything. He began by building and racing his own Top Fuel car, with Tommy Dyer behind the wheel. The Ed Pink racer is shown here at Riverside Raceway in the early 1960s. *Author's Collection/Courtesy of Edelbrock Corporation*

me a lot about the business. After running a general garage for a time, I discovered that engine building was my passion.

I opened a shop close to the Edelbrock plant on Jefferson Boulevard in Los Angeles. I swear that I spent as much time at Vic's shop as my own. I came to realize that the dry lakes were not the answer. Drag racing came into the picture and it had advantages. There were a lot of drag strips closer to the Los Angeles area, and promoters began paying a few bucks for Top Eliminator.

I was still doing general repair when I built my first fuel dragster in the late '50s. It was a Joe Itow chassis with a blown 392 Chrysler. I had Tommy Dyer driving. As soon as we started racing, Vic Senior, Bobby Meeks, and Don Towle jumped in to help me. Lou Baney, Art Chrisman, and many of the early fuel racers helped me over the rough times. Vic Senior would check on me every Monday, asking, "How did you do?"

He once asked me, "Why do you race fuel? It's too expensive." I told him I loved it. Every once in a while, I would come back from lunch and find a 55-gallon drum of nitro in front of my door. It would be from Vic Senior to help things along.

When I finally decided that engine building would be my life, I opened a shop in Tony Nancy's complex in Sherman Oaks. Before Vic Edelbrock, Sr., passed

Called the "Old Master," Ed Pink started building engines in the days of the flathead, working with pioneers like Vic Edelbrock Sr., Bobby Meeks, and Ed Iskenderian. He built his first Top Fuel dragster in the late 50s. Pink went on to become one of America's great engine builders not only in Top Fuel and Fuel Funny Car but the Indy 500 and sports cars. *Tom Madigan Collection/Courtesy of Edelbrock Corporation*

In the late 1960s, Detroit automakers saw the benefits of Top Fuel racing and jumped on board with sponsorships. As part of their effort, Ford produced an SOHC engine for selected teams to use against the tried-and-true Hemis. Connie Kalitta's team, shown at the 1965 NHRA Winternationals (foreground), was among those using the mighty Ford. *Don Brown*

away in 1962, he gave me a dynamometer from his shop on Jefferson Boulevard so I would be able to test engines before giving them to a customer.

My second Top Fuel effort was a Ken Fuller chassis with my engine. I partnered with Louie Senter of Ansen Automotive, and we had Tommy drive the car until we sold it in '63. I moved from Tony's complex to a new shop and met an aspiring chassis builder named Don Long. The two of us realized that we both needed to create reputations. So,

Don built a super-lightweight, new-generation-style chassis and I put together the best engine I could. We hired Mike Snively to drive. The car made all of us players in the Top Fuel game.

By the late 1960s, owning and maintaining a Top Fuel dragster and running a full-time business became too much, and I gave up owning my own car before I burned out.

Next, a huge step in my career, I got involved with Lou Baney and the SOHC Ford Top Fuel program.

Above and right: By the mid-1960s, Ed Pink had become one of the most sought after engine builders in the Top Fuel class in California. Noted for his meticulous workmanship and his ability to make horsepower, Ed Pink was in direct competition with the legendary Keith Black. The Pink vs. Black rivalry became notorious. *Tom Madigan*

What Ford wanted was someone to conduct an engine development program, not just a race deal. They wanted to sell engines. Both Pete Robinson and Connie Kalitta were running the engine, but they were racers and I was an engine builder, so Ford wanted me to provide information they could pass along to their other race teams.

The car ran strong, first with Tom McEwen driving and later Don Prudhomme. In the end, Baney ran out of money and Ford pulled out of the program.

When the 426-cubic-inch Hemi hit Top Fuel, things got serious. The new engine had a stronger block, more cubic inches, and the head flowed air much better than the 392.

By the late '60s to early '70s, my business was a combination of completed engines and custom machine work. The car magazines were making a big deal out of the (Keith) Black and (Ed) Pink deal. One example was at the 1969 NHRA Springnationals in Dallas, Texas. In the Top Fuel final, it was Prudhomme in a Keith Black Chrysler on Goodyear tires with Hilborn injectors and Pennzoil, against Kelly Brown with a Pink SOHC Ford on M&H tires, Valvoline oil, and Enderle injectors. The Snake won with a 6.70 ET vs. Kelly's 6.71 ET.

In reality, Black and I were good friends, and Sid Waterman and I are still good friends. All the hoopla was in the press. There was plenty of business to go around.

However, as the 1970s kicked into high gear, the Top Fuel picture changed radically. Funny Cars hit and suddenly I was building Funny Car engines: Super Shops, Larry Huff and Soapy Sales, Berry Setzer, Gas Ronda, Don Schumacher, The Blue Max were all running my engines.

Then, another change took place that seriously affected business. The crew chiefs on the various teams began rebuilding their own engines. With the new all-aluminum blocks and replacement sleeves, teams were rebuilding between rounds. They didn't need me. It got to the point where I was spending my time answering questions on setup and fuel systems, not building engines.

Manufacturers of speed equipment quickly realized the small-block Chevy was going to be very popular with racers. Soon, the market was flooded with parts, and the Chevy became the budget racer's salvation. Although, sometimes one wasn't enough. *Don Brown*

I also had a problem with some of the manufacturers who sold parts to me, as an engine builder, and to the crews for the same price. You couldn't make any money on parts. I began exploring other options. I began building some super-street engines, engines for Bonneville, for the new Formula 5000 open-wheel series, and Vel's Parnelli Jones Indy team connected me to Cosworth and I started building Indy engines. I made a transition from drag racing to track racing.

In 1980, when Ed the Ace McCulloch won the NHRA Nationals in the Super Shops Funny Car, that was my swan song in drag racing. I must say, Top Fuel racing was a great time in my life and my career.

The people I worked with, like Baney, Louie Meyer, Lou Senter, Tommy Dyer, Don Prudhomme, Tom McEwen, Tony Nancy, Tommy Ivo, Barry Setzer, Don Schumacher, the crew from Edelbrock, they were awesome to be around. I was lucky enough to be in drag racing when it was coming of age. I loved it.

THE WHIZ KID

Paul Pfaff is what you call a renaissance man. He learned from the pioneers of the dry lakes, from men like Bobby Meeks and Art Chrisman, and then went on into the modern era to make his name. Pfaff ran a flathead Ford at old Santa Ana and began learning the engine building trade. When most builders put their emphasis on the Hemi Chrysler, Pfaff went another direction and became a small-block Chevrolet aficionado. He was a master of the working man's race engine.

Paul and I went to the same high school in Los Angeles. We became friends after a chance meeting at Santa Ana drag strip in 1955. In the early 1960s, Pfaff and his partner, Dave Sowins, built the engine for my own dragster. Sowins became my crew chief and mentor. As recently as 2001, Paul and I built a small-block Chevy engine as a project for a magazine article. Our friendship has spanned 50 years.

At his shop in Huntington Beach, California, we talked about Top Fuel racing and the Chevy small-block heritage.

PAUL PFAFF

I was very lucky. I started drag racing when the pioneers of the sport were still active: Art Chrisman, Jazzy Nelson, The Bean Bandits, Fritz Voight, Don Yates, Mickey Thompson, and Calvin Rice. Guys like Bobby Meeks and some of the other older guys were always ready to help a kid get started. We ran a lot of nitro in the early days, and the notes I took would

help me later. I became a Los Angeles County Fireman. Firemen have off time, so I joined forces with a close friend and fellow fireman named Dave Sowins to go drag racing and build a backyard business building engines.

Right away, Dave wants to build a dragster. We welded up our own chassis and began running a flathead Ford on fuel. First Dave drove, then Don Yates took a turn, but the flathead had seen its day. The Chevy small block was introduced in 1955 and became an instant hit for a lot of reasons: it was cheaper and easier to get than a Hemi, more manufacturers were building parts, and the factory was producing packages that put out good horsepower.

We met up with a fellow named Sig Erson, who was general manager at Iskenderian Cams. Both Sig and Ed Iskenderian wanted to get the Chevy market, and they helped us tremendously to put together a strong small block. At the same time, Neil Leffler came into the picture. Neil had come to California from Ohio with a fuel-burning coupe. He stayed and went to work on GMC diesel trucks. Then Neil began reworking the GMC blowers to work on a fuel-burning dragster engine.

When the small-block Chevy hit the market in 1955, it became an instant success and was the engine of choice for the budget racer. This Texas-based dragster is a good example of the small block in action. *Don Brown*

A very young Roger Wolford stands by a very early dragster, built by Dave Sowins and Paul Pfaff with a body by Eddie Potter. Pfaff & Sowins built their engine-building business around the small-block Chevy. During the ban on fuel, engines with a 259 cubic-inch limit could run a supercharger and fuel to run against unlimited blown gas dragsters. *Roger Wolford Collection*

If two blown Chrysler Hemi engines worked up front, why not put two in the rear? This odd pairing of two rear-mounted engines did not prove to be popular, but it was a sight to behold while it ran. *Don Brown*

If two blown Chrysler Hemi engines worked for the teams who ran MoPar, then two blown big-block Chevy engines should have worked for those who loved the Bow Tie. *Don Brown*

We started running the local strips with the late Gary Smith driving, then Roger Wolford. From the very beginning, everything we did was an experiment. We tried all the injectors: Scott, Enderle, and Hilborn. We went from a two-speed transmission to high gear only. Dave ported and polished the heads by hand, and Isky and Sig ground a new cam about every week.

Then Isky came up with not only the camshaft, but lightweight aluminum rods to replace the old hand-boxed steel rods we were running. Every manufacturer in the hot rod parts business knew the Chevy small block was going to be a popular engine, so they all created something to improve performance. The Chevy worked. Some teams ran two, others a single, but the point was you could go Top Fuel racing on a workable budget.

Our first car was way too short, too heavy, and out of date, so Roger Wolford went from just driving to car building and we built a lightweight chassis with a longer wheelbase and better handling. Sowins did most of the assembly work and the week-to-week maintenance, and we split the engine-building duties. Wolford was a terrific driver and he learned to slide the clutch and make runs with very little tire smoke.

When we raced the Chryslers, especially at night, the drivers would blow the tires off and we could tip-toe out and win. As time progressed, we continued to learn more and build better chassis and began working with racers like Mickey Thompson, Gene Adams, Wes Cerney, Jim Brissette, and John Garrison. We thought Keith Black was god, but he would always offer an opinion about your problems if you asked. This despite the fact that he was a Hemi guy.

Everything we tried was trial and error, like chassis development. One night after racing Long Beach, Roger decided the car didn't handle good enough so we went home and cut the chassis off in the front and added two feet of tubing and raced the next day at San Fernando. That's how we learned.

Running nitro was the same thing. You've heard the old saying that ignorance is bliss, well, we didn't think we could hurt anything by using nitro so we would run 65 to 80 percent and not worry until things started blowing up. You would simply adjust.

When you race nitro, it gets in your blood.

I don't care what anyone says, California was the hotbed of Top Fuel and everybody looked west for developments. Of course, you can never leave out racers like Garlits, Kalitta, The Greek, and Joe Schubeck. They did their own thing, but they learned from the West Coast.

The other thing that was great about those days was the fact that most of the racers were friends and shared information. Except for the occasional fist-fight, everyone got along. When the big money came in, it took the sport out of the hands of the budget racer and, coupled with the Funny Car invasion, Top Fuel lost a lot of its blue collar appeal.

In my opinion, the '60s were the best time because we started out with nothing and, from the '50s to the '70s, we had to do everything on our own. Fun was first on our list of concerns, then came winning.

Pfaff & Sowins gave up Top Fuel racing in the late 1970s. Roger Wolford went on to drive Funny Cars and the occasional Top Fuel car. Paul now builds racing engines for offshore powerboats. Dave Sowins passed away in 2006.

WORKING MAN'S RACER

If any one character can best exemplify the meaning of the working man's racer, it would be Roger Wolford. Roger can, and has, done it all, from chassis builder and mechanic to driver and touring professional. He worked for Mickey Thompson, toured with Jack Chrisman, and was outstanding as a Top Fuel driver.

I have known Roger for over 40 years, and always found him to be a straight shooter, outspoken and fearless. So, when he offered a few remarks, I jumped at the chance.

ROGER WOLFORD

I was a farm boy from Kansas who was smart enough to know that if you wanted to go Top Fuel racing, California was the place. I came out in the late '50s and went to work for Scotty Fenn at Chassis Research.

As a kid in Cleveland, Ohio, "Gentleman" Joe Schubeck dreamed of coming to California and racing against those he had seen on the pages of *Hot Rod* magazine. His dream came true, and Schubeck became one of the best Top Fuel drivers in the country. *Don Brown*

Scotty was way ahead of his time. He built a good chassis for the time and he was the first guy to come up with safety hubs for dragsters that really worked. He was consumed about safety and building safe cars, but most people just thought his ideas were odd.

For a while I ran my own dragster, but then I met up with Pfaff & Sowins and started driving their Chevy car. Most of the teams back then worked 40-hour weeks and raced on weekends. It was fun, but you had to be dedicated and be ready to spend nights in a garage and not in front of a television.

Pfaff and Sowins were hard racers and they wanted to prove their abilities so other racers would use their engine-building service. After we pulled our thumbs out of our asses, we started building longer chassis and better engines so we could run with the bad boys. The Chevy was always the underdog and we would get our dress blown up on a regular basis, but every now and then we would hook up and dust off a Chrysler with some big-name driver.

The '60s got to be wild, but the small teams got along and learned together. It was weird—when you raced someone, they were the enemy. But if you broke a part, that same team would loan you what
continued on page 223

For the working-class Top Fuel racer, the Chevy engine became the powerplant of choice. Aftermarket manufacturers offered racers plenty of parts and, if conditions were right, the Chevy produced enough horsepower to beat the Hemi. Paul Pfaff and his partner, the late Dave Sowins, were key players in building fuel-burning Chevy engines in the 1960s. Pfaff continues building engines today at his shop in Huntington Beach, California. *Tom Madigan*

Roger Wolford came to California from the midwest to drive Top Fuel dragsters. He accomplished his goal, driving many top flight cars. Shown here, Roger substitutes for Jack Chrisman while Chrisman recovers from injuries received in a racing accident. Wolford also put the Chevy small block in the history books as the driver for Pfaff & Sowins throughout the 1960s. *Roger Wolford Collection*

THE LADIES TAKE A BOW

Racing in any form would never have succeeded without the participation of women. This story would not be true to life without mention of the countless contributions of women. Going back to the earliest days of hot rodding, women have been there, first as a support group and later as bona fide competitors. Every wife and girlfriend, mother and sister who has been involved in a racing family knows firsthand how difficult and demanding the sport can be, and deserves a show of respect. To those women who have stepped out into the world of racing as competitors, the ovation should be even more pronounced. For these reasons, the following acknowledgement is long overdue.

Sadly, this tribute to women in drag racing cannot be as long as it should properly be, but as your author I decided that the only reasonable way to handle the situation was to acknowledge those women I have met personally or whose stories I experienced as part of my career as a magazine journalist. The following is dedicated to all the women who love racing, as competitors and spectators both.

VEDA ORR

I discovered the story of Veda Orr while doing research for a book documenting the history of the Edelbrock Corporation. Veda was the wife of Karl Orr, a pioneer dry lakes racer and founder of a precursor to the modern speed shop. Veda was a true trendsetter in those early days of racing on the California lake beds. Dating back to the mid-1930s, Veda, dressed in coveralls, could be found at the lakes actually working on her husband's race car. According to the late Dean Batchelor, also a veteran of the dry lakes, Veda was the first woman known to have officially run for time there.

She was a member of the Albata Car Club, a very unusual occurrence for a woman at the time. She became close friends with the likes of Ak Miller, Vic Edelbrock, Sr., Wally Parks, Alex Xydias, Jack McGrath, and Manny Ayulo. All great stuff, but one thing about Veda stuck in my mind and made her story so compelling. During World War II, while the racers went off to defend our country, not only did Veda take over the job of publishing the SCTA official newsletter, but she took responsibility for writing letters to the boys fighting overseas. She held hot rodding together during some very difficult times. After the war Veda produced a booklet called the Lakes Pictorial, filled with photos of dry lakes events plus sensational drawings by famed artist Dick Teague. Ask any old hot rodder what was the one thing they remember about the war and most will say the letters from Veda Orr.

PEGGY HART

Old C.J. Pappy Hart would always go out of his way to help a young racer get a grip on things. In my eyes, he was a true gentleman of the sport. However, C.J. had some competition when it came to handling a situation. Pappy's wife, Peggy, was not only his right hand at the track but she could pull on a crash helmet and race with the boys, handing out her share of whippings.

When the gates to the Santa Ana drag strip opened in June, 1950, Peggy was there. And when they closed in 1959, she left with Pappy and headed to Long Beach, where the pair managed Lions Associated Drag Strip for several years.

Although Pappy got most of the magazine ink for his pioneering management of the first commercial drag strip, Peggy got her accolades from the racers. Like Veda Orr and many of the other women of early hot rodding, she raced. Not only did Peggy Hart drive the dry lakes, but she ran a gas dragster and competed at the Bonneville Salt Flats. Peggy was involved with racing for more than 45 years and should rightfully take her place as a female pioneer in the world of motor sport.

JUDY THOMPSON

Although my wife, Darlene, and I dearly loved Mickey Thompson's second wife, Trudy, she came into Mickey's life long after he had given up managing drag strips.

His first wife, Judy, who has related her story within the pages of this book, was another of the true female pioneers in California drag racing.

Every driver I interviewed who raced Long Beach in the late '50s and early '60s remembers Judy as being one of the true lovers of the sport. She worked every job at the track, including announcing, ticket taking, and refereeing Mickey's nightly conflicts with the drivers and crews. But her single most memorable tradition was the post-race picnic spreads she offered those who hung around to bench race after the real racing was done. Many a Saturday night, Judy offered racers and crew members baloney sandwiches, chips, and cold beer. Then, as the crowd enjoyed their racer food, with the scent of nitro lingering in the ocean mist-filled air, the evening's events could be relived. Every driver who ever raced a Top Fuel car at Long Beach remembers those nights and their fondness for Judy Thompson.

PAULA MURPHY

Paula Murphy remains not only a great human being but one hell of a race driver. Murphy was very underrated in the early days of her career, but she proved critics wrong with her accomplishments. Paula drove sports cars in the 1950s, she raced at Bonneville, and she drove a jet dragster and a Top Fuel Funny Car.

Paula was one of the first drag racers to promote a major sponsorship (STP), and she made her name appearing at major events around the country. There is one fact that very few racing enthusiasts are aware of: as part of an ad campaign, Paula Murphy drove a car around the world in a team promoted by National Car Rental. My old buddy, the late Johnnie Parsons (1950 Indy 500 winner), was on the same team, and he told me that Paula was awesome when it came to driving through the most difficult situations.

SHIRLEY SHAHAN

Although I didn't actually meet Shirley Shahan until she was near the end of her driving career, I witnessed her abilities from afar as a spectator. As a staff member of *Popular Hot Rodding* magazine, I got to sit in on an interview with Shirley as part of a feature on her career. She was a true California racer, born and raised in the farming community of Tulare. Shirley made her name in the Stock and Super Stock classes. She was never afraid to race the big boys. My friend, Kenny Stafford, who went on to become a Top Fuel superstar, told me he raced Shirley in the stock car ranks. While he was checking out how cute she was, Shirley put him on the trailer.

A Chrysler PR man named Sam Petock gave her the name "Drag-on-Lady," and it stuck throughout her career. Shahan had many high points in her career, but one of her best moments was taking the Super Stock title at the first U.S. Fuel & Gas Championships in 1959 at Bakersfield. Shirley raced until the early 1970s, but she remains one of the pioneers in promoting women in the sport of drag racing.

BARBARA HAMILTON

I never had the opportunity of working with or interviewing Barbara Hamilton, the first woman to gain an NHRA license to drive a supercharged car, but she can be considered another milestone in the history of women and drag racing, and as such deserves mention.

LUCILLE LEE

As with Barbara Hamilton, I never got the chance to interview Lucille Lee, a pioneer female driver in Top Fuel. Lucille opened the door for women to gain access to a chance to compete with the men in Top Fuel. She warrants recognition for her actions.

BARBARA PARKS

As I attended the memorial service for Barbara Parks at the NHRA Museum, during the testimonials presented about her life, I suddenly realized just how important a part she had played in the development of the NHRA and its National events.

Her husband, Wally, founder of the NHRA, looking frail and showing each his 93 years, had crawled from a hospital bed to attend his wife's memorial and tell the world that Barbara was the rock of his life.

Kenny Bernstein, one of the bravest Top Fuel drivers ever, choked up as he spoke of Barbara. Don Prudhomme talked of how much she did for drag racing, its sponsors, and young drivers on their way up. He ended his comments by adding that when Barbara was young she was hot, and the drivers paid attention when she talked.

Barbara was there from the beginning. She worked every job that needed to be done. She stood by her Wally as the NHRA grew into a major racing organization. She knew drag racing inside and out, and understood the importance of sponsor support.

For a young journalist covering National events, Barbara was always there with a kind word. As long as you played by the rules, she would make your job easy.

LINDA VAUGHN

My first meeting with Linda Vaughn came in 1970 at the Popular Hot Rodding Championships, held at U.S. 131 Dragway in Martin, Michigan. Over the years, we have remained friends. In my opinion, Linda did more for drag racing and its image than any other promotion ever conceived.

She wowed the crowds as Miss Golden Shifter, putting George Hurst and his company front and center in the eyes of young men between 18 and 65. She was the show. She gave drag racing sex appeal, glamour, and image. Men and women cheered her, and Linda had the wonderful capacity to put hero drivers in their place with just the pucker of her lips and a smile. Over the years, Linda has represented major corporations such as the NHRA and SEMA, but they all seem to blur into one image—Linda waving to the crowd.

Off track and away from the maddening crowd, Linda Vaughn is a caring and thoughtful person, never turning her back on anyone she calls a friend. Linda gave drag racing its soft side.

SHIRLEY MULDOWNEY

And then there is Shirley Muldowney. I actually handled some press release work for the ad agency BBDO, who represented Dodge and Shirley with her Top Fuel car. From our first conversation, it was clear that here was a champion. Indeed, Shirley was three times the NHRA World Champion in Top Fuel.

Shirley believed that there should be no distinction between men and women behind the wheel of a Top Fuel dragster; a racer is a racer. The truest statement that can be made about Shirley is the fact that she neither asked for nor received any special treatment when she rolled to the starting line. She raced and beat the best drivers in the business. She was never intimidated by Don Garlits or Don Prudhomme or any other top driver. She proved herself a Champion through her own courage, and that is the best you can say about any racer. She was tough, fierce, and fearless on the track, and a class act off it. Shirley Muldowney is the reason young women compete in Top Fuel racing today.

In today's world, women in racing are commonplace. But in the early days of drag racing, women were considered helpers and decoration. The boys didn't want to be upstaged. It took the courage and determination of the women mentioned here and countless others to change attitudes. Something for which the boys should be eternally thankful.

While the beautiful Linda Vaughn made the drag racing scene more sensual, she also brought a touch of class to the mass of fans packed in the stands. She helped promote products from manufacturers like Hurst, and she opened the door for young women to become part of the sport of drag racing. *Don Brown*

A FEW BITS AND PIECES

Every book, every story, has fragments left out, bits that won't fit, pieces for which there can be found no room. The tale of California Top Fuel from 1950 to 1970 is no exception. The story could go on and on. Many voices could have, and should have, been heard. In the end, the door of opportunity had to be slammed shut, the publisher could allow no more and pulled the plug on the page counter. I abandoned the struggle, then had second thoughts. There had been tape recordings made and voices kept calling. I just couldn't leave things as they stood. What made the situation even worse was that the voices came from friends, and I could not disregard their efforts. So, the following segment contains a few comments from interviews conducted that somehow fell between the cracks.

WEED

Tim Kraushaar (Weed) became a fixture at local Southern California Top Fuel meets throughout the 1960s. Weed worked as a starter, announcer, pit crew go-fer, driver, and car owner. He lived the '60s surrounded by nitro and burning rubber.

TIM KRAUSHAAR

Around 1967, Top Fuel in California really started happening. Guys figured out how to make big horsepower, and the manufacturers were putting out better and more sophisticated parts.

You got to remember that, in the '60s, three or four guys, working average 40-hour-a-week jobs, could pool their disposable income and build a Top Fuel car. Couple that idea with the fact that prize money got better, and you had the groundwork for a lot of cars being built.

There was a time when California was the Mecca for Top Fuel racing. There were eight drag strips within a 200-mile drive of Los Angeles, and we could race 45 weekends a year. The back Eeast teams had to come west.

In the '60s race car builders did not have CNC machines, computers, laser measuring devices. Everything was done on a Bridgeport, a lathe, hand-operated drill press, or gas welded in a garage. You had to be creative to race in the '60s.

To offer some idea of how things went in the '60s for the hard-working racers, the guys without much money, here is a little example. When I worked at Lions Drag Strip, every Saturday night after the racing was over, either C.J. Hart or I would wander through the Top Fuel pits with a pocket full of money and we would hand out a hundred here and fifty there to the teams who went out early or didn't qualify. That's the way it was done. Or, we would head for Nick's, a bar & grill on the corner of Wardlow & Cherry, and buy dinner and drinks for all the racers who hung out after the races.

THE RACK MAN

Don Rackemann has always been a larger-than-life figure, sporting the best in men's apparel, diamond pinky rings, Rolex watches, and hot wheels. He made Top Fuel racing in California colorful. He is still brash and outspoken, and in many ways proved to be the forerunner to today's corporate wheeler-dealer. He has always been the money man.

There was no way of telling our story without the rack man offering his two-cents.

DON RACKEMANN

Man, I started at the very beginning, hanging out at the Piccadilly Drive-In when I was 14 years old. It was 1945, the end of World War II and the GIs were coming home, looking for action. Hot rodding was a big deal.

I once watched Lou Baney dust off an outlaw motorcycle racer in a street race on Washington Boulevard in West Los Angeles, with about five hundred spectators watching. I was hooked on street racing and hot rodding from that point on. I built my first hot rod when I was 15 years old.

We would street race seven nights a week, sometimes for money and other times just to kick somebody's butt. Finally, I opened up a shop in 1950 and partnered up with Lou Baney, because he had a bigger name than me. We called it Lou Baney Automotive.

Less than a year after Santa Ana opened, Lou Baney and Louie Senter got a rent agreement on an old airport site in Saugus and opened a drag strip. I went to work, and learned how to run a drag strip. At the time, Saugus was in the middle of nowhere, so Baney would put up a $25 Savings Bond for Top Eliminator and that brought out all the big names. In 1951 twenty-five bucks was real money.

When Mickey Thompson and Wally Parks backed the ban on fuel, I was part of an outlaw group called Drag Racers Inc., and we raced at tracks that didn't recognize the ban. We were not going to stop running nitro. We ran Bakersfield with the Smokers before it became the March Meet.

In the early '60s, I bought Fontana Drag Strip from a fellow named Dean Brown. Things were going great, but we had a wind problem, and in the winter it was colder than a well-digger's ass. I decided to make a killing and put on a huge promotion booking the Greek and the Greer/Black and Prudhomme cars for a winner-take-all match race. I had to pay them both to show up, and I spent a ton on advertising. Wouldn't you know, we held the race on the weekend President Kennedy was shot. Nobody showed, and I lost my ass.

We actually opened Fontana on July 4th and, as the crowd started in, the cops busted me for a total misunderstanding concerning the bank financing for the track. I ended up facing some crazy judge and got a year in the slammer. We got everything straightened out, but the story went through the drag racing world that Rackemann wrote bad checks.

While I was in jail, Mickey Thompson bought me out of Fontana, and then a judge friend of mind found out what the crazy judge had done to me and he got me released so I didn't have to serve the whole year.

Doris Herbert, sister of Chet Herbert and wife of Kent Enderle, owned *Drag News* newspaper, and I ended up working for her as an ad salesman. After a disagreement with Doris, I went to work for Wally Parks and his *National Dragster* paper. Then Doris offered to sell me *Drag News*, so I quit Wally but Doris changed her mind and I had to work for her as an employee. Later, I started my own paper, called *Motorsports Weekly*. Things didn't work out for my paper and, in 1974, Doris finally relented and I bought out *Drag News*.

In the early '70s, Bob Kachler promoted a deal with the Continental Baking Company, and I signed on to put together two funny cars called the Wonder Wagons. It was one of the first big sponsorship packages at the time. Only McEwen and Prudhomme had the Hot Wheels deal.

In the end, due to the escalating costs of racing, Don Rackemann gave up drag racing ownership but continued to play a part in its history. Today he remains one of the most colorful figures from Top Fuel's early days.

CAT HERDER

Transplanted from the East Coast, Doug Kruse came for the1961 U.S. Fuel & Gas Championships in Bakersfield and stayed. He became one of the most sought-after Top Fuel fabricators and car builders. Kruse played a critical role in the growth of California Top Fuel racing throughout the 1960s. He worked with all of the famous chassis builders, including Ken Fuller, Don Long, Woody Gilmore, and John Buttera. But, Doug Kruse also played a pivotal role in trying to organize Top Fuel drivers into an association, something akin to herding cats.

DOUG KRUSE

It was obvious to me that California was the place if you were into Top Fuel racing. When I decided to stay, I went to work for Robert Ryan Johnson (Jocko to everyone in the business), and slowly developed my skills in pounding out aluminum bodies and building race cars to the point of opening a shop of my own.

The mid-1960s was the major transition period when Top Fuel cars went from the old-style, 2-inch tube main rails and making everything too heavy into the world of super-light, chrome-moly tube, super-light parts, longer-wheelbase chassis, and real, hand-pounded, full bodies. Cars went from backyard-builder to purpose-built race machines. After 200 miles per hour, race car builders began to realize that pushing through the air had problems, so they began to look at aerodynamics and the use of basic wings for downforce.

When Mickey Thompson resigned as the manager of Lions Drag Strip, issues cropped up between the racers and the new administration. I had meetings with racers like Tom McEwen and Kenny Stafford, and realized that they were very close to boycotting the track. But, instead we formed a group called United Drag Racers Association (UDRA), and convinced the Lions Club of Long Beach to hire C.J. Hart as manager. This solved much of the problem. The UDRA went on to sponsor professional drag races at different tracks and eventually went nationwide.

With costs going up and pressure from Funny Cars taking away some of the popularity of Top Fuel cars, I decided to put together an event called the Professional Dragster Championship, open to only dragsters—Top Fuel, Top Gas, and Junior Fuel—to be held at Long Beach. It was my concept to have all of the touring professionals like Garlits, The Ramchargers, Kalitta, and Karamesines racing California cars like the Snake, McEwen, and Safford. By having all dragsters, the race would have substantial prize money. The fans loved it, and we had the largest crowd ever at Long Beach. We had 93 dragsters going for a 64-car show. But, it was not enough to change history. Funny cars and rear-engine dragsters took over, sponsors demanded more, and the cost of racing spiraled upward. Professional drag racing began to bend to the demands of the big dollar.

From my personal standpoint, the "60s allowed the car builder the freedom to innovate and that's what I enjoyed the most.

continued from page 215
you needed. Throughout the early '60s, most teams were like a clan of cave dwellers—everyone contributed to the cause. There were exceptions, Ivo, and the Greer, Black, and Prudhomme car, for example. They ran hard, and Tommy Greer was noted for following the true democratic principle—if it's broke, throw money at it.

When Keith Black, Ed Pink, Sid Waterman, and Dave Zeuschel started building racing engines commercially, there appeared to be the beginning of a division between teams. Black sometimes had five or six cars running his engines, all with different setups. He could gather way more information than anyone else. It was like the multi-car teams in NASCAR. It was hard to run against that type of information. As it turned out, we had the friendly guys and the rest of the world. It got down to where you helped your friends and screwed the rest.

Round money was what kept the little guys going; there were no big sponsor dollars until the late '60s early '70s. Costs did go up and, if you didn't win a couple of rounds, you went home broke. The money guys looked down a little at the rest of us, so it was very rewarding when you dusted one off. But, hey, we all wanted to race.

Another point about the '60s that has been convoluted over the years is the story of friction between the back Eeast racers and the West Coast racers. Most of that is bullshit. The racers from east of Phoenix made it a point to come to California, especially in the winter months. They couldn't race at home, so they came to California. We had the advantage of good weather and the fact that a lot of the manufacturers were local.

It was great fun to hang out with Garlits or The Greek, Jimmy Nix, Vance Hunt, Kalitta, Schubeck. There were a bunch of guys who came out to get new equipment, test, bench race, and brain pick. Even the dreaded Northern California racers would spend time down south. Although, one thing that pissed off the Northern guys was when we referred to any racer north of Bakersfield, or north of the Ridge Route, as Frisco Racers. They hated that.

In the late 1960s, the wheels started coming off for the home builder. Detroit car companies started putting money in drag racing, big sponsors like Mattel Toy and the Funny Cars took the spotlight.

In the true spirit of a Working Class Racer, Roger Wolford built his own cars, drove them, and did all of the rest of the labor connected with racing a dragster in the days when it was a grassroots sport. His first fuel-burning dragster, shown here in 1957, was powered by a flathead Ford and ran speeds around 130 mph. *Roger Wolford Collection*

SEMA started up and suddenly chassis had to be certified. Parts were being made for the rich guys, but the days of being able to make your own pieces were over.

I drove for Neil Leffler and we tried to making a living off of round money, but that didn't work. I finally got together with Ed Lenarth and we built the Holy Toledo Jeep Funny Car. We learned, and so did many of the budget Top Fuel racers, that you could build a Funny Car, back the motor down so it would live, and put on a show for the promoters by doing burnouts and make more money than running a dragster. Promoters would pay California cars appearance money plus travel expenses. Suddenly you could make a living again.

Top Fuel became the place for big budget teams; Funny Cars were in and they were what the fans came to see.

Still, when it is all said and done, I loved running Top Fuel back in the days when you had to handle your own act, build your own stuff, and money didn't matter.

SURFER-TURNED-RACER

The 1960s were a difficult time. There was a war the country didn't want, a battle over civil rights, and a generation of young people filled with disillusionment. To combat the stress, the culture embraced free love, flower power, drugs, and rock and roll. Freedom of expression came of age in California Top Fuel racing, creating a broad band of characters and forming a new culture that would define the sport for the next decade.

A validation of this profile can be found in a

For the working class racer, earning a living and supporting a family came before racing. But for some, like Roger Wolford, work and racing blended. Wolford worked for Scotty Fenn, the first commercial chassis builder. Later, in 1962, Roger worked and drove for Mickey Thompson when Mickey was running his Pontiac program in Top Fuel. *Roger Wolford Collection*

Top Fuel in California was Number One in new ideas throughout the 1960s. Some of them worked, while others had a few bugs to be worked out. In 1967 at Fremont in Northern California, Noel Black tried a twin-engine, four-wheel-drive Top Fuel car. Weight and aerodynamics obviously caused problems. *Steve Reyes*

California-born 1960s Top Fuel racer named Jim Busby.

In reality, Jim Busby took the California image far beyond the boundaries of the Golden State. He became an international sports car racing champion, winning the famed 24 Hours of Le Mans three times in his class. He lived in Europe as a Porsche, BMW, and Mazda factory driver. He retired to become a Vintage car racer. He now represents Ferrari in North America and drives a 2001 Ferrari Formula One car. Busby also operates one of the most notable restoration shops in the country. And, appropriately enough, the shop is located in Laguna Beach, a town that is the very essence of the California lifestyle.

Now in his sixties, Jim Busby remembered the days when he would go surfing in the morning and Top Fuel racing in the afternoon.

JIM BUSBY

I was born in Pasadena. Hot Rod City we used to call the town, because it was inundated with street rods, race shops, and stripped down roadsters. I began to engage in street racing at age fourteen, without a driver's license, and never looked back. I built my first Top Fuel car at age 19. It was an old Scotty

Fenn K88 once raced by Emery Cook.

As the '60s progressed, I began to get serious about Top Fuel racing, and several of my friends joined with me and we became the Beach Boys Racing Team. The team consisted of Hank Westmoreland (who drove most of my cars), Bob Ekelberger, Bill Karges, and me.

Our logo was legitimate because we would actually go surfing and then tow the race car to the track with our surfboards still in the van. We were sometimes confused with the Surfers racing team of Tom Jobe, Bob Skinner, and Mike Sorokin. There was also Don "The Beachcomber" Johnson, who ran a Top Fuel car around the same time. It was all part of the California image and it helped promote drag racing around the country.

I must say that we did not become a successful team without help. Going back to my first dragster, Bruce Crower, Ed Donovan, and chassis builder Don Long helped me throughout the years and, as we got more serious, Hank became a huge factor as both driver and crew chief. Although I drove for a long time, once we started touring and running NHRA Nationals events, Hank was the man.

Carl Schiefer, who I had known for years, introduced me to Dick Smothers of "The Smothers Brothers" TV show and, through Dick's connections, we secured sponsor money and built a new Roy Fjastad chassis with an Ed Pink Elephant Hemi. The car became the Smothers Brothers Beach Boys Special. It turned out to be a very good combination and, as a touring California car, we got our share of appearance money and won a few races along the way.

What I liked about Top Fuel racing in the '60s may not be the same for other people. Some call the period "the old days." That is not the case. It was a time of tough, innovative racing conducted by racers who worked regular 40-hour-a-week jobs. Contrary to what some people think, the cars were not junk. They were sophisticated race cars running faster than anyone could have imagined. It was those with high levels of skill and innovation who won races. And, before the cost of Top Fuel went off the chart, there was room for wild experimentation. For example, we took a Don Long chassis and installed two Ford 255-cubic-inch four-cam Indy engines with turbochargers and ran Top Fuel. You couldn't do that today.

Unfortunately, innovation was not enough. Money overcame ingenious thought and I sold the Smothers Brothers car to Dwight Salsbury and went road racing.

Despite racing at Le Mans, driving a Formula One car, and traveling the world road racing circuits, my heart has a special place for a foggy Saturday night at Long Beach when Top Fuel cars would send header flames four feet in the air and shock waves five miles into space.

A MAN OF IDEAS

Known as a period of experimentation, Top Fuel chassis builders of the late 1950s and throughout the 1960s and 1970s laid the groundwork for the cars of today. The names most often connected with innovative chassis design begin with Scotty Fenn's Chassis Research, and continue with Jim Nelson and Dode Martin, the Dragmasters. Both Fenn and the Dragmasters were well ahead of their time and took dragster racing to a higher level.

They were followed by a host of names,

When Top Fuel chassis builders discovered chrome-moly steel tubing, it meant they could build lighter and stronger chassis. Northern California chassis builder Pete Ogden illustrates the meaning of "lightweight." *Steve Reyes*

Before the front-engine dragster gave way to the rear-mounted version, builders tried many combinations to get more speed and more horsepower. Running two blown Hemi engines was one way, and, in the case of Motes and Williams, it worked well. The team ran strongly in Top Gas. *Don Brown*

including Rod Pepmuller, Lefty Mudersbach, Joe Itow, Roy Steen, Frank Huszar, Tommy Ivo, Don Garlits, Pete Ogden, Ron and Gene Logghe, Joe Schubeck, Roy Fjastad, Don Long, Woody Gilmore, Jim Davis, and Ken Fuller. There were others, but those mentioned have crossed my path over the years. Fuller was one of the first to introduce lightweight, small-diameter, thin-walled tubing in chassis design, and he created his own unique, cocoon-style roll cage to protect the driver. He can also take credit for building many of the era's most famous cars.

In 1964, Fuller built a chassis for my dragster. I can testify firsthand to the quality of his workmanship and his ability to help those who have trouble helping themselves. In person, Ken Fuller is outspoken and to the point. He tells things straight up, without adding a sugar coating, and has always been somewhat controversial in his thinking. Fuller now lives in Northern California and he's still creating new ideas. I used our long-time friendship to coax him into offering his take on the Top Fuel scene during the heyday of the 1960s.

KEN FULLER

The short version of the story is that I got interested in drag racing after my discharge from the service. I was a structural aircraft mechanic in the Navy, so when I got out, I took a job welding at C&T Automotive. Working with tubing and all of that welding started me thinking about chassis design. My first car was for Don "The Beachcomber" Johnson and Daddy's Auto Body shop. It was way lighter than the other cars around and it did very well from the get-go.

Then I built a chassis for Tommy Ivo, powered by a single Buick engine. A short time later, I built a twin-engine Buick car for Ivo, and things started happening once that car hit the track. I moved into a shop at Tony Nancy's complex and he had me build a roadster chassis for him. My business picked up, but Ivo and Nancy wanted to keep me a secret. And, between the two of them, they kept me building new cars. I actually built Ivo's four-engine car.

To digress for a moment, after I built the Ivo single-engine Buick chassis, all of my customers who ordered a chassis wanted the skid-bar, or trapeze design, roll bar. I didn't like it, but that is what was in demand. Then I built a chassis for Ernie Alvarado (Ernie's Camera Shop) and for Rod Stuckey and used my own design for the roll cage. I believed that keeping the driver packed tightly in the car with his arms inside the cage was the way to go. So, after Ivo and several early cars, I went to that design. Also, I was a firm believer in using chrome-moly tubing and gas welding the connections.

My original plan was to have a shop specializing in engine installations and building custom headers. That went out the window quickly and I became a chassis builder. During this transformation period, two situations really helped establish my reputation. First, I rebuilt the Rod Stuckey car into the Greer, Black, and Prudhomme car. Second, several of the teams from Northern California, namely Ted Gotelli and Master & Richter, ordered cars and suddenly I was in demand.

At the same time, I figured that one way to improve my business was to run my own car. I teamed up with Dave Zeuschel to build an engine and got Don Prudhomme to drive the car. It was a good combination—we won the Bakersfield Fuel & Gas Championships in 1962.

I worked hard to build the type of car the customer wanted, but at the same time I made a conscious effort to make everything I built look better and work easier than any other builder. I figured if it

A new face in the race, the rear-engine Top Fuel dragster had taken hold, and by 1971, the front-engine design was fading quickly. The rear-engine car had advantages, like clear vision, no fear of facing a fire, and better traction. Here, Jeb Allen, in the "Praying Mantis," puts a holeshot on a front-engine car. *Don Brown*

looked good, it would sell. I built cars for some hard runners, including Kenny Stafford, The Greek Chris Karamesines, Roland Leong, Danny Ongais, McEwen & Adams (The Shark Car), Sid Waterman, and a bunch of others. I even built some oddball cars like the Magwinder, a rear-engine car I built for Chuck Jones with a chassis made from magnesium tubing that weighed a little less than 1,450 pounds with a blown Chrysler in it.

As the '60s progressed, chassis concepts went to longer wheelbase designs. Fuller concedes that he followed the trend of longer wheelbase extensions, but while doing so, he also placed an emphasis on better diagonal bracing of the chassis main rails, rear end placement, front end design, and engine location.

KEN FULLER

A chassis is really just something that keeps the engine off the ground.

I tried to build cars that were easy for the teams to run and to maintain. There were a lot of long-wheelbase cars that didn't handle, so obviously just sticking long pieces of tubing between the rear end and the front axle was not the answer. My main concern was always to keep the driver safe.

By the mid-1970s, two things changed the sport in my eyes. First, Top Fuel went to rear engine. I built about five rear-engine cars, one was for Tony Nancy. The second was liability problems for chassis builders. The cars were going really fast and I didn't want a big lawsuit. One bad deal could put you out of business. In fact, the liability insurance coverage cost ten times more than I was getting for a chassis. I never did charge enough for my chassis.

Another disappointing situation I got tired of was the fact that I would build a car for a customer, make it as good as I could, so when it left my shop it was a top-of-the-line race car. The next thing I knew, the team would thrash the shit out of it doing things that were, in my opinion, stupid, then want me to fix it. That crap got old in a hurry. I gave up building Top Fuel cars and turned to restoration work building roadsters and hot rods. Right now I'm building a car for Bonneville.

I always liked Top Fuel because there was no argument about it. Best guy won. No sniveling. You had no excuses for losing except that the other driver beat you. That was Top Fuel in the '60s. Now they limit things, like engine sizes and fuel percentage. I would still like it to be unlimited—run what you brung.

CHAPTER EIGHTEEN

THE LONER

He may have been called The Loner, but Tony Nancy had many friends. When he went to Top Fuel, pals like Woody Gilmore, John Buttera, Keith Black and Paul Southerland all helped build his race car. *Steve Reyes*

The time has come to complete the task.

Endings always seem to show up at the least anticipated time. But, all stories must end, so new ones can commence. So it is with our story of Top Fuel drag racing in California from 1950 to 1970. True, that time in history has long passed and is never to return. If you lived the experience, consider yourself lucky. If not, you missed two of the most colorful decades on record. The only question posed at this point is, what is the most appropriate path to our conclusion?

Once set in motion, an ending cannot be changed and it must remain final.

So, I decided to end this story with a personal experience. I feel that by using something embedded in my spirit, the essence of all that has been told so far will somehow be made more enduring to the reader.

Anthony "Tony" Nancy was the last Top Fuel dragster driver to win the U.S. Fuel & Gas Championship in Bakersfield, California, driving a front-engine machine. He did it by beating his closest and dearest friend, Harry Hibler, in the final round. It was nothing personal, just the way California Top Fuel drivers did their job.

Known by everyone in racing as the Loner, Tony Nancy was an old-school guy—tough, stubborn, fearless, a hard racer who never gave an inch. He truly lived by the code "never blink and never lift." He was, in effect, the epitome of the Top Fuel driver circa 1950-1970. Of course, there was much more to Tony Nancy than Top Fuel. He was a California kid, hot rodder, street racer, war hero, a self-taught restoration artist, and the type of knight in shinning armor who would defend a lady's honor or help a child in need.

Very few ever got to know Tony completely; Harry Hibler, Tom Sparks, and John Wolf are a few who I knew who did. I was a friend of his for 40 years, and it took 35 of them to get through his protective shield. One thing was for sure—you either played fair and true, or he would jump in your face.

I met Tony in the early '60s at his shop in Sherman Oaks. He had a big reputation as the best for boat and car interiors. His shop was the place for racers to hang out. He rented stalls to others in the business, including chassis builder Ken Fuller, and engine builder Ed Pink. If you were a name in Top Fuel racing, you hung out at Tony's shop.

The perfection displayed in his work drew the Hollywood car crowd to his door. Steve McQueen (who Tony once tossed out of his shop for being disrespectful), James Garner, Burt Reynolds, Clark Gable, Gary Cooper, Dean Martin, and John Wayne all brought their cars to Tony. The cars, too, were famous: Rolls Royces, Bentleys, Lamborghinis, Maseratis, and his specialty, Ferraris.

An easy way to place Tony in the proper perspective would be to imagine a portrait of a typical California hot rodder, shortly after World War II. That would be Tony Nancy.

He started as a kid, riding his bicycle to the shops of Eddie Meyer and Frank Kurtis, straining to witness the building of racing cars. He would get teased by Indy drivers like Jack McGrath, Manny Ayulo, and old man Vukovich. Eddie Meyer would sometimes rub a knot on his head for getting too close and bothering the workers. A neighbor named

Long before he turned to Top Fuel, Tony Nancy was a California superstar in Top Gas. Tony (foreground) is shown here overcoming a challenge by George Boltoff for the Number One spot on the Drag News Mr. Eliminator List at San Fernando drag strip in 1964.
Tony Nancy Collection

In 1969 Tony Nancy switched from Top Gas to Top Fuel and became an instant success. His most significant victory was, of course, the Top Fuel title at the U.S. Fuel & Gas Championships at Bakersfield. Tony was the poster boy for California Top Fuel drivers; he was fast, quick and did it on a budget. *Tom Madigan*

Greg Fisher took Tony to the El Mirage dry lakes to watch the hot rods run and, from that point on, he was a racer.

At fifteen, Tony built his first hot rod. At age 16 and nine months, Tony's world took a hard turn. Like many boys raised by a single parent (his mother), Tony took to the streets and got a little wild. A local police official suggested that he join the Marines to avoid jail time. Underage, he forged papers and went away to serve in a Police Action called Korea. In a moment of quiet some 40 years after his war experience, he uttered a few words to me about his struggle to stay alive in a foxhole filled with his dead comrades. In his home, there was a wooden box filled with metals for bravery—none of which he ever displayed in public.

After an apprenticeship at a famous Hollywood Cadillac dealership, Tony became a master at the art of interior restoration. He opened a shop specializing in race car and boat interior design. Work was one thing, but racing became his passion.

His first real race car was a 1929 Ford roadster with a blown flathead Ford on fuel. The engine

A dragster in modified roadster sheet metal is what Tony called his Ken Fuller-chassis, Oldsmobile-powered 22 Jr. car at the NHRA Winternationals. Here, Tony accepts the trophy for Best Engineered Car of the Meet in 1962. *Tony Nancy Collection/NHRA Photo*

Before making his mark as a California Top Fuel gunslinger, Tony Nancy had a long list of accomplishments in Top Gas dragsters. He built two rear-engine cars, Wedge I and II, back in the 1960s. He crashed Wedge I in Ohio. Powered by a blown Plymouth Hemi, Wedge II was more successful despite being a handful to drive. Before his passing in 2004 Tony restored Wedge II to its original beauty.
Don Brown

belonged to racing pioneer Tom Sparks. Next, with chassis builder Ken Fuller doing the welding, Tony built a lightweight roadster powered by a Nail Head Buick V-8. Addicted to competition, Tony again joined forces with Fuller. They brought in aluminum craftsman Wayne Ewing and built a 1925 Model T Modified Roadster powered by another Buick, but this time with a supercharger. The car was a sensation, and Tony became feared as a competitor. He made 1962 a winning season, topping off the year with a class win at the NHRA Winternationals.

Still not satisfied, he again called on Ken Fuller for a chassis. This time, he added race car designer Steve Swaja and a close friend, named Jimmy Summers, to complete a full-bodied slingshot dragster powered by a Wedge-head Dodge.

The car and Tony became one of the most successful gas-powered dragsters in the country. So

good, in fact, that Tony stayed number one on the *Drag News* Mr. Eliminator list for nearly two years.

During that period, Tony wanted to push the limits of car design, so he again called on Steve Swaja to design a revolutionary car. Chassis builders Roy Steen and Frank Huszar turned the design into reality, and pioneer race car body builder Emil Deidt, at the time in his late seventies, was called upon to create a full body. The car was a radical, rear-engine dragster called the Wedge.

There would be two versions, Wedge I and II. Although there had been previous attempts at building rear-engine cars (the Speed Sport Roadster and the Chuck Jones Magwinder were two examples), the Wedge cars were the first true dragsters. Don Garlits, who built the first fuel-burning rear-engine dragster, will tell you that Tony laid the groundwork for the later designs.

During and after the Wedge period, Tony always ran conventional front-engine dragsters too—cars powered by Oldsmobile, big-block Chevy, and, finally, Chrysler Hemi engines.

Despite the fact that every car ever built by Tony Nancy was featured on the cover of *Hot Rod* magazine, and that he had strong ties to Goodyear, Cragar, Valvoline, Wynn's Oil, Revell Toy Company, Paul Schiefer, Kent Enderle, and many speed equipment manufacturers like Forged true pistons, Tony remained a California racer. He chose to race on his own terms and to stay close to his business. He once said, "Many of my friends like Prudhomme, McEwen, and Garlits went full-time professional racing and they got some big bucks from sponsors. I decided to stay in California and run my business. I toured when it was convenient for me. Looking back, I may have missed some opportunities, but that's life."

Top Fuel drivers are not like your everyday, regular people. They tend to be ultra-competitive,

He not only raced hard in California, he competed around the world. Tony Nancy toured the world, promoting American drag racing in places like England, Australia, Japan, and Italy. Here, Tony gets set to run his car at the famed Monza race track in Italy. His crewman is a staff member from CalTex (Texaco Europe), the fuel supplier for Tony's car. *Author's Collection*

Tony Nancy didn't switch to Top Fuel until 1969 but, once he started running Nitro, he went to the limit. The Loner won Bakersfield in 1970, was runner-up at the Winternationals in 1970, and set the top speed record for Top Fuel in 1972 with a 236.22 mph blast. *Steve Reyes*

The Loner ran a rear-engine Top Fuel car off and on until he retired from competition in 1979. He always said he loved the old days best, when you could do everything on your own. *Steve Reyes*

The late Tony "The Loner" Nancy gives the fans a California-style burnout in his 1970 Top Fuel dragster. This was the first car Tony ran in Top Fuel. *Steve Reyes; Tom Madigan collection*

ego oriented, and they push their own limits and those of fellow drivers to the breaking point. Their mantra is: Always pushing, never lifting. In 1970, although he never really wanted to go full-time racing, Tony was pushed into building a Top Fuel dragster. It was something the Loner had never done. Said Tony, "Prudhomme talked me into it. He wanted to see me run with the big dogs."

Tony picked the most talented people in drag racing to help. Woody Gilmore and John Buttera built the chassis, Paul Sutherland pounded out the full body, and Keith Black supplied his aluminum block and heads. Black also offered instructions for working with nitro, but Tony insisted on building the engine himself.

The result was one of the most stunning Top Fuel cars ever. Fear was something that Tony had left on the snow-covered hills of Korea, so going from Gas Man to Fuel Man was a simple step. Tony rocked the Top Fuel world by taking runner-up at the Winternationals in his first national event.

On a personal note, in my 50-some years of going to the drag races, I have seen many fearsome machines. But when I worked as a crew member one time for Tony's Top Fuel car, there was something unreal about the experience. When he rolled to the starting line, the car shook the ground harder than the others, the header flames defied reason, and Tony drove with pure, unadulterated desire. He willed the car to record speeds, while never showing the slightest sign of weakness. He was more than fearless—he was devoid of the very concept of fear.

Far ahead of his time, Robert "Jocko" Johnson built a couple versions of his streamlined dragster, one of which was driven by Jazzy Nelson. This photo, taken at Fremont Drag Strip in 1965 shows Emery Cook behind the wheel. *Steve Reyes*

In March, 1970, Tony brought his machine to the only race that mattered to a Top Fuel driver, the Smokers Fuel & Gas Championships at Bakersfield. Tony took on the best and he did it like a Top Fuel driver would dream of doing it—no holds barred, fight to the finish, big loads of nitro, big balls, oil blowing, blower tossing, old school, never lifting off the throttle, mean-ass Top Fuel dragster racing. It was a simple choice of run hard, or lose and go home to Mommy. In the end, he had to put his best friend on the trailer, but that's the way it was in Top Fuel.

Tony's reign of terror in Top Fuel continued throughout the early 1970s. He set ET records at several major strips and, in 1972, he shattered the top speed record, running 236.22 miles per hour.

By the mid-1970s, big money found its way into Top Fuel and Tony battled reality for a time. He built a rear-engine car and collected some sponsor money, but he never went big time. He retired in 1979.

Tony admitted that he always liked the old days best. He once said, "The guys like Art Chrisman, Jazzy Nelson, Calvin Rice, Tom Sparks, Emery Cook, and Lefty Mudersbach were all drivers, owners, and mechanics. Those guys were my heroes. They built their own chassis and engines. Back in the old days, you had to be smarter and cleverer than the other guy, not richer. Don't get me wrong, Top Fuel is still very exciting, but for me it was just more fun when you could do everything on your own."

Although front-engine Top Fuel cars died of natural causes in the mid-1970s, Tony Nancy lived on until Veterans Day, November 11, 2004.

This book is dedicated to the memory of Tony Nancy for two reasons: he was my friend for over 40 years; and he was a great example of a California dragster driver and car builder. He was not really a Loner, he just believed in his own ability to do things his way. *Tom Madigan*

Tony Nancy is gone, the front-engine Top Fuel car is gone, and the years between 1950 and 1970 are gone. The journey of this book is over and the stories told will never be lived again. But it was a great time to be alive.

SOURCES AND REFERENCES

High Performance/ Dr. Robert Post
Hot Rod Pioneers/ Ed Almquest
The American Hot Rod/ Dean Batchelor
Diggers—Funnies—-Gassers & Altereds/ Bob
    McClurg
Quarter-Mile Chaos/ Steve Reyes
Dragster and Funny Car Memories/ Don
    Montgomery
The Top Fuel Handbook/ Chris Martin
The Loner/ The Story of a Drag Racer/ Tom Madigan
Hot Rod Magazine various issues 1955-1970

"Bakersfield '67"… Drag Racing Magazine/ Ralph
    Guldahl Jr.
"U.S. Fuel & Gas Championships '66"… Drag Racing
    Magazine/Ralph Guldahl Jr.
NHRA Motorsports Museum Archives/Greg Sharp
Primedia Archives/ Matt Stone
National Dragster/March 1970… "Tony Nancy Wins
    Bakersfield"
Petersen's History of Drag Racing/ Petersen
    Publishing/Lee Kelly/Dave Wallace Jr. Editors
Heroes of Hot Rodding/ David Fetherston

THANK YOU TO THE FOLLOWING FRIENDS FOR THEIR HELP IN THIS PROJECT

Jere Alhadeff
Bud Barnett
Don Brown
John Bowser
Blake Bowser
Tin Beebe
Jim Busby
Gigi Carleton
John Clinard/Ford Motor Co.
Art Chrisman
Bob Creitz
Jim Deist
Edelbrock Corporation/Jan
    Schield
Jerry Forsberg
Ken Fuller
Jim Fox
Ralph Guladahl Jr.
John Glick
Don & Pat Garlits
Tom Hanna
Harry Hibler
Dennis Holding
Ed Iskenderian

Tommy Ivo
Ed Justice Jr.
Parnelli & Judy Jones
Bob Joehnck
Lee Kelly
Doug Kruse
Tim Kraushaar (Weed)
Roland Leong
Ed Lenarth
Darlene Madigan
Dode Martin
Bob McClurg
Dave McClelland
Tom McEwen
Jim McFarland
Bob Muravez
Don Montgomery
Bill McNatt
Jim Nelson
Paul Pfaff
Don & Lynn Prudhomme
Robert E. Petersen Archives
Tony Pedregon
Cruz Pedregon

Frank Pedregon
Dr. Robert Post
Ed Pink
Don Prieto
Don Rackemann
Eric Rickman
Steve Reyes
Chuck Ridgley
Matt Stone
Joe Schubeck
Kenny Safford
Greg Sharp/ The NHRA Wally
Parks Motorsports Museum
Judy Thompson
Tony Thacker/ The NHRA Wally
Parks Motorsports Museum
Tom Voehringer
Jim White
James Warren
Dave West
Sid Waterman
Norm Weekly
Dave Wallace Jr.
Roger Wolford

ACKNOWLEDGMENTS

Every book I have ever read has some type of special space where the author thanks everyone who helped put a project together. This book offers the same but with a twist. Added to the long list of acknowledgements of those who were involved in this project are a few of my thoughts about the meaning of the project and why the use of a testimonial-style format was important.

About 99 percent of those who offered content to this story I call friends. Most of the contributors I have known for 30 or 40 years, so it was not just a case of interviewing characters as targets of opportunity but, rather, wanting to record the lives of people who have been a part of my life. I wanted the characters to tell their stories in their own style and as if they were members of a family, because drag racing is one oversized family. My intent was to encourage the reader to get to know those involved, and the way to accomplish this was to offer some insight into why they fit so perfectly as pieces of the story.

Drag racing is a visual and sensual sport, therefore without great photos the story of Top Fuel in California circa 1950-1970 would have been diminished. The photographers who supplied the drama for this book are not only great artists, but friends who genuinely wanted to help make this project a success.

Don Brown, once a competitor of mine in our early days as magazine editors, was first to offer his collection of photos to me. Steve Reyes, who is considered by most to be one of the great action photographers in drag racing, once taught me the basic rules of covering a National event; he overwhelmed me with his generosity and his involvement in this story. Both Jere Alhadeff and Bob McClurg are themselves top-of-the-line cameramen and have authored their own action books on drag racing, but when I needed their help they never hesitated. Ed Justice, Jr., was a young teen when he would come to the races and stand in with the professionals shooting his share of the action. Ed went on to run Justice Brothers Inc., a leader in racing lubricants.

As for the featured pioneers of Top Fuel drag racing in California, I much appreciate their unselfish attitude toward this project. A special thanks goes out to: Don Prudhomme, Tom McEwen, Tommy Ivo, Bob Muravez, Art Chrisman,

Kelly Brown, Don Garlits, James Warren, Kenny Safford, Jim Nelson, Dode Martin, half of the Frantic Four (Jim Fox and Norm Weekly), and Roland Leong for taking time from their busy days to sit down and record their stories.

The same gratitude goes to engine builders Ed Pink, Sid Waterman, and Paul Pfaff, and to car building artists Ken Fuller, Doug Kruse, and Tom Hanna.

There were others who had an impact, including Bob Joehnck, the man who made me promise not to change his story by adding fluff. Roger Wolford and I go back to the early 1960s, but time and space caused us to lose contact for nearly 40 years. When our mutual friend Dave Sowins passed away, we reunited at the memorial service and picked up our conversation as if no time had passed. Roger filled in many gaps from those days gone by.

And then there is Ralph Guladahl, Jr. (Digger Ralph),who actually wrote much of the history of Long Beach as a journalist and part-time public relations man for the track. Ralph supported this project from the get-go and offered countless memories about Top Fuel racers, most of which could not be printed unless wrapped in a plain, brown package.

As an example of just how involved my life has been with those who told their stories, consider that Paul Pfaff and I went to the same high school and when I went drag racing it was Pfaff who helped me learn the rules before something bad happened. Even further back, Ed Lenarth and I were playmates as four-year-olds in Cleveland. And speaking of Cleveland, Joe Schubeck, a friend for 40 years, came west and made a name in Top Fuel. Schubeck also played a role in a scenario few, if anyone, have heard about.

When my wife, Darlene, fell ill to cancer, Schubeck saved her life by setting up an appointment with a doctor who was a friend of his at the Cleveland Clinic, then paying our way back and forth, and offering his condo and car for our use while we were fighting the problem.

Hard-nosed "Hand Grenade" Harry Hibler was just recovering from a near fatal motorcycle accident when this project began. Despite much pain, Harry jumped at the chance to help lay out the groundwork, by contacting many of those interviewed and by offering his own special story. The same level of enthusiasm came from Bob Muravez, who knows everyone and anyone who has ever pulled on a helmet, face mask, and goggles and climbed into a Top Fuel car. I found out that no one ever says no to Floyd Lippencotte Jr.

Special thanks go out to two pioneers who are not only friends but who have worked all their lives to save lives. I did not get a chance to record their stories, but I know firsthand what they have done. I'm talking about Jim Deist and Bill Simpson. From the late 1950s to the 1970s and beyond, Deist and Simpson realized that, if the hazards of the sport where not overcome, the sport of drag racing might die because of public opinion and the sheer madness of using Nitro as a fuel. If was their combined efforts that saved many a drag race driver from the violent nature of going fast in the quarter-mile.

In some strange way, I feel the need to thank Mickey Thompson and Tony Nancy for their stories, even though their words were recorded many years ago and neither is with us today. I discovered that Top Fuel racing had penetrated my soul when the voices of these two old friends came back to life on tape.

As for regrets I have a few. I wish with all my heart that I could have recorded the stories of Keith Black, Denny Milani, Mickey Brown, Gary Gabelich, Dave Sowins, Steve Carbone, Mike Sorokin, Mike Snively, and Bruce Woodcock. I know that I will see them again in another time and place. I know that their spirits are around watching over this story.

Tom Madigan 2007

INDEX

Adams, Gene, 95, 128, 130, 131, 213

Alexander, Bill, 110, 111, 163, 201, 203

Alsenz, Bob, 16, 20

Arfons, Art, 35, 108, 155, 167

Arnett, Joaquin, 12, 20, 44, 78, 101

Austin, John "Tarzan," 123

Baca, Dennis, 40, 189

Baker, Eddie, 86, 87, 99

Baney, Lou, 20, 101, 133, 135–137, 148, 151, 153, 163, 194, 196, 197, 208

Batchelor, Dean, 33

Bean Bandits, The, 12, 20, 28, 29, 33, 44, 64, 78, 87, 101, 211

Bedwell, Cliff, 28, 44, 47, 49, 87

Beebe, Dave and Tim, 182, 183

Bivens, Jerry, 100, 136, 201

Black, Keith, 47, 115, 136, 145, 149, 151, 153, 175, 176, 178–181, 184, 188, 196, 197, 203–205, 208, 213, 223, 234

Bowles, Charles Sr. and Chuck, 63

Brissette, Jim, 194, 195, 198, 213

Broussard, Danny, 100, 136, 188

Brown, Kelly, 149, 191–199

Brown, Mickey, 88–90

Bruckman, Rich, 90, 91, 93

Bynum, Jack, 75, 76

Cagle, Gary, 64, 101, 179

Cannon, Frank, 29, 30, 35–37, 129

Carbone, Steve, 163, 201, 202

Chrisman, Art, 20, 29–37, 55, 64, 87, 101, 129, 130, 161, 164, 172, 211

Chrisman, Jack, 32, 33, 36, 37, 47, 91, 101, 136, 215

Chrisman, Lloyd, 32, 33, 36, 37

Coburn, Roger, 154, 165

Coelho, Manny, 28, 87

Collett, Gordon, 70, 132, 167

Cook, Emery, 28, 44, 47, 49, 87, 101, 235

Cortopassi, Ed, 28, 204

Davis, Eddie, 87, 99, 136

Davis, Jim, 174, 175

Deist, Jim, 65, 66, 90, 187

Dixon, Larry Sr., 152, 201

Donovan, Ed, 132, 133, 141, 199, 204

Dragmasters, 20, 50, 51, 54–58, 105, 130, 178, 179, 225

Edlebrock, Vic Sr., 13, 14, 17, 22, 41, 42, 53, 99, 106, 118, 206, 207

Ewell, Jack, 109, 162, 201

Ewing, Wayne, 46, 135, 136, 149, 232

Fenn, Scotty, 44, 49, 50, 120, 214, 215, 224

Fisher, Greg, 100, 136, 231

Fjastad, Roy, 106, 149

Force, John, 115

France, Bill, 41, 77

Frank, Nye, 109, 110

Fuller, Ken, 46, 98, 105, 107, 109, 110, 121, 122, 130, 136, 142, 143, 145, 147, 149, 151, 153, 161, 176, 179, 188, 189, 204, 208, 226, 227, 230, 231, 232

Gabelich, Gary, 61, 71, 73, 74, 77, 81, 132, 163, 201

Gaide, Don, 106, 108, 158

Garlits, Don, 34, 36, 45–47, 70, 71, 75, 77, 89, 93, 108, 123, 125, 126, 131, 139, 149, 153, 155, 160, 162, 165–175, 181, 198, 199, 202, 213, 232

Garlits, Ed, 126, 130, 168

Garrison, John, 135, 213

Gilmore, Woody, 46, 136, 194, 234

Goldstein, Leroy, 163, 201

Gotelli, Ted, 149, 175, 204

Greer, Tommy, 137, 142, 149, 151, 179

Guladahl, Ralph Jr., 92, 163–165

Haines, Bob, 149, 175, 202

Hale, Sammy, 149, 175, 201

Hamilton, Barbara, 218

Hanna, Tom, 46, 135, 136

Harris, Leonard, 89, 90, 110, 129, 130

Hart, Cloyce "C. J./Pappy," 12, 19, 20, 33, 51–53, 83, 92, 93, 95

Hart, Peggy, 216, 217

Hashim, Ernie, 47, 165

Heath, Melvin, 16, 34, 108, 110

Hernandez, Fran, 17, 78, 206

Hibler, Harry, 60, 62–77, 81, 89, 12,

203, 229, 230

Hubbard, Vic, 175, 204

Hunt, Vance, 132, 173

Huszar, Frank, 46, 62, 64, 65, 194, 232

Iskenderian, Ed "The Camfather/Isky," 39–47, 49, 99, 160, 168, 171, 207, 211

Ivo, Tommy, 47, 57, 61, 62, 71, 77, 101, 106, 107, 116–125, 130, 143, 147, 149, 180, 182, 183, 190

Joehnck, Bob, 13–17

Johansen, Howard, 45, 101

Johnson, Don "The Beachcomber," 100, 106, 113, 120, 136, 163

Kalitta, Connie, 93, 132, 136, 155, 167, 173, 175, 208, 213

Karamesines, Chris "The Greek," 47, 70, 71, 93, 98, 132, 149, 155, 158, 163, 165, 167, 173, 213

Kraushaar, Tim "Weed," 220

Kruse, Doug, 46, 135, 136, 222

Laris, Danny, 87, 99

Lee, Lucille, 218

Leffler, Neil, 81, 211, 223

Lemons, Tommy, 168

Leong, Roland, 58, 150, 151, 153, 163, 175, 177–181, 184, 185, 188, 189

Lindley, Kenny, 20, 100, 136

Lions Clubs, 86–97

Lippencotte, Floyd Jr., 77, 101, 102, 104–115, 163, see also Muraviz, Bob

Logghe, Ron and Gene, 132

Long, Don, 46, 136, 151, 153, 188, 189

Malone, Art, 131, 132, 168, 172, 190, 192

Martin, Dode, 20, 50–53, 55–58, 130, 151, 178, 179, 225

Mather, Bernie, 164, 165

McClelland, Dave, 6–9

McCurry, Tom, 106, 149

McEwen, Tom "The Mongoose," 47, 61, 76, 77, 91, 95, 96, 100, 110, 127–141, 148, 149, 153, 163, 173, 182, 183, 189, 196

McGrath, Jack, 106, 107

Meeks, Bobby, 17, 22, 206, 207, 210

Miller, Ak, 22, 23, 53, 78, 106

Miller, Marvin, 154, 165

Morgan, Darrell, 62, 65

Moss, Jack, 18, 35, 38, 64

Moss, Sterling, 120

Mudersbach, Lefty, 29, 101, 161, 204

Muldowney, Shirley, 199, 219

Mulligan, John "The Zookeeper," 163, 182

Muravez, Bobby, 77, 101, 104–115, 130, 147, 149, *see also* Lippencotte, Floyd Jr.

Murphy, Paula, 75, 217

Nancy, Tony "The Loner," 9, 47, 61, 63, 66, 71, 77, 81, 118, 123, 143, 145, 107, 168, 207, 208, 228–235

Nelson, Jim "Jazzy," 13, 19, 20, 28, 29, 47, 50–59, 87, 98, 99, 151, 178, 179, 211, 225

Nickelson, Dyno Don, 66, 136

Nix, Jimmy, 70, 129, 132

Ongais, Danny, 57, 58, 151, 178

Orr, Veda, 216

Palamides, Romeo, 28, 122, 123

Parks, Barbara, 218

Parks, Wally, 21–23, 53–55, 84, 87–89, 106, 171, 174

Pedregon, Cruz, 78–81

Pedregon, Frank Jr., 78–81

Pedregon, Frank Sr., 77, 78–81, 112, 149

Pedregon, Tony, 78–81

Pepmuller, Rod, 106, 108, 123, 149, 180

Percell, Joel, 100, 136, 151

Peters, John, 102, 109–111

Petersen, Robert E. "Pete," 21–23

Peterson, Gary, 66, 67

Pfaff, Paul, 20, 47, 210–215

Pink, Ed, 107, 115, 135, 136, 141, 148, 151, 153, 194–196, 204–209, 223, 230

Postoian, Setto, 108, 155, 167, 172

Potter, Eddie, 81, 118, 201, 212

Prudhomme, Don "The Snake," 61, 67, 76, 77, 81, 96, 101, 106–109, 123, 133, 136, 139–141, 143–153, 161, 163, 174, 178–182, 184, 185, 189, 192, 197, 208, 233, 234

Rackemann, Don, 220, 221

Ratican, Don, 106, 158

Reath, Joe, 108, 129

Rice, Calvin, 20, 28, 29, 34, 35, 87, 211

Ridge Route Terrors, 65, 77, 154, 165

Road Kings club, 61, 106–108, 149

Robinson, Pete, 58, 70, 93, 111, 155, 163, 167, 208

Ronda, Gas, 133, 136, 208

Roth, Ed "Big Daddy," 26, 81

Ruth, Jerry, 132, 163

Safford, Kenny, 106, 107, 146, 149, 158, 163, 182

Schiefer, Paul, 184, 187

Schubeck, Joe, 70, 93, 108, 132, 155, 167, 173, 213

Schubert, Zane, 75, 81

Schwartz, Marvin, 74, 75, 168

Scrima, Ron, 92, 130

Senter, Louie, 20, 208

Shahan, Shirley, 217, 218

Shelby, Carroll, 151

Simpson, Bill, 65, 66, 90, 162, 187

Smith, Clay, 41, 78

Smokers Car Club, 36, 46, 89, 160, 161, 163

Smyser, John, 74, 77

Snively, Mike, 151, 162, 163, 181, 184, 185, 188, 189, 208

Sorokin, Mike, 162, 163, 181, 184

Sorrel, Bob, 46, 135, 136

Sowins, Dave, 47, 118, 211, 212, 214, 215

Stuckey, Rod, 66, 142, 149

Swaja, Steve, 124, 125, 232

Swingle, Connie, 168, 175

Tapia, Bobby, 78, 81, 201

Thompson, Judy, 84, 85, 87, 93, 95–101, 113, 217

Thompson, Mickey, 29, 35, 36, 47, 51, 56–58, 65, 66, 78, 82–101, 108, 113, 129, 130, 136, 163, 173, 204, 205, 211, 213, 224

Towle, Don, 17, 206, 207

Vaughn, Linda, 219

Voight, Fritz, 34, 87, 98, 99, 211

Vukovich, Bill, 107, 160

Wallace, Dave Sr., 62, 81

Ward, Glen, 57, 128

Warren, James, 154, 165

Waterman, Sid, 115, 136, 204–206, 208, 223

Waters, Tony, 164, 172

Winfield, Ed, 14, 41, 42

Wolford, Roger, 49, 50, 212–215, 223, 224

Woodcock, Bruce, 90, 201

Yates, Don, 20, 87, 204, 211

Zeuschel, Dave, 47, 115, 123, 136, 143, 147, 149, 153, 161, 204, 223

Zoucha, Rich, 59, 203